3·29·14

Terrence Moore Speaker at meeting Ft. Wayne
Education Resurrected

Defining the purpose & Content of Education in the USA & How To Make it so
ARE you willing To Challenge them!

The Story-Killers
A Common-Sense Case
Against the Common Core

Terrence O. Moore

*To my wife, Jennifer,
lover of great stories*

"But why is it prohibited?" asked the Savage. In the excitement of meeting a man who had read Shakespeare he had momentarily forgotten everything else.

The Controller shrugged his shoulders. "Because it's old; that's the chief reason. We haven't any use for old things here."

"Even when they're beautiful?"

"Particularly when they're beautiful. Beauty's attractive, and we don't want people to be attracted to old things. We want them to like the new ones."

—Aldous Huxley, *Brave New World*

CONTENTS

Preface

If you are a parent of children in school these days, most likely you are confused. No doubt, there are a lot of things to be confused about, from the curriculum to the fuss over school lunches to the obscure jargon that schools use to describe the most obvious things. But the issue that has you the most perplexed is something called "the Common Core." Though everyone seems to be talking about it, no one can tell you exactly what it is.

So you begin to ask questions: of your children's teachers, of the school principal, of a couple of school board members you know, even of a state legislator who serves on the education committee and happens to live in your neighborhood. What you get back are radically different, even contradictory, answers. The teachers simply call the Common Core a curriculum. They refer to it as the "Common Core curriculum," or assert, "We're doing the Common Core now." They say matter-of-factly that all their lesson plans must be "aligned" to the Common Core and show you the new books the school has received bearing the image of the Common Core: two white C's in a ball of red. The principal of the school tells you, in more measured words, that the Common Core is not a curriculum but rather a standardized exam. She assures you that the students will be well-prepared for this exam throughout the year. So you should not worry; your children's elementary school will still be highly-rated and a "blue-ribbon" school. You ask the principal if she has actually seen a sample of one of these exams. She admits that she has not, but she still has confidence in the "professional educators" she has hired and her thirty years as a "career educator." The school board members say less about the testing. They insist that the Common Core is only a set of "standards"—a term that seems deliberately obscure, at least as they use it. Thus teachers and schools will still have the

i

"flexibility they need as professional educators to develop and deliver the most up-to-date, high-level instruction" to your children, say the board members. The higher you climb up the ladder of school accountability, the more of what you hear sounds like talking points.

You arrange a brief conversation with the state legislator living in your neighborhood via his wife. (You like the wife; the husband is a pure politician and always positioning himself for the next election.) He speaks in more grandiose terms. He refers to *extensive* hearings that took place prior to the state adopting Common Core. You do not remember them, though you keep up with that sort of thing. He goes on for some time about a *park assessment* or something like that. He uses repeatedly the phrases "rigorous standards" and "college and career readiness." And he, like the school board members, insists that the Common Core is only a set of standards and therefore will not inhibit "flexibility in implementation" at the state level and in the various districts. Above all, the Common Core is not a curriculum and does not tell "professional educators" how to teach.

Well, there it is. There is nothing to worry about—according to the people in charge. And yet the assignments you see your children bringing home seem sillier than the ones you did not like very much last year. The worksheets, whether in math or English, often have written at the top the words "Critical Thinking." Yet the work below seems neither like thinking nor very critical. You were already wondering whether your children, who knew how to read before going to school, were being challenged enough. Now you know positively that they are not. Yet here is the astonishing thing. You have looked into the local private schools in your area: a Catholic parochial school and a small non-denominational Christian school. And they have adopted the Common Core! Other than home-schooling (something else you are considering), where is a parent to turn in order to get her children out of the curriculum/testing/standards monolith that promises the world but delivers really silly math and English exercises for her children?

Not satisfied with the answers coming from the professionals, you begin to investigate this mystery called the Common Core. Your confusion does not subside immediately. A web-search of *Common Core* produces lots of articles, both for and against. The people who write these articles all seem to have impressive credentials and to work for institutes with high-sounding names.

Yet the debate suffers, in your mind, from two contrary but equally frustrating defects. Either the argument consists in a lot of generalities about how the country must have a great education system to remain competitive in a "twenty-first-century global economy" (a phrase you grow to hate), or it is so technical and apparently scholarly that you have no idea how these high-sounding phrases bear on your children's school lessons, really the principal thing that interests you. Sometimes you suspect that this discussion takes place in a language created by a professional class who deliberately confuse the public so that nobody can really know what they are doing with education in this country. Your biggest complaint is that no one ever explains things in real, human terms—about what the Common Core really is, about what good schooling ought to be.

Be that as it may, you come up with two interesting pieces of information. The first is, despite claims to the contrary, the Common Core has never been tried in any school or by any state. The Common Core should have been "field-tested" in different kinds of schools, you learn, before any state—to say nothing of the whole country—ever adopted it. The second feature of the Common Core that strikes you as odd concerns the English Standards specifically. What the new program boils down to, it would appear, is having students reading less literature and more "non-fiction" or "informational texts," that is, readings that are not literature or cast in the form of stories. This first feature of the Common Core seems to you disingenuous and even dangerous. You know how long it takes for a new drug to get on the market before it receives approval from the FDA. Yet here is the educational medicine, so to speak, that all the nation's children will be taking every day, seven hours a day—and no clinical trials have been done. The stratagem of reducing the amount of literature children read also seems risky. Your children love to read books, especially stories. You have read them hundreds of stories since they were toddlers. Yet they never seem very excited about the things they read at school, probably because the stories are not that gripping. So the Common Core's solution to that problem seems to be to *take away stories* rather than teaching better stories or, equally important, doing a better job of teaching stories. What's a parent to do?

Your further researches into the Common Core yield even scarier results. The whole question takes on the appearance of a murder mystery or a conspiracy. You find out, contrary to what the state legislator who lives down the street says, that the Common Core was adopted by over forty states in a rush—with very little public debate. Further, this happened at a time when the states were hurting financially because of the recession, and "Race to the Top" money was given to those states that did adopt the Common Core. You learn that most of the money that funded the original writing of the standards came from the deep pockets of Bill Gates. Perhaps related to this fact, the Common Core will have students working far more with computers, even while studying English and math, two subjects that you would think would be largely free of "screen time." More troubling, you come across some articles about data-collection and mining. The annual state exams, and the constant computer work and testing that take place prior to these standardized exams, will collect a lot of information on your children that will extend beyond a single test score once a year. There is also a ton of money to be made off these exams. It seems that the people behind the Common Core also have a hand in running the tests and stand to gain financially. You find out that "park assessments" really refer to a testing agency known as PARCC. The other people who stand to make out like bandits are the textbook publishers. If that's not enough to get one wondering, it turns out that the actual writing of the *Standards* was done in complete secrecy. People who took part in the committees or "work groups" had to sign letters of confidentiality promising that they would never divulge any of the proceedings. Apparently, that is not standard practice in the writing of standards. In fact, transparency and public debate are (or were) thought to be essential to forming good schools and curricula. Finally, you cannot for the life of you figure out why large multi-national corporations such as Exxon-Mobil would be offering expensive advertising in print and on television in favor of the Common Core. When has a giant corporation ever taken such an interest in a school curriculum before?

As interesting and intriguing and downright scary as some of these findings are, what you want to know is how this new Common Core will affect your children directly. On that question, your research uncovers much less. You do try to read the Common Core documents. But you really cannot make heads nor tails of them. They are written more like the U. S. Tax Code than a treatise on teaching literature. It occurs to you that the people

iv

who supposedly know the most about teaching students to read and write should be able to compose a more interesting guide to teaching English. In fact, the authors of these bureaucratic documents do not write about books in a way that speaks to common sense, and they seem uninterested in literature for its own sake, that is, in reading great stories. Dissatisfied, you decide to undertake the unthinkable: to visit the local public schools. You want to see first-hand how this new education is affecting the classrooms and real children.

Getting into the schools is harder than you first thought it would be. What you want to do is simply visit a few classes in your local high school and middle school and the elementary school in which your children are already enrolled. You know not to ask to see the Common Core in action. Doing so would raise too many red flags. So you call the schools to see whether as a parent whose child is enrolled in a local school you would be able to visit schools to observe what your children should expect to encounter in the future. "Why would you do that?" is the first response. "Our schools are blue-ribbon schools, some of the best in the state." You say vaguely that you would like to know more about how the middle school and the high school will prepare your children for the future. The person, usually a secretary, puts you on hold. That person comes back with an answer, usually one of two: "Due to increased security . . ." or "We can't have the learning process disrupted." After being made to feel like either a crazed gunman or a nuisance rather than a concerned parent, you ask to speak to a principal, who begins by offering similar excuses. Finally, you have to call the district and remind those venerable bureaucrats that you are a taxpayer and a parent of enrolled students who could easily dis-enroll them tomorrow. Through cajolery and coercion, you manage to gain entrance into the public schools in your area. You did not know it would be like trying to visit schools in North Korea.

What do you see? At the elementary level you are struck by three things. First, the students are treated almost like babies in the way the teachers talk to them. Everything is said in a sing-song voice and in single syllables as though the students, even in the fifth grade, are toddlers. You did not talk down to your children when they were younger, and you wonder why teachers, of all people, would do that in a school. Do they just expect so little of children that age, or is this the way the teachers really are? You had always liked your children's teachers (and still do), but you had never heard them talk for an extended period nor about anything remotely academic. Not that there is much academic going on in your children's school. That is the second thing you notice: how little time is devoted to actual teaching. There are long stretches when the students read silently or work on a worksheet. There are projects that keep the students occupied. Far more time is spent on the computer than you had realized. And the students seem to go to the library regularly, though the books they bring back are not impressive. What you've come to see, though, are the effects the Common Core might be having on reading. This is the third thing that you notice, during what goes by the name of "whole-group instruction" or "read-alouds." The books simply are not very challenging. Several times you found the teachers reading books to the students that you read to your children when they were three or four—and not Dr. Seuss or *Cinderella* or *Jack and the Beanstalk*. The classics or the recent classics (in the case of Dr. Seuss) are not on the menu. Rather, the books being read to students are those published only a few years ago, and they seem to lack "meat." They are wholly devoid of a gripping story. When you ask where these books came from, the teachers say that they are a part of the Common Core.

When you visit the middle school, you begin to notice a pattern. While in elementary school the students are simply exposed (you hesitate to use the word *read*) to books that seem beneath them, in the middle school students do *occasionally* encounter books that rank as good literature. Yet the students never spend more than a single class period on them. The teachers will ask a few, predictable questions. The students, when they are even interested, offer a few predictable answers, and then the class moves on to another book (or portion of a book) the next day. Were you to visit only one day of a given class, you would never suspect this quickie-mart method of teaching literature to be in effect. You would simply assume that the class was on that given passage for that day. Instead, what you find in the English classes is a "one-day-Twain-next-day-Alcott" approach that must leave the students (to the extent they are paying attention) unsatisfied.

Not that a work of either Twain or Alcott would be read on most days. The other noticeable trend is the appearance of selections that are not literature at all. You are not surprised by this novelty since the introduction of "informational texts" is touted by the advocates of the Common Core and criticized by its detractors. The teachers (who, by the way, are not loath to have you in their classrooms, unlike their administrators) explain it by saying that they are teaching more "non-fiction." Some teachers do not seem to be bothered by the change, while others have misgivings. For your part, you find it rather jarring to see a middle-school English teacher trying to make sense of tedious documents such as the California Invasive Plant Council's *Invasive Plant Inventory*.

Your biggest worry is what happens at the high school.[1] You spend a fair amount of time there. What you observe seems miles away from preparing students for college and careers. In fact, it is nothing less than a spectacle. You realize this one day when you are walking down the halls and see a number of students dressed up as monsters. You ask one of them why they are dressed in this way (the day is nowhere near Halloween), and he responds that it's for class. They are doing "monster biographies." You visit the class to see what this could mean. Sure enough, the students, one by one, stand up to read a monster's biography. Actually, they are *auto*biographies. Each student has created his own monster and has a tale to tell—invariably a ridiculous one. The class doesn't manage to get through all the monster stories, so they will continue the next day. On the way out, you ask the teacher what kind of assignment this was. She replies that it is a "Common Core exercise in critical thinking and writing." With a forced smile, you thank her for allowing you to sit in. "This has been very enlightening."[2] Though at first you have to laugh at this nonsense, your laughter turns to anger when you realize all the things these students should be learning in a high-school literature class.

Another class you visit is positively alarming. The students take turns reading aloud (mostly in a monotone) a short story called "The Story of an Hour." It is about a woman who is informed that her husband has died in a "railroad disaster." At first she is shocked and grieved. After a few moments, though, she recovers. She is overcome by a different emotion. She says under

---

[1] Academically speaking, that is; you know to worry most about the moral influences of middle school.
[2] See Prentice Hall LITERATURE, Teacher's Edition, *The British Tradition*, volume two, Common Core Edition (Upper Saddle River, N.J.: Pearson/Prentice Hall, 2012), 766. I shall explain this monstrosity—a real assignment—in chapter seven.

her breath, over and over, the word "free, free, free!" When the class has finished the story, the teacher writes on the board "Compare and Contrast," and invites the students to compare the woman's situation before the accident and after.[3] The students dutifully say that before the woman hears of her husband's death, she thinks she is in a loveless marriage and that her future is very dark. On receiving the news, she can again think about a happier life and "being her own person" and "living only for herself." The teacher leads the class to heap a lot of criticism on "nineteenth-century marriage." One girl remarks, "This may seem kinda weird to say. But it's like, maybe divorce is better because nowadays you don't have to live your life anymore hoping your husband will die." You leave the class thinking, "My God, what are they teaching these kids?"[4]

In many of the classes you detect a definite political bias. You first notice it in a class reading an "informational text." It is an editorial from *The New York Times* in 1999. The piece begins, "The Berlin Wall was bound to fall eventually." While the teacher pauses to tell the class that this is the "main idea," you think to yourself, "Is that true? Who was saying in 1980 or so that the Berlin Wall would come down eventually?" You lived back then and do not remember *The New York Times* making that pronouncement. The next sentence appears to set things on track. "But that it came down as bloodlessly as it did 10 years ago this week is largely a tribute to one leader." You are actually surprised to hear that. Will this class actually give credit where credit is due? You had always heard that public schools were extremely Left-leaning. The next couple of lines, then, hit you like a thunderbolt: "Today Mikhail Gorbachev is a political pariah in Russia and increasingly forgotten in the West. But history will remember him generously for his crucial role in ending the cold war and pulling back the Iron Curtain that Stalin drew across Europe in 1945." What? You continue to listen for one name to emerge from this editorial. It does not. After the editorial is read, the teacher goes into her spiel on "the main idea" and "background information" and whether the text is written for "a general or a

---

[3] There is a wrinkle here that I shall not divulge until chapter eight.
[4] Prentice Hall LITERATURE, Teacher's Edition, *The American Experience*, volume one, Common Core Edition (Upper Saddle River, N.J.: Pearson/Prentice Hall, 2012), 628-633.

specific audience."[5] What bothers you is the decidedly political point that is being made by this editorial, one that does not recount events *as you remember them*. You wonder whether you should ask a question or intervene in some way. The students in this class were born in the late Nineties. The teacher herself seems to be in her mid-twenties. Who knows what "information" she was fed at school and in college? At last the discussion turns to the place of Gorbachev in bringing down the wall. Just when the teacher finishes her short encomium on Gorbachev, who showed how "one person can make a difference," a boy at the back of the class, who has been whispering to another boy the whole time, calls out. "I thought Reagan was the reason the Soviet Union fell." The teacher is clearly taken aback. "Well, you know, Reagan *was* president, and he, like, met with Gorbachev. But what this article says is that Gorbachev was the cause. That's the *main idea* of the article. And, you know, we will read about Reagan in a couple of days. And what we'll see is that when Reagan spoke to the students at Moscow State University he *restrained his strongly anti-communist sentiments.*[6] And he used *simple* language. And he was a good *salesman*. So we'll be looking at those rhetorical devices and techniques a little later." The boy in the back row looks at his companion and shakes his head. As you leave the room, you ask the teacher whether what you just saw was "a Common Core lesson." "Yes," she beams. "Isn't it great to see all this critical thinking?" "Oh, yes, great." You think to yourself, "So Mikhail Gorbachev was the enlightened reformer who, single-handedly, transformed the world, and Ronald Reagan was just along for the ride. All that talk of an 'evil empire' and the challenge to 'tear down this wall' probably just got in the way. But he gave a simple, moderate speech at Moscow State University!"

Later that week you see students read part of the script of George Clooney's and Grant Heslov's *Good Night, and Good Luck* pitting Edward R. Murrow versus Joe McCarthy. You are surprised to see that movie surface as *literature* in a school. What you notice most, however, is the scorn heaped upon not only McCarthy but the very notion that there might have been

---

[5] Prentice Hall LITERATURE, Teacher's Edition, Grade Ten, Common Core Edition (Upper Saddle River, N.J.: Pearson/Prentice Hall), 403-404.
[6] Ibid., 449-451.

communists in Hollywood and in America attempting to do harm. The teacher sets the tone by using the phrase "right-wing extremists," which gets repeated no fewer than a dozen times. What occurs to you, in light of the other class that expunged Reagan from the historical record, is that there really were Communists in Hollywood. Reagan himself cooperated with an FBI investigation. Insurgents threatened to throw acid in his face, and he had to carry a gun for self-protection. There were actual riots outside the gates of Hollywood studios, and bombs were set off in cars and in homes of those who opposed the communist-instigated strikes. Those who tried to cross picket lines were assaulted. In the classrooms of America these actual events have been not just ignored but turned into one big laugh at the expense of those stupid (or evil) "right-wing extremists."[7]

In other classes you notice so-called discussions that are not necessarily biased, but do offer a strange view of history. In one class, the students are reading an excerpt of some document written by a journalist or a historian—you are not sure which—who seems to claim that the Declaration of Independence "means different things to different people." The teacher keeps repeating this phrase. The Declaration "can mean different things to different people." The teacher also says that "these are only ideas, and depending on how or where people live, they can interpret ideas differently."[8] Long after the class has ended (which the teacher told you was indeed "a Common Core lesson"), you cannot get those phrases out of your head: "different things to different people" and "only ideas." Does *life* really mean different things to different people? Does *liberty*? If they do, then how could a nation ever defend life or liberty? And what does the word *only* in front of *ideas* suggest? Are ideas not important? Are they subject to *any* interpretation *anyone* wants to give them? Did the Founding Fathers believe that? Why was the line, "We hold these truths to be self-evident," not brought up in the class? Self-evident

---

[7] Prentice Hall LITERATURE, Teacher's Edition, *The American Experience*, volume two, Common Core Edition (Upper Saddle River, N.J.: Pearson/Prentice Hall, 2012), 1240-1249. In fact, the real hero of the story, who both stood up to the communists infiltrating the unions and helped to clear the names of those actors who were falsely accused of being communists, was Ronald Reagan. See *An American Life*, chs. 14-15. Do not expect George Clooney to produce a picture showing Reagan in a positive light, though.

[8] LITERATURE, Grade Ten, 560-564.

truths would not seem to be open to just any interpretation. Such questions did not come up in the class—for a simple reason. The students were not reading the Declaration of Independence itself, just someone's interpretation of it, further mediated through a school textbook.

Another of the curiosities you witness in this Common Core business is the result of almost never having students read a story that takes more than a day to cover. Following that questionable practice leads to reading a *lot* of authors, many of whom you have never heard of, a good many who are living today, even in units of the books that are historical in nature. "Are these authors on the same level as Shakespeare or Melville or Poe?" you wonder. One of these modern authors writes about tortillas quite a bit.[9] The teacher, a rather young woman, tells the class that the author is one of the leading "Chicana writers in the country" and that she read "a lot of her stuff in college." The teacher also tells the class several times that this author "is always pushing the envelope" in her poetry. The immediate reading makes no impression on the students whatsoever. The "discussion" is, well, like eating a cold tortilla in which the butter doesn't melt. But you decide to look up this author that night, especially since you have been wondering who some of these ultra-modern authors are. You cannot believe what you see and what you read! "Pushing the envelope" is putting it mildly: "I am the lust goddess," etc. Critics call this author's poetry "provocative," but you prefer "sick," "vulgar," and "trashy." You study up on this author and find out that she is recommended in the Common Core documents themselves twice and featured in several of the textbooks. The selections in the textbooks do not strike you as literature so much as personal commentary from a Hispanic perspective, but the treatment of her work by the editors is glowing. Is the purpose to get students hooked on this author so that her more provocative writings might be read?

Some of the things you see students being assigned are just plain silly, much like the monster autobiographies. The final straw comes when you visit a tenth-grade literature class. Though you hoped to see a discussion, you find instead students drawing, while chatting to each other, of course. From the assignment on the

---

[9] In addition to my treatment of this author in chapter eight, see also LITERATURE, Grade Ten, 104-106.

board, you see that they are working on sketches of a "city of men" and a "city of cats." The teacher is self-conscious about your being there, only to see students doing some low-grade art work. Finally, he announces, "Okay, class. Let's finish up those sketches and start our literary *analysis*." Another five minutes pass. The literary analysis starts with the teacher asking students to "compare and contrast" (there is that phrase again) the city of men and the city of cats. For a while, the students are reluctant to offer examples, so the teacher prompts them. Under *men* he writes the words *malls* and *movie theatres*, followed by students' suggestions of *houses* and *schools*, and, with the teacher offering leading clues, *hospitals*, *libraries*, and *work* (which the teacher translates to *office buildings*). Then the teacher asks what a city of cats would look like. He seems to want the students to say that cats would prefer to live in nature. He's looking for answers such as *fields* and *meadows*. One girl raises her hand. "But, like, we have a cat, and he just lives with us." The teacher is clearly at pains to convince the students that cats would prefer to be in the wild, and cities have made life much tougher for cats. "See, the author shows that cats symbolize what has happened to nature as a result of progress." (You notice that the teacher seems to be reading from a script.) He continues. "They may also represent the passage of time when there was no distinction between the city of men and the city of cats. They were able to live side-by-side." After that oration, ten hands go up in the air, and several students blurt out, "We have a cat" and "Yeah, we do, too." It is clear both the teacher and the author (and the textbook editor and maybe the architects of the Common Core) are not getting their point across. The students are supposed to be convinced that there has been so much progress that cats and men can't live together any longer![10]

Before you leave the classroom, you write down something that appears on the board under the heading RL-9-10.3.:

---

[10] The reader who thinks I am making all this up should consult page 385 of Prentice Hall's tenth-grade LITERATURE book. One of the questions asked of students is, "Why is the city uninhabitable for cats?" In the margin of the Teacher's Edition, the answer is supplied: "The city is uninhabitable for cats because people have built huge structures and machines that are dangerous to cats." One of those machines, in the words of the actual author, is "the mortal traffic of cat-crushing automobiles."

Determine a theme or central idea of a text and analyze in detail its development over the course of the text, including how it emerges and is shaped and refined by specific details; provide an objective summary of the text.

You later learn that the mysterious code stands for "Reading Standards for Literature, grades 9-10, Standard 3." So there you have it: a genuine Common Core standard being adhered to in a public high school in your district. College and career readiness awaits your children. They, too, can dress up like monsters, learn that a husband's being killed was preferable to being stuck in a nineteenth-century marriage, be informed that Mikhail Gorbachev had the idea of ending the Cold War and pulling down the Wall, read modern Hollywood actors' version of the Red Scare, be told that the Declaration of Independence can mean anything you want it to because Jefferson was writing *only* about ideas, read a lot of either forgettable or "provocative" modern authors, and be told that the modern city of man has virtually destroyed cat civilization. But all that is only the tip of the iceberg.

As you try to take in everything you have seen in the ostensible literature classes held to the Common Core English Standards, you formulate three basic questions. What is this thing called the Common Core? How is this educational mayhem taking place under our very noses and in the name of school reform? Where is this unaccountable authority going to take us? That is, unless we do something to stop it.

Note to the reader: I write with urgency. The Common Core is a pressing issue. While I think the reader would profit from reading the whole book, those actively involved in the growing resistance movement may want to start with chapter five, which contains a sustained critique of Appendix B (the list of readings recommended by the Common Core) or chapter eight (which analyzes an actual Common Core high-school textbook). Nonetheless, I would urge the reader who approaches the book in this way to circle back and read the remaining chapters. The *Common Core Standards for English* is a deliberately confusing document and must be understood thoroughly in order to expose completely its absurdity and clear political bias. That exposure is what I hope my book accomplishes.

Introduction
Brave New Core

Aldous Huxley's *Brave New World* is a story about a futuristic dystopia in which the few members of a ruling class control the rest of the society through technology, infant and childhood conditioning, and people's lower appetites and constant craving for fun. It is a world in which families no longer exist; children are "decanted" rather than born; and ideas of "mother, monogamy, and romance," long since abandoned, are looked upon in horror. Since there are no families, and birth control has been perfected, men and women "have" each other indiscriminately and frequently, usually after a night in a dance club so loud no one can speak and after taking an all-purpose drug called "soma." The people *do* work since they must be occupied during the day. Their work is both highly routine and technologically advanced. The residents of this world zip about in helicopters and marvel at all the latest gadgetry, most of it designed to keep them from engaging in genuine conversation. They frequently attend movies, called "feelies," whose technological advances allow the spectators to *feel* as much as they see the film. The plots of these films are simplistic, not based on any discernable literature, of which the society has none, and nearly always end up with several men "having" the starlet.

The social make-up of this world is a permanent hierarchy, with no movement up or down. People's intelligence and even their height, products of the decanting process, are designated by various Greek letters. Alphas are at the top; they and the Betas just below them control all the rest of the society, with Gammas, Deltas, and Epsilons being given all the menial work. The Alphas run the industries and also the considerable propaganda machine necessary to provide social stability, which includes the feelies, the

1

newspapers, and the conditioning centers. None of the Betas or anyone below (nor even most Alphas) gives a second thought to the information churned out for general consumption by the various class-based newspapers; the radio; the Bureaux of Propaganda by Television, by Feeling Picture, and by Synthetic Voice and Music; and the originator of them all, the College of Emotional Engineering.

Education, too, is class-based. Children are conditioned by "hypnopædia" (schooling while sleeping or under hypnosis) from their cradles. Older children are taught to enjoy pleasures appropriate to their given class, including sexual pleasure by at least the age of seven. The Alphas and Betas are the most advanced readers of the society. They learn to read through the use of simple sentences such as "The cat is on the mat." Their advanced reading, though, other than the newspapers, seems to consist in technical manuals used at work, such as *The Chemical and Bacteriological Conditioning of the Embryo. Practical Instructions for Beta Embryo-Store Workers.*

The motto of the world state—to which everyone belongs since individual countries have been eliminated—is Community, Identity, Stability. The occupants of this world (they could hardly be called citizens) have only a vague sense of history. They worship a god whose chief messenger on earth was Ford—or Freud; they conflate the two—and whose will is for people to have untold amounts of fun and to be efficient, orderly, and just like everyone else. Individual opinions do not really exist, and anyone who engages in argumentation becomes suspect and can easily be transferred to a less populous region, such as Iceland. There is almost no distinction among government, industry, and culture. They are all controlled by the same people at the apex of the Alpha class.

Since ordinary people are satiated in their appetites and have no ambitions that could make them unhappy or disturb the society, there are no great passions or dreams, and therefore no real culture exists to shape and give voice to those passions. The people of this modern society have no longings for the heroic or the beautiful or the noble and are incapable of imagining these qualities in human beings. Therefore they are dumbstruck when one of their own— who was *born*, not decanted, and who grew up on a reservation in New Mexico without modern conveniences—comes to London and begins to question their ways. He is an oddity to them.

What makes him particularly odd besides his strange circumstances is his education. He, unsatisfied with *The Chemical and Bacteriological Conditioning of the Embryo*, takes to reading (through an accident) the complete works of Shakespeare in his youth. At the time he begins the book, a native man from the reservation is visiting his mother regularly to meet his (and her) physical desires, and the young boy—listening to the voice of nature and not to the hypnopædia and other forms of conditioning he would have undergone—knows what is happening is wrong. The first words the boy reads cut like a knife:

> *Nay, but to live*
> *In the rank sweat of an enseamed bed,*
> *Stew'd in corruption, honeying and making love*
> *Over the nasty sty.*

These words from *Hamlet* make the boy, whose name is John, want to kill the man who is sharing his mother's bed but who is not his father. Subsequently, all of John's natural tastes and passions and emotions—love, anger, a sense of beauty and of the good—are formed by his intensive reading of Shakespeare. Hence the title of Huxley's book. After John is discovered, once he learns that he will be taken back to the modern society, he quotes from *The Tempest*:

> *O brave new world that has such people in it.*[11]

Little does he know that that world and those people would be his undoing.

Huxley published this story in 1932. He considered such a world the more probable route mankind would take in their march towards tyranny. In a famous letter to George Orwell, he wrote the following:

> The philosophy of the ruling minority in *Nineteen Eighty-Four* is a sadism which has been carried to its logical conclusion by going beyond sex and denying it. Whether in actual fact the policy of the boot-on-the-face can go on

---

[11] The original in *The Tempest*, Act 5, scene 1, reads "such people in 't!"

indefinitely seems doubtful. My own belief is that the ruling oligarchy will find less arduous and wasteful ways of governing and satisfying its lust for power, and these ways will resemble those which I described in *Brave New World*. . . In other words, I feel that the nightmare of *Nineteen Eighty-Four* is destined to modulate into the nightmare of a world having more resemblance to that which I imagined in *Brave New World*. The change will be brought about as a result of a felt need for increased efficiency.

In other words, Huxley thought the "ruling oligarchy" would figure out that people are more easily ruled through their appetites and pleasures than through their fears. Further, such a tyranny could be embarked upon in the name of "efficiency," or, today we might say, "a twenty-first-century global economy." Of course, Orwell was right, too. At least he was right about one course the world could take, the one offered by the Soviet Union. It was the part of Huxley (and perhaps Ray Bradbury) to explain the ways in which the free West could bring about its own moral and political demise.

The pressing question of the moment is obviously, how right was he? How far down the path toward Huxley's futuristic dystopia have we travelled? That question is easier to answer if we consider the state of affairs in the realms of morals, culture, and politics in the year 1932 compared to 2013, just over eighty years later. How different is our world when contrasted with that of our grandparents?

What was the state of the family in the 1930's? Do we need to trot out the illegitimacy rate (or "out-of-wedlock births" as it is called euphemistically) or statistics in the decline of "intact" families to make the point? How did our grandparents date (or, rather, court) each other, and how does our children's generation go about that business? In what ways has entertainment changed? True, not all the movies are quite as pornographic as Huxley predicted, but the Internet has taken care of that. Reality television is something even the prophets of decline could not come up with. Today's music probably has less of a big-band sound than would "Calvin Stopes and His Sixteen Sexophonists," but are the effects any different than the songs of Rihanna? Would Huxley be surprised by Miley Cyrus's twerking? How about the growth of a rigid caste system? Did the Founding Fathers, did our grandparents, so frequently talk about the "middle class" and "the top 2%" or create social programs to cater to a permanent underclass?[12] Who rules in America? Is it "We the People"?

Our idolatry of technology is something most people do not want to talk about. There is not a moment of the day when ninety percent of the population are not compulsively texting, checking their smartphones, or updating their facebook page. So dependent have we adults become on the devices we did not have thirty years ago that we do not consider the potential effects of throwing those same devices promiscuously into the classrooms of our children's schools. Perhaps we should dwell on this line from Huxley, which comes when Linda (the mother) is instructing John how to read the instructional manual:

> "I'm afraid you won't find it very exciting," she said. But it's the only thing I have." She sighed. "If only you could see the lovely reading machines we used to have in London!"

Reading machines. At this moment, the nation's classrooms are being equipped with "workstations" where students can prepare for standardized testing, clicking their way through most of the school day. We are so enamored with our technology that we have forgotten the moral and intellectual and political foundation that has made our economic and technological advances possible.

And what about our Brave New World of education? Sex education for children as young as seven? That is already happening. Aside from what is required by mandated state exams, sex education (under the cover of "health") is the one thing most states and districts are interested in. The class basis for education is stronger than ever. In bigger metropolitan areas like New York and Boston and Atlanta, affluent parents pay tuition starting at $15,000 per year for thirteen years prior to sending their children to college where they will pay even larger sums starting at $40,000. Let us do the math on that. A family with three children could easily spend half-a-million dollars in pre-college tuition

---

[12] I realize that Huxley was British and that his novel was set in Britain, but I am transferring these themes to their American context.

costs. Even when sending their children to less expensive schools, parents would likely pay seventy- to a hundred-thousand dollars per child. Everyone else attends the public schools. Suburban parents throughout the nation, like unworried Betas in Huxley's tale, send their children to the "good" suburban schools, where their children receive the best of the worst.

What do those children read in public schools (and increasingly in private ones)? For the past two years, in place of what used to be called *literature*, the nation's schools have been swiftly turning students to non-fiction or "informational" texts. This clear change of direction, running against the long course of Western education, is being done under the guise of "career readiness." In other words, move over Shakespeare; make room for *The Chemical and Bacteriological Conditioning of the Embryo*. Skeptical readers may think I am exaggerating. But how otherwise can one explain the appearance of a South Florida EPA report in an American *literature* textbook? And what is the reason for this exchange that is supposed to take place based on another reading, according to the Teacher's Edition of that same textbook?

> **About Government Forms**
> Before going over the Virginia Department of Historic Resources form, discuss with students their own experiences with government forms. One common experience may be a learner's permit or driver's license application.
> **Ask**: What kinds of information are typically sought by government forms? Why do you think governments require this information?
> **Possible response**: Based on their experience with application forms, students may mention name, address, phone number, age, and other contact identifying information. In the case of licensing, for example, a government that grants an individual permission to drive needs to be able to identify and contact that individual.[13]

---

[13] *The American Experience*, volume one, Teacher's Edition, Common Core Edition (Upper Saddle River, N.J.: Pearson/Prentice Hall, 2012), 561.

Why should this "informational" discussion take place in a literature class? How does a discussion that begins about race relations during the Civil War era turn into the reading of a pamphlet of the American Archaeological Institute, which morphs into a discussion about filling out government forms? Are the publishers trying to require teachers to get students into the habit of filling out government forms? Would Huxley be surprised? If a people are going to be ruled over by a bureaucracy, presumably they must be *conditioned* into filling out its many forms, and even enjoying doing so.

Discounting artistic hyperbole, I believe we are about halfway down the road to the Brave New World of Huxley's imagination. To be sure, we still have distant memories of good things. Yet we hardly know how to act on those memories. And what common sense we have left is often overcome by ideology. In the state of California, for example, it has recently been determined that children can choose what sex they wish to be, thus giving them "equal access" to either male or female restrooms in schools. Is this the sign of a healthy society? Is this the sign of a people recovering or losing its common sense?

The scheme of education proposed in the Common Core is the vehicle that can take us the rest of the way. I do not make that statement lightly. Any ruling oligarchy, as seen in any fictional dystopia, rules through the abuse of language. The abuse of language necessitates the takeover of the schools, where language is taught. The Common Core, itself a textbook case in the abuse of language, is a complete consolidation and nationalization of a public education in America that has already been injected with imbecility and indoctrination for half a century. Once they complete the consolidation and nationalization, the ideologues and bureaucrats of the Common Core will be able to *program* students' thinking about the world: what they think about politics, about economics, about history, about religion, about families, about goodness, and about love—and what they do not think about these things. The architects and authors of the Common Core will be able to program students in this way because they will control the stories children and young people read and the way they read them. The authors of the Common Core will likewise be able to keep the nation's children from reading stories, particularly traditional stories, that run counter to the political ideology and ambitions of the ruling class the authors of the Common Core represent. Simply put, the Common Core (and the current public schools on the whole) will be the educational arm of the progressive state. While such a design may sound like the stuff of science fiction (Huxley's College of Emotional Engineering) the desire to control people through controlling their education is a phenomenon with a long history. As Plato pointed out in his *Republic*—a book never read in today's high schools, nor usually even in college—whoever writes the stories shapes—or controls—the minds of the people in any given regime.

The design of the Common Core is not to instruct, educate, enlighten, and improve the minds and souls of young people by teaching them the great stories of our Western and American tradition. It is not to teach them to be free people living under the rule of law. It is not to teach them to be good and to love the beautiful. It is not to teach them to find true happiness. It is not to teach them to pursue truth. Those are the traditional aims of education in this country but not the language of the Common Core. Rather, the purpose of the Common Core is to remove all trace of these ideas. The Common Core is a design to smear the Western and American tradition with the brush of sexism, racism, and all the other charges we have come to expect from the political Left against this country's long history of freedom. The Common Core is likewise an effort to provide a sub-standard, limited, and superficial education for anyone who attends a public school. Finally, the Common Core is a program that directs people to be preoccupied with only the functional aspects of human existence and to have almost no interest in the higher aims of life. All this is to be done in the name of progress or, as it is stated nowadays, "college and career readiness for a twenty-first-century global economy."

The means by which the Common Core will effect these illiberal ends is by killing the great stories of our tradition. The great stories are, first, the works of literature that have long been considered great by any standard of literary judgment and, second, what we might call the Great American Story of people longing to be free and happy under their own self-government. The Common Core will kill these stories by a deadly combination of neglect, amputation, misinterpretation, subtle and not-so-subtle criticism, and a further dumbing-down of the nation's classrooms. On the ruins of the old canon of literary and historical classics will be erected a new canon of post-modern literature and progressive

8

political doctrine. Simultaneous to this change, fewer and fewer works of literature will be read on the whole. Great literature will be replaced with "information" masquerading as essential "workforce training." Much of this information will read like bureaucratic orders to a compliant and unthinking populace, as we have seen in the bald instructions to teachers to encourage students to like (or at least get used to) government forms and data-collection.

What will be the results of this educational regime? Two by-products of this form of schooling we already see in America today. First, young people, who are not armed with the great stories of literature and history, will have their views of goodness and happiness formed by the false stories produced by the mythmakers in Hollywood and other parts of our popular culture. Just consider the view of sex and the relations between the sexes promulgated in movies. Second, the American people will know little about the forms of self-government the Founding Fathers created to secure our freedom and security and to allow us to pursue and attain happiness. Ill-versed in the ideas and habits of self-rule, we shall look increasingly to a supposedly benevolent, omni-competent, and all-providing state, run by an unknown and wholly unaccountable bureaucracy of "experts." Parents who do not follow politics will wonder what such designs have to do with the schooling of their children. What they may not understand is the extent to which those in charge of the Common Core regard the nation's children as belonging far less to their parents and far more to a vague, amorphous entity denominated *society*. And that society cannot be left to itself, as individuals working out their own greatest happiness without doing harm to others. Rather, it must be directed, or programmed, with all the latest ideas and fads.

The reason the stories that were once read in this country come into play is the old adage "the best defense is a good offense." The offense of truth has always been a telling of great stories: stories that show men and women at their best or, alternatively, the ends we come to when we pursue our worst inclinations. Without stories of the good, human beings do not know what the good is. Without stories where the good guy is the hero, young people have no one to root for and nothing to believe in. Those stories, therefore, must become the target of the men (and women) who think they know how to rule over us better than we know how to rule ourselves.

Of course, the architects of the Common Core (and the people who are supporting the Common Core) do not say such things out loud. If they were clear about their intentions, the American people would handily reject the Common Core and its authors and its rich supporters. The authors of the Common Core will not say, "While we went to exclusive college-prep schools and to selective colleges—and that is where we shall send our own children—we don't think *your kids* are up to that. So we will give them what they need to become at least somewhat productive members of society." Nor will they say, "While you may still have an unthinking patriotism and reverence for the Founding Fathers, and still believe in outmoded ideas like love, virtue, faith, and the traditional family, we know better. We learned all that was rubbish in our Ivy League colleges that you couldn't get into. So we are going to replace what used to be called the classics gradually with newer books that all hinge on race, class, and gender—and expose love, virtue, faith, and family as being no better than superstitions." Nor will they say, "All this school choice that is cropping up all over the nation makes us uncomfortable. Voucher programs are giving private, religious schools public money. Some charter schools are opting for a classical curriculum that undermines the progressive ideology's heretofore unchallenged grip on the schools. And we don't know what to make of all these crazy home-schoolers. Why don't those women just get jobs like they're supposed to and leave their kids to us? So to stop all this fracturing of our education system, we need to institute some kind of all-encompassing control of schools that can't be undone at the state and local levels. That means nationalized standards, i.e. nationalized testing, i.e. nationalized curriculum, i.e. nationalized programming of your children to think the way we want them to think and to set their horizons only so high as we want them to." No, you will not hear such things coming from the architects and the supporters of the Common Core because they are not honest people. So we must judge them by their actions and not by their words.

What the Common Core does (as opposed to what its authors say it is going to do) are the things I just mentioned. While holding up the illusion of reform, the Common Core continues to gut the school curriculum beyond what has already happened over the last several decades. But the Common Core goes well beyond the ordinary educational claptrap. It is designed as an all-encompassing—and eventually computerized—system that will view children and young people less as human beings in need of intellectual and moral development than as consumers of information and future workers in highly specialized fields requiring little thought beyond those fields. Perhaps it would be going a little too far in saying that the arch-testers of the Common Core regard your children as mindless robots, but the element of programming in the system is unmistakable. Therefore, the first phase of the Common Core (the one I shall deal with mostly in this book) consists in beginning to remove the *humanity* out of the disciplines of learning that used to be called the humanities.

This contention is not a matter of speculation or opinion, by the way. On page five of the introduction to the Common Core English Standards, the authors reproduce a chart that clearly illustrates the demise of the humanities. It shows children in grade 4 reading 50% "informational" texts vs. literary texts, by grade 8 reading 55% informational texts, and by grade 12 reading 70% informational texts and only 30% literature. Thus literature is on the wane in public schools. The words under this chart could not be clearer: "The Standards aim to align instruction with this framework . . ." Admittedly, the authors of the Common Core insist that *some* of this reading will take place in other classes. But that insistence raises many questions. Are the *English* standards designed to control what gets read in other classes as well? How can those readings be imposed without anyone knowing what the history or science "standards" might look like? Why are the *literature* textbooks now being crammed full of informational texts and English teachers saying that they are teaching more and more "non-fiction"? If not 70-30 by the senior year, what is the ideal percentage of *literary* texts that would be read in the *literature* class? None of this is made clear in the Standards. Indeed, for an *informational* text whose purpose is to advocate the use of *informational* texts in the education of young people living in the *information* age, there is far less straightforward *information* than one might expect to be found in these so-called standards.

At the moment what the Common Core produces is confusion. No one—no legislator, no education department official, no district administrator, no teacher, no alleged school reformer who supports the program—can say what the Common Core is exactly. No one can point to a Common Core school. No one can show what the effects of this program have been on actual students. No one can

11

say with any precision whether the Common Core, which we are told is only a set of "standards," is a change in philosophy from current educational practices, and if so, whether it is a good change in philosophy. Although the authors of the Common Core claim their system does not dictate any specific curriculum, and that states and local school districts will be free to decide what works best for them, everyone in the schools is acting as though it *is* a substantial change in curriculum, and the phrase "Common Core Curriculum" rings through the halls. Worse still, the engine driving the whole enterprise—standardized testing—remains a mystery. Could someone tell us how this situation is anything other than a few unnamed Alpha-plusses telling the rest of the society that we need this change in the name of efficiency—and the details will be worked out by the really *smart* people who understand the intricacies of education?

Concerned parents who try to read the official documents of the Common Core would become even more confused. Much of the language used in those documents is standard educational jargon. Cutting through that language, a discerning reader would see that the authors make large claims in the introduction about "college and career readiness." Yet the documents that follow are exceedingly boring to read. How will this boring writing be translated into meaningful school reform that will make students "college and career ready"? What will be the visible differences between what is going on in schools today compared to schools under the direction of the Common Core? What will change? More important, what will remain the same? What would a Common Core *lesson* look like?

That these questions are not answered in these documents—and that they were never even asked by state legislatures—we should find appalling. I spend a lot of time working with teachers in new classical schools, many who have come from progressive schools of education. I have to be very clear with them about how the traditional way of teaching is completely different from how they have been trained to teach. Moreover, for a charter school to be approved by an authorizing agent in this country (be it the state or a district) its founders have to be painstakingly clear about what the school will teach and how it will be taught. There is no such clarity in these documents. It is as though the authors of the Common Core have said to the nation, "We'll write some educational jargon so it will look as though you are adopting a *rigorous* education, but as to what the actual teaching or learning will look like, or what will be taught and learned, or how what is taught will be tested, well, you'll just have to trust us." In fact, the authors of the Common Core turn their lack of transparency into a virtue. They assure us, "The Common Core is not really a curriculum," and "The Common Core will not dictate how you teach," and "Matters of curriculum and instruction will still be left in the hands of the states and districts," and "School choice will not be compromised." "We're just giving you a set of standards and making a few suggestions about what kinds of books you should have the children read. And, of course, we will be overseeing all the testing through our good friends at PARCC and Smarter Balanced. But we're really not going to change everything—honest." Just how gullible do they think we are?

Our confusion is made worse by our no longer knowing what a good education looks like in the first place. Without a standard by which to judge these "standards," it is hard, nay, almost impossible to evaluate them in any way. It is as though this discussion about the Common Core is taking place in a vacuum. If we do not know what our educational health looks like, then we have no way of evaluating the remedy that is supposed to bring us back to health. The Common Core documents do not help us out in this regard. For all the jargon about "college and career readiness," the Common Core Standards do not tell us what an education is or what an educated person looks like. They invoke phrases; they do not make an argument. Sometimes the hardest person to argue with, as we are finding out the hard way, is the person who says nothing.

The confusion that results from reading these documents I believe is intentional. The documents strike me as deliberately confusing. Either the authors of the Common Core are woefully bad writers who have no idea what they are doing in the realm of teaching reading and literature, or they have constructed an inelegant, bureaucratic, disorganized, and overly complex manual whose purpose is to erode (and eventually erase) the teaching of traditional literature courses in this country, while making the general public believe that they are requiring more rigor in reading. In other words, there may very well be an art to technical, bureaucratic obscurity and deception, and the authors of the Common Core Standards have mastered that art.

My intention is to bring clarity to the confusion, to shed light on the current darkness. With a little patient investigation, the Common Core English Standards can be interpreted and the inevitable results of this educational bureaucracy exposed. My investigation, I should point out, is concerned with just one portion of this hostile takeover of the nation's schools. Many other things are going on that are no doubt disturbing, such as the invasive data-collection and mining that promise to be a large component of the testing that the Common Core will usher in. My argument, however, will be confined to the academic effects of the Common Core on the English classes, which is what students will encounter. My intent is to expose exactly what will be taking place in the classrooms in both the immediate and the distant future based on what the Standards are already doing and are promising to do.

Put into proper perspective, the real aims and effects of the Common Core are not impossible to figure out. The Common Core English Standards impose on schools:

- insufficient, utopian, and radical aims of education;
- a set of substandard academic standards;
- a pseudo-science of textual "complexity" disguising the real intent of requiring students to read things that would not be found in a traditional literature class;
- superficiality and bias in the choosing of those "texts" for reading, to the disadvantage of the true classics;
- simplistic and mind-numbing ways of reading any good literature that remains in the curriculum;
- the continuing dumbing down of English classes;
- and a tyranny of textbooks that ensures teachers will force on students the absurdities and bias that is the strange brew of the Common Core.

More simply put, the unstated but nonetheless unmistakable intent of the Common Core is to erase any remnant of traditional learning in the English classes of our public schools. As such, the architects of the Common Core are nothing short of story-killers. They are deliberately killing off what is left of the great stories of Western literature. Those who should be doing everything in their power to rekindle the imaginations of young people, who spend too many hours catatonic in front of a computer or television

14

screen, are doing quite the opposite. The authors of the Common Core must believe either that the young men and women of today are not capable of understanding and enjoying the stories that constitute their cultural and moral inheritance or that our children should not be reading them—at least not in their entirety—in the first place. The first motive is a case of inexcusably diminished expectations. The second is a case of deliberate sabotage. Although some readers may disagree with my thesis, I believe that the second is the more likely cause.

The naïve reader may wonder, "Who? Why? Who would do such a thing to children and why would they do it?" To answer that question fully to the satisfaction of everyone would take an entire book on the history of progressive education in this country and the progressive movement as a whole. The simple answer would be to invoke Plato's lesson again: he who controls the stories of a society holds the reins of power. On the other side of the equation, imagine how powerless one is who does not know his own story, or any story about the thriving of human beings. Through stories we know who human beings are. We know how they—we—flourish and, alternatively, how we wither and perish. In stories we find ourselves, as individuals and as a people. Without stories—without the narratives that reveal the sources of human happiness and flourishing—we are lost. As human beings, we must learn who we are and how we ought to live. And that learning comes largely through reading and studying stories. In the absence of great and inspiring stories, too many of us become satisfied (or "wretchedly content") with the treadmill of minimally challenging work and mindless play—day after day, year after year. Moral complacency and political indifference are the result. That leaves the door open for the ambitious and the arrogant to rule over us. If we forget (or are made to forget) "life, liberty, and the pursuit of happiness" and "a city upon a hill," we may well give up on ourselves as Americans: as ordinary men and women doing extraordinary things.

There has never been a great people without great stories. And the great stories of great peoples often dwell on the subject of greatness. They dwell on the subject of plain goodness as well: the goodness that is to be found in love, marriage, duty, the creation of noble and beautiful things. It is patently obvious that the authors of the Common Core are uncomfortable with these great stories of the great and the good. They are plainly uncomfortable with great literature. And they are even more uncomfortable with what might be called the Great American Story, the true tale of a free, moral, and enterprising people pursuing their individual and corporate happiness in a self-governing republic under the rule of law. That entirely unique story in the history of the world has had an ax taken to it in the Common Core English Standards, and the Social Studies Standards are waiting in the wings to finish off what's left of our heritage and our self-understanding.

The authors and promoters of the Common Core are expecting us not to care. They are expecting us not to fight for our stories. They are hoping we shall not notice or not be bothered by the withering away of Shakespeare and Austen and Melville and Twain. The arch-testers are expecting us either to be fooled or to take the cavalier attitude of "What's a little Milton when we have a *twenty-first-century global economy* to worry about? How much can the memory of Washington or Franklin mean to us when we're busy making our students *college ready?*" They are counting on us to trade our poetry gladly for the "literary non-fiction" of training manuals and political propaganda and guilt-inducing multicultural mush. They fully expect us to shrug with thoughtless indifference. Do not be fooled. *The fate of our stories is the fate of the nation.* The alleged Alphas behind the story-killing Common Core know that plain truth if they know nothing else. That is why they are at pains to hide the stories that expose their schemes best. While U.S. General Services Administration, Executive Order 13423: Strengthening Federal Environmental Energy, and Transportation Management is an "exemplar text," the name Aldous Huxley is eerily not to be found in the Common Core English Standards nor in the most popular Common Core British literature textbook. *O brave new core that has such readings in it*!

Chapter One
Insufficient, Utopian, Radical Aims

Before considering any other aspect of the Common Core Standards, we must figure out what the authors of the Common Core think an education is. If the aims the authors of the Common Core put forth are flawed or limited in any way, there is a good chance that their educational program will be flawed and limited. In examining the ends of the Common Core, we must be equally clear on what we think an education is. As useful as a thorough critique might be, if there is no better idea before the public, then the authors of the Common Core win by default. Let us begin our inquiry, then, by examining the aims of education presented by the Common Core. Since everyone loves the expression "critical thinking" these days, let us subject these standards to a little critical thinking.

To their credit, the authors of the Common Core, while they are not completely clear on their aims of education, certainly repeat the same phrases concerning their ends again and again. The principal phrase they use is "career and college readiness." On the first page of the introduction to the English Standards, they use that phrase or some variant at least six times in what cannot be more than seven hundred words. It appears throughout the rest of the document, too. Some people might say that the repetition of the phrase produces clarity. Others might say it makes the document sound like a broken record, or that the phrase is like a bad cough that won't go away. Either way, these are their ends of education: *career and college readiness*.

The other phrase that is only slightly less important is "twenty-first-century globally competitive society." Anyone who pays attention to what is said about education today has heard this phrase countless times. In fact, it seems to be the only thing that most of the politicians and bureaucrats can say when addressing education. "We have to prepare our young men and women for a twenty-first-century global economy," say all the talking heads. The twenty-first-century global economy, you see, is a very scary thing. It is much scarier than the *twentieth-century* global economy that we grew up in (though there is no Soviet Union and no Cold War). So we need to do whatever it takes! Of course, no one ever really defines what the twenty-first-century global economy is.

I wish to make the case that the ends of "college and career readiness" for a "twenty-first-century global economy" are actually shortsighted ends for education. In fact, those who speak in this way are making a fundamental mistake by confusing education with job training. I have to make this case in a way, though, that doesn't come across as either hopelessly professorial (and therefore irrelevant to a twenty-first-century work force) or as horribly snooty, as something straight out of the mouth of Frasier Crane. This is not an easy case to make these days, so I hope the reader will have some patience. The funny thing is that the people in power on the political Left do not have to be convinced of this. Though they talk a great deal about education as jobs training, they send their children to exclusive private schools where they are taught to master language. (Will the Sidwell Friends School where the Obama children attend, as did the Gore children and Chelsea Clinton before them, be adopting the Common Core?) These children go on to exclusive, private colleges and universities where they continue to master language (and are taught how to abuse it for their own purposes). Those who have any semblance of power on the political Right are usually the ones who do not want to hear about true liberal education. They lead the chant for "job skills in a twenty-first-century global economy." In so doing, they undermine their own political positions (and principles if they have any) and sell the minds of their youngest constituents short.

Slyly but unmistakably, the phrase "twenty-first-century global society," whatever others may mean by it, is being used by the authors of the Common Core to bring about radical, progressive ends of education, ends that would not be supported by the majority of parents if they knew what was really going on in the schools. Thus the insufficient and radical ends of education pursued by the Common Core Standards will make the nation's public schools both less and more than they should be: inferior schools academically, and officious, overreaching schools politically and socially. The remedy to these shortsighted and radical ends is a traditional, classical, liberal education.

Before we can explain what a liberal education is, we must expose the flagrant errors and inconsistencies in the present way of thinking. As it turns out, the hackneyed phrases used by the politicians and bureaucrats and modern "educators" are really hollow at the core. First, there is *college and career readiness*. Let us consider for a moment just how limited and narrow those ends are. To be sure, parents want their children to have "good jobs" one day. And many children will end up in college. But should those two purposes be the leading—indeed the only—reasons parents send their children to school—and that children want to be in school? To gain a wider perspective on the possible aims of public education, we should look at a document from our educational past. Here is a selection from the Massachusetts School Law of 1789:

> Whereas the Constitution of this Commonwealth hath declared it to be the duty of the General Court, to provide for the education of youth; and whereas a general dissemination of knowledge and virtue is necessary to the prosperity of every State, and the very existence of a Commonwealth:
>
> Section 1. Be it enacted by the Senate and House of Representatives, in General Court assembled . . . That every town or district within this Commonwealth . . . shall be provided with a School-Master or School-Masters, of good morals, to teach children to read and write, and to instruct them in the English language, as well as in arithmetic, orthography, and decent behaviour . . . And every town or district containing two hundred families, or householders, shall be provided with a grammar School-Master, of good morals, well instructed in the Latin, Greek, and English languages . . .
>
> Section 4. Be it further enacted by the authority aforesaid, That it shall be and it is hereby made the duty of the President, Professors and Tutors of the University at

Cambridge [Harvard], Preceptors and Teachers of Academies, and all other instructors of youth, to take diligent care, and to exert their best endeavours, to impress on the minds of children and youth, committed to their care and instruction, the principles of piety, justice, and a sacred regard to truth, love to their country, humanity, and universal benevolence, sobriety, industry and frugality, chastity, moderation and temperance, and those other virtues which are the ornament of human society, and the basis upon which the Republican Constitution is structured. And it shall be the duty of such instructors, to endeavor to lead those under their care (as their ages and capacities will admit) into a particular understanding of the tendency of the before mentioned virtues, to preserve and perfect a Republican Constitution, and to secure the blessings of liberty, as well as to promote their future happiness; and the tendency of the opposite vices to slavery and ruin.

Wow! What do we make of this formulation of the aims of education compared to the limited way lawmakers and school administrators talk today?

We could spend pages on this document, but let's hit the high points. The first thing to note is the year: 1789. This frame of education was established the same year the national government under the Constitution came into being. This school law, then, put into place a form of schooling that would have been the educational equivalent of the Founding Fathers' view of justice and political order. The Constitution referred to in this document, however, was the Massachusetts Constitution of 1780 written by John Adams. Thus, education was recognized as being a state and local matter. What were the aims of that education? Well, prosperity was one of them. The law clearly defines the prosperity "of every State and *the very existence of a Commonwealth*" to warrant the establishing of what we would now call a public system of education. The House members and Senators of Massachusetts in 1789 were at least as worried about the *political* well-being of their Commonwealth as the economic well-being.

We could, then, easily compare this feature of the 1789 law to the Common Core and recognize nearly the complete absence of any political concerns in the latter. Is that because our political well-being is wholly assured nowadays? Or are schools just no longer institutions that inculcate political wisdom?

Notice what the economic and political well-being of the Commonwealth depends on, according to the Massachusetts law: *knowledge* and *virtue*. Are those the same desired ends that leap off the page of the Common Core documents? Is going to college the same thing as "knowledge"? There is, admittedly, one sentence in the entire introduction to the Common Core English Standards that suggests knowledge is an end to education. I leave it to the reader to decide whether this usage emerges out of the spirit of the document or is an afterthought and window-dressing and a sop to potential traditionalist critics. And what of virtue? Where does that appear in the Common Core? The educational founders of Massachusetts did not just invoke the word *virtue* generally as we often do today with the word *character* or, more often, *values*. They spelled out what they meant by virtue. Imagine a public document written today with the words "piety, justice, and a sacred regard to truth, love to their country, humanity . . . chastity, moderation and temperance." How many different activist groups would come to the fore to attack such language? Do people even use or understand this vocabulary anymore? Chastity? Temperance? Huh? Do not fail to notice that it is the duty of both schoolteachers and professors at Harvard to inculcate such virtues. Are piety, love of country, and chastity currently on the academic menu at Harvard? Are they taught in the suburban public schools of the Boston area?

We should just briefly mention two other particulars about the Massachusetts School Law. The first is that it provides for instructors in Greek and Latin. How might teaching those two "dead languages" lead to young people having knowledge and virtue, which in turn secure the prosperity and well-being of a commonwealth? The Common Core utters not a word on the teaching of Latin or Greek, though classical schools around the nation are proving once again that knowledge of classical languages leads to the mastery of our native tongue. Second, we should notice that the 1789 lawmakers tell us what happens when these ends are not pursued, when young people do not acquire the ennobling virtues that "preserve and perfect a Republican

21

Constitution": *slavery* and *ruin*. Now we could play the modern, historicist card and say that the lawmakers of Massachusetts were being hyperbolic since they had just been through a revolution and all, and people were much more moralistic in those days, but it's not the sort of thing we should worry about now. Or, we could take to heart this lesson taught to us by these Founding Fathers of America and of American public education, a lesson pertaining to a fundamental principle of commonwealths—whether in 1789 or the twenty-first century. Knowledge and virtue must be the ends of education, and if those ends are not attained, the future of our civil society is put in jeopardy. Should we not still take the words *slavery* and *ruin* seriously today? The authors of the Common Core do have a political objective. As we shall see below, it is not remotely close to the political objective of the Founding Fathers.

Before getting into the nitty-gritty of the Common Core documents, we should pause to notice that the aim of "college and career readiness" turns education into an instrument rather than an end in itself. Doing so is a mistake that the Founding Fathers never made, nor has ever any liberally educated person. Saying that the aim of education is college and career readiness implies that once we have gone to college and gotten a job, we have practically done with our education. This is tantamount to saying we have done with our political, moral, aesthetic, and, in general, *human* lives. We are now just cogs in a machine called the twenty-first-century global economy. And, as mere workers, we have no business in the politics and culture of the nation, except to receive what others have thought and done and written for us. Maybe that is exactly what the Founding Fathers meant by *slavery*.

The next perplexity to consider is whether college and career readiness are the same things. If the school's job is to get students ready for college—which the students will attend for four or more years (and pay a lot of money for)—wouldn't it be the college's responsibility, at least in part, to make students *career* ready? Or might it be the case that the college is supposed to offer a "higher" education, and the professions and careers will provide well-educated college graduates the training relevant to each occupation? Either way, it would not be left to the *schools* to make students *career* ready but instead only *college* ready. By lumping college readiness and career readiness together so casually, without stopping to explain either one, the authors of the

Common Core throw us off the scent of what constitutes genuine college readiness.

But, you may say, not every student goes to college. Many students after graduating high school go straight out into the work force. That is true. So is "career ready" really a euphemism to describe students who will not go to college? If that is the case, then we must face a question that is suppressed by the catchy phrase "college and career ready." Does making students ready for a *career* compromise preparing them for *college*? If so, if these are two separate things, then should there be two different plans or curricula: a "career plan" and a "college plan"?

The Common Core documents are silent on the matter. The authors of the Common Core want us to believe that college readiness and career readiness are one and the same, even though their descriptions of careers do not sound like anything one would ever do in college. There could be a hidden agenda here. Reliable people think that the ultimate purpose of the Common Core is to corral students into their "appropriate occupations," and that some of the data that will be kept on children starting in the early grades will create a system of "tracking" children. The schools would not be willing to tell us about that now, and the Common Core authors deny those plans. Yet the public high schools have been tracking students for decades, as do the elementary schools through their levelled reading programs. Should we be surprised to learn that the Common Core will track children through technology and an inferior curriculum?

I must state emphatically that I am against programs that track students into college-bound and career-bound "paths." I am against them for two reasons—one philosophical and one based on experience. The philosophical reason is that we are all human beings and American citizens and therefore everyone in this country deserves a genuinely liberal education up through high school. The reason based on experience comes from my own family and from my running a classical school for seven years and helping set up other such schools around the nation. In the age of our grandparents, most people did not go to college. Whereas my paternal grandfather went to college and then to medical school, my grandmother graduated high school and then went to work (in part supporting my grandfather while in medical school). Though my grandfather was smart and certainly knew things, my grandmother seemed to know *everything*: language, books, geography, history, baseball statistics, you name it. Reading on her own no doubt added to what she knew, but she had the advantage of living at a time when graduating high school still meant something because students still learned things while there. Similarly, not all the students I have taught at one of the most rigorous classical schools in the country went on to college. Some students did not have either the academic abilities or the inclination for college. Some wanted to get a job right after school and go to college later. Others went into the military. Yet these students worked hard in school and loved having discussions about the great things that happen in great books. They learned far more history, science, language, and math than they would have in most college "core" classes. In my opinion, a genuine liberal education at the high school level is just as important for students who will *not* go to college as for those who will. It is relatively easy to pick up job skills and training at a trade school or on the job itself. Yet it is becoming increasingly difficult to obtain a liberal education—even in college.

The Common Core's conflation of "college and career readiness" matters. The undue emphasis the Common Core places on *career* readiness reveals that skills-based training, rather than liberal education, is where the story-killers' hearts really lie. The direction they are taking the study of English already indicates that "as new evidence emerges" they will increasingly turn education into training, learning into "information," and students into future "workers" sitting in front of computer screens for most of the day. That spirit is evident in statements like this one on page 4:

> Most of the required reading in college and workforce training programs is informational in structure and challenging in content.

Once again we see the conflation of college and "workforce" training (with no evidence at all to justify it). No one bothers to ask the obvious questions. Do you mean to say that in order to prepare students for the modern workplace we should re-make schools in the image of the modern workplace? Rather than teaching them to read with Kipling and Poe and Twain and Stevenson, should we hand them factory and office manuals to read à la *Brave New World*? Those questions would lead to the follow-up question: If workforce training is what we were really after, then why would we not turn our children at age thirteen over to industry? Presumably, the leaders in industry know a lot more about what constitutes the *training* needed to make young men and women members of a "productive workforce." Why wait until age eighteen? These are questions the authors of the Common Core will never answer simply because they expose their entire program as being utterly illiberal and shortsighted. They will also not ask them since they know what the answers are. The biggest complaint of industry is *not* that young people come into the workforce without proper *training*. Rather, the biggest complaint against today's workers (other than their lack of a work ethic) is that they cannot read on anything close to an adult level.

The fatal flaw in the reasoning behind the Common Core (specifically the requiring of so many "informational texts") consists in the unsupported claim that to prepare today's students for tomorrow's jobs, we must teach students to read using the kinds of materials they will most likely read on the job. There is, admittedly, a certain plausibility behind this argument. Unless you work at a publishing house or are an English professor, you are not given stories to read at work. Would that we could all read gripping novels and get paid for it. Nonetheless, the notion that young people should learn to read by reading the kinds of things they will one day read at work is mere supposition. We can prove the opposite by looking at the history of literacy in this or any country in the Western world.

The places where literacy has been highest have had two characteristics: high church attendance combined with emphasis on the Bible and widely available schooling with an emphasis on traditional learning. The two places historians often point to that had nearly universal literacy are colonial Massachusetts and eighteenth-century Scotland. Colonial Pennsylvania also had high rates of literacy. Common sense tells us why these societies achieved high literacy. Not only were the methods of teaching reading then far better than those widely used today, but people actually had a book to read. And in what does that book consist? The Bible is mostly composed of *stories*. There is also law and poetry and letters that are highly theological. The bulk of the Bible, though, is devoted to stories or histories. On the surface, these stories are fairly simple. Most any child can master the basic facts. Read closely or intensively, however, the Bible is an extremely complex and multi-layered literary work. Large, highly philosophical commentaries have been written on Genesis alone, one brilliant one by a modern scholar who admitted to thinking there was not very much to the book before he started digging into it.[14]

Alongside the reading of the Bible in Western and American education has been the classical tradition, the study of seminal Greek and Roman works, usually read in their original languages. These, too, are stories, whether literature or histories. One famous book, Plutarch's *Lives of the Noble Greeks and Romans*, was what we might call the Western world's bestselling history textbook for centuries. It was the Founding Father's primer in understanding human action. Plutarch was read by boys *before* they went to college, and they read these biographies throughout their lives. The obvious question to ask is: Was the generation of the Founding Fathers better readers than our generation?

There are probably three ways to consider that question, and two in particular concern our present inquiry. First, which society achieved the highest rate of overall literacy, that is, how many people could read? There will always be a great deal of debate about that question because it is hard to compare two societies separated by two centuries. We can consider the two other factors, though. In which society does the *average* reader read better? And in which society do advanced readers read better? In these latter respects, it seems obvious to me that colonial and Revolutionary Americans were far more literate. The best way to figure that out is simply to look at what both the average Americans and more advanced readers used to read and then compare those readings to what Americans read today.

Well, that comparison is not that hard. All we have to do is take one of these "texts" from the colonial period and see how well modern Americans comprehend it. Plutarch's *Lives* is still in print, so you can test your own ability to follow a "complex" narrative of an historical figure—such as Pericles or Caesar—by reading one, realizing that Plutarch would have been read by fifteen-year-olds.[15] Or give a fifteen-year-old Plutarch's life of Caesar to read to see how he does with it. Further, we can easily examine the articles

---

[14] Leon R. Kass, *The Beginning of Wisdom: Reading Genesis* (New York: Free Press, 2003). Preface.
[15] Plutarch's *Lives* is, not surprisingly, *not* one of the books recommended in Appendix B of the English Standards.

that were written in newspapers in the eighteenth century (to include Franklin's *Pennsylvania Gazette* and *The Federalist*) and compare them to today's newspaper articles. Which are more complex? There is no contest. Today's students struggle with Plutarch. Students today, even those who go to church regularly, struggle with the deeper meaning behind the prima-facie "simple" stories from the Bible. Getting them to understand a *Federalist* paper is like pulling teeth. And clearly eighteenth-century journalism is written at a far higher level than the simplistic "pieces" cranked out by the modern media, which must be written at the sixth-grade level so that newspapers do not lose half their audience. Ditto for political speeches: President Obama's 2012 State of the Union Address registered at an eighth-grade level.[16]

The things I just mentioned were read by *average* readers in the Revolutionary period. If you want to know what the "advanced" readers were capable of, then take out a speech or philosophical work of Cicero and read it—*in Latin*.

Yet the authors of the Common Core insist that students should read far more recently written, *informational* texts, such as newspaper articles. In other words, we have a long history of young people being brought to a very high degree of literacy through reading *stories* in their youth. Yet to counter the declines in both average and advanced reading over the last half-century, brought about by our abandoning the serious teaching of those stories, we want to use the same "texts" (articles written at a sixth-grade level) that are a product of that decline. Ergo, the literacy for the twentieth-first-century global economy will be built upon the cracking foundation of our present semi-literacy. Was there not once a famous story-teller who said something about not building a house upon sand?

What is equally clear is that the authors of the Common Core have no understanding whatsoever of what makes students *college* ready. They do not really say what a college is. They quote no study, no college president, no college professor confirming that the nation's colleges are crying out for students to read more "informational" as opposed to "literary" texts. They even overlook studies that have been done that show students who are avid readers of literature in high school perform better on college exams

---

[16] Byron Tau, *Politico*, 1/25/12. On the scale used, this was the third lowest score of any State of the Union address since 1934.

and in their college classes.[17]   These studies are simply validating common sense and the practice of good schools over the centuries. I know this to be true based on the performance of my freshmen every year. The students who can really read great books, students who have been to a classical school or home-schooled with a classical curriculum, take to reading complex historical documents and even difficult works of philosophy like fish to water. The students who have not carefully studied great works of literature struggle with these difficult readings.[18] In short, the authors of the Common Core are simply wrong about what constitutes true college readiness, and they may not be levelling with us on what they really mean by career readiness.

Admittedly, there is a difficulty in making this argument. To many in the general public (and most of the politicians) the debate over literary texts and "informational texts" seems like six of one and half a dozen of another. Won't they both be complex texts? Can't young people learn to read using a variety of sources? We shall deal with that argument head-on a little later. For now, we should realize that the texts that will be taught in schools, and the ways in which they will be taught, will not deliver the much talked-about and never explained "critical thinking."   Recently, I saw a specimen of the future when I visited a fifth-grade class in a Michigan school. The teacher was using one of the new textbooks pointing towards the 50/50 distribution of literary and informational texts. It was also clear that the readings were chosen for their brevity so as to reproduce testing conditions. The reading *du jour* was a sappy, forgettable piece about the training of seeing-

---

[17] "Reading Between the Lines: What the ACT Reveals About College Readiness in Reading," 2006. See esp. pp. 6-7. This study is clouded with some of the same opaque reasoning found in the Common Core documents. Nonetheless, the list of qualities found in a complex text described in this section and in the body of the study around page 17 describes more accurately the attributes of serious literature. The quotations of Dr. Sandra Stotsky are also helpful. See also the 2009 PISA (Program for International Student Assessment) results. Two clear trends seem particularly telling. First, girls across countries read better than boys, and part of the reason can be attributed to girls reading more fiction than boys. Second, students of either sex who read fiction for pleasure become better readers. OECD (2010), *PISA 2009 Results: Executive Summary* and OECD (2011), *Education at a Glance*, 100-103. The study indicates that "the strongest readers" are "those who read fiction." I thank Erin Tuttle for pointing me to these studies.
[18] I refer to students in public high schools who may be assigned great books but are not really taught to read them carefully and for their intrinsic meaning. I shall discuss this phenomenon in chapter six.

eye dogs. The text indicated that the seeing-eye dogs were trained to stop at red lights. After reading this revelation, the teacher unleashed her great exercise in critical thinking. "Okay, class, why does the seeing-eye dog stop at red lights?" The painfully obvious answer was, "So the blind lady does not walk out into traffic and get hit by a car." The class was dead silent. Finally, after trying various hints, the teacher told them the answer. This was not a case of the children not being able to figure out this marvel of low-level thinking. Rather, they were bored out of their minds. Meanwhile, at classical schools around the country, fifth-grade students are having Socratic discussions on great works of literature, learning intensive grammar, and sometimes already starting formal Latin. Which students will be more college and career ready seven years hence?

For all the lip service in the Common Core documents about making students "college and career ready," the approach being taken will do neither. Rather than focusing almost exclusively on these byproducts of a good education, they should spend more time on the education itself. A large part of a good education consists in learning to read, to love, and to invest oneself in good stories. The Common Core's pedestrian preoccupation with what will happen when children turn nineteen undermines the powers of imagination and of observation that are essential to good reading. One is reminded of the famous poem by Robert Frost, "Stopping by Woods on a Snowy Evening":

> Whose woods these are I think I know
> His house is in the village though;
> He will not see me stopping here
> To watch his woods fill up with snow.
>
> My little horse must think it queer
> To stop without a farmhouse near
> Between the woods and frozen lake
> The darkest evening of the year.
>
> He gives his harness bells a shake
> To ask if there is some mistake.
> The only other sound's the sweep
> Of easy wind and downy flake.

The woods are lovely, dark and deep.
But I have promises to keep,
And miles to go before I sleep,
And miles to go before I sleep.

Human beings in general, and children in particular, find happiness in watching "woods fill up with snow," that is, appreciating the beauty that is in nature. The Common Core, though, plays the part of the horse in our educational scenario. The horse cannot see why a man would want to stop and look at something with no purpose, "without a farmhouse near." So the animal "gives his harness bells a shake," as do the authors of the Common Core with their constant incantation of "college and career readiness." Driven onward by the constant threat of standardized testing, told incessantly by their worried teachers that they "have promises to keep" (doing well on the standardized tests, getting a job, going to college), the children are not invited to look at the woods, "lovely, dark and deep." Thus they miss out on the beautiful things in the world. When they do turn nineteen, colleges and employers find out that they do not read very well. Why not? Because schools have not given the students anything worth reading nor taught them how to appreciate things that are lovely, dark and deep. Their minds and souls lie dormant.

The paradox of modern education is that the more emphasis we place on college and career readiness, the less college and career ready students become. This paradox makes no sense to the modern, data-driven, shortsighted, utilitarian educators. We mentioned a storyteller who once warned us about the house built upon sand. He also said something about finding one's life by losing one's life.[19] That lesson applied to education means that in order to find oneself in the world—knowing how the world works, being able to get a job—one must first *lose oneself* in stories. One must learn how to read stories before learning how to "read the world," so to speak. To fixate children's minds (and teachers' minds) on the mirage of college and career readiness, as the Common Core clearly means to do, is not only a case of putting the cart before the horse, but also of putting the horse in charge of the cart and of the man supposedly driving the cart, to draw on

---

[19] Matthew 10:39 and elsewhere. But shhh! . . . we can't bring Him up in a public-school setting.

Frost's poem. Doing so reveals a failure to understand the human things and a complete ignorance of reading and liberal education. Reading is a profoundly *human* enterprise: it requires the whole man or woman or child, not just the part that wants a job in the distant future. The Common Core will *never* make a nation of readers by marching to the dreary drumbeat of college and career readiness.

Let us turn now to the other favorite, hackneyed, and unexplained phrase of the day: the dreaded *twenty-first-century global economy*. The first thing we must recognize is that this phrase is used repeatedly in order to scare us. If the *twenty-first century* (which we cannot predict) is looming out there, then we will do everything we can (and spend as much money as we are told to) to prevent it from eating us alive. The phrase is also used in order to make us look "forward" in our notions of education, never to the practices or wisdom of the past. When we have the twenty-first century in front of us, why would we ever look back to the eighteenth or nineteenth centuries, or even the twentieth— ancient history essentially? When we examine the phrase closely, however, we see its emptiness. When has the future *not* been scary? In 1776, when the Founding Fathers pledged their lives, their fortunes, and their sacred honor in declaring "That these United Colonies are, and of Right ought to be Free and Independent States"? In 1860, when Abraham Lincoln was elected president, on the eve of the Civil War? In 1914, before the U.S. was drawn into two world wars, sunk into a fifteen-year Depression, and, coming out of these events, later caught up in an unpredictable Cold War, facing a hostile adversary armed with both millions of soldiers and a large nuclear arsenal? Oftentimes looking to the past makes looking to the future seem less scary.

The phrase "global economy" is equally misleading. Its use implies that America has never really been in a global economy, that it is something new and different, so we need a new kind of education. No one pauses to consider America's long history in the global economy. In fact, America has no history that is not a part of the global economy. When in fourteen hundred and ninety-two Columbus sailed the ocean blue, he was doing so as an attempt to find a shorter passage to the Indies and the Orient. In other words, he was trying to speed up trade and communications in a Fifteenth-Century Global Economy! In the seventeenth century when English settlers came to America, they did so for two main reasons: religious freedom and economic advancement. The latter, requiring trade with the mother country, took place in a Seventeenth-Century Global Economy! The Seven Years' War that resulted in the massive debt that resulted in the taxes that resulted in the American Revolution? Yep, the Eighteenth-Century Global Economy. And so on. The phrase "twenty-first-century global economy" actually says nothing about our future. It speaks volumes on our ignorance of the past.

Of course, in addition to trying to scare us, the educational demagogues who employ the phrase "twenty-first-century global economy" also reveal their idolatry of technology and "information." On the first page of the English Standards, we are told, "As a natural outgrowth of meeting the charge to define college and career readiness, the Standards also lay out a vision of what it means to be a literate person in the twenty-first century." That is an astonishing statement. It claims that the literacy of the present is different from the literacy of the past and implies that the literacy of the past is outmoded; the old literacy has gone the way of the horse-and-buggy. This sentiment is found throughout the document. On the very next page we find a sentence beginning with the phrase "To be ready for college, workforce training, and life in a technological society," etc.

Many people simply go along with this kind of language. They see technological changes around them. Ways of communicating are very different now. So everything must presumably change, including education. This pervasive spirit is the modern hubris, or at least one important branch of the modern hubris. Right now the big move in schools is to provide every child with a laptop or a Kindle. Supposedly we can click or web-surf our way into twenty-first century literacy. The notion of a newer, different, and superior form of literacy exposes a futuristic, technological Utopianism. It puts a blind faith in machines at the expense of the human mind.

Though it would take perhaps another book to make the entire case against the modern idolatry of technology in education, we should outline some of the fundamental mistakes. First, common sense attests that those of us who learned to read and write way back in the twentieth century did not all of a sudden become illiterate in 2000. Maybe the Y2K scare was also supposed to bring a great crash in the nation's reading, but it didn't. The only crisis in literacy has been the result of schools not teaching students to read properly since about 1960. Furthermore, as an antidote to our hubris, we should imagine the result of historical figures coming to our century to measure the *standards* of our "twenty-first-century literacy." How would most of us, to include the supposedly educated, fare in a conversation with any of the Founding Fathers? We can simply read their writings to see how that conversation would go. On the other hand, how many of the Founders would be at a loss for very long in our world? Do we really think it would take Benjamin Franklin much time to figure out how a computer works? After sitting down with one for a week, he would likely tell us ten improvements we could make. Wouldn't he, armed with an arsenal of clever sayings and his own genius for turning a phrase, own *twitter* after a month? As for the quality of people's writing in our twenty-first century, try this little test. Read all of the Common Core English Standards. Then read Benjamin Franklin's essay "Proposals Relating to the Education of Youth in Pensilvania." Which is a better example of writing, The Common Core Standards or Franklin's Proposals? Which is more "research-based"? Which would lead to a better education? Well, Franklin's academy was the embryo of the University of Pennsylvania. The verdict is still out on the Common Core. The point is, even with all of modern technology at their disposal, self-proclaimed school reformers can still put forth a poorly-written, illogical, confusing, inelegant monstrosity.

Besides twenty-first-century literacy being in no way superior to (or even different from) pre-twenty-first-century literacy, or just life in general in the years B. M.,[20] the call to revolutionize the nation's classrooms with technology must be thought highly suspect. To begin with, we have a demonstrable track record of things going wrong when schools embrace any new technology. Take math. Young people today cannot do simple arithmetic in their heads. The people who work at fast-food restaurants (overwhelmingly the young) are perplexed whenever we hand them extra change so as to get an even dollar back. You may think such innumeracy is confined to fast-food clerks. Not so. I was once buying a stamp in a college mail room that only had a change box rather than a register. I gave the student working there a dollar to buy a single stamp. He fumbled around for a while. He could

---

[20] Before Microsoft.

not figure out how much change I should get back. The older lady who ran the mail room was as astonished as I was. On my way out, I could not resist. "I hope you're not a math major," I said. "No. Finance," was his reply.

Why is that? Why can young people not do simple arithmetic in their heads? There are two reasons: the way math has been taught in this country for about forty years (made worse after the math wars in the Nineties)—and *calculators*. The two reasons go hand in hand. The teachers do a poor job of teaching math from books that have very little math in them, and they let their students use calculators to solve the simplest problems. Forget about fractions. It is much easier to convert fractions to a decimal on the calculator. It is, of course, not the calculator's fault that young people do not know arithmetic. It *is* most certainly the schools' fault for allowing students to let the machines do their thinking for them. We have forgotten that long before there were calculators, there was this powerful force called the human mind: the original calculator.

An even more devastating experiment with technology in the schools has been television. Hardly anybody now remembers the outlandish promises made back in the Sixties and Seventies regarding how television would revolutionize America's schools. Supposedly, teachers would integrate interesting, path-breaking "programming" into their lessons, combining the insights of world-renowned scholars with more hands-on instruction in the classroom. Of course, anyone who went to school in the Seventies knows how laughable these promises seem now. What really happened was that teachers turned on the televisions and then sat behind their desks. The programming was not that spectacular. So the students learned less than their parents had, much less than their grandparents. Yet no one has bothered to follow up on whether all the promises of revolution have come to fruition. Obviously, no one with any authority over schools ever said we need to take those televisions out of the classrooms and insist that teachers get back to serious teaching.[21] The televisions are still there. Too often the teaching is not.

Our preliminary reports about the new technology's effects on the classroom indicate that computers are a lot more like television

---

[21] The effects of television on education and the nation's thinking in general have been addressed by, inter alia, Neil Postman in *Amusing Ourselves to Death*.

than anyone is willing to admit. I shall offer a couple of illustrations and allow the reader compare them to her own. A year or so ago one of my students told me what high school really amounts to these days. "The teachers are so lazy!" she said. "They put everything on Power Point, then sit behind a desk clicking away." What she meant was that the teachers do not teach. I saw a specimen of this "clicking" in a freshman honors English class in an affluent suburban district. The class appeared to be one of the first taught on *Romeo and Juliet*. The students were watching the large screen in front of them. On display were selections from the movie *Romeo + Juliet* starring Leonardo DiCaprio. These scenes were punctuated by supposedly alluring and thought-provoking phrases that the teacher had spliced in, such as "Was it Love or Passion?" and "Too Young for Love?" The most salient point of the entire episode lay in one small fact that most people would not have noticed. Not a single student in that class had a copy of Shakespeare's *Romeo and Juliet* out on the desk in front of him. Now some people will maintain that this class, after such a powerful introduction to the play, will go on to have intense, energetic, thought-provoking discussions about this memorable tragedy. But that is a scene that I have yet to see coming out of, to quote a phrase from the arch-testers, the "setting, characterization, or plot" of the modern American classroom.

The truth is the introduction of computers and other forms of the new technology into the classroom has done nothing to improve students' learning. It is true that art teachers can now much more easily show their classes great paintings and sculptures by using the internet. It is likewise true that history teachers can employ actual speeches of Churchill or Reagan using videos found on the web. Ninety percent of the time, though, that is not how the computer is being used. Back in the late Nineties we were told that a new kind of classroom discussion would unfold. While teachers were presenting material to their classes, students at their individual "workstations" would be scouring the web for further "information" to supplement their teachers' lessons. From their "research" the students would come up with amazing questions that might either add to their fellow classmates' knowledge or even stump the teacher, thus leading to more research. Of course, it took about a week for sensible teachers to see that these promises were a high-tech windmill. What the students really do behind their computers is surf the web for things unrelated to the discussion at hand (often requiring family-friendly safety filters) and enter into chat rooms with each other or with students in other classes. The "information" passing back and forth among the students is not something along the lines of, "Mr. Testprep forgot to mention the Zimmerman Telegram in the causes of America entering World War I," but rather, "This is boring, dude."

The youngest children are not spared some highly questionable effects of technology. Recently, some early elementary teachers were telling me how often their students speak in text-ese: BFF, TMI, and host of other three-letter codes. One teacher said that she caught a kindergarten student saying "WTF." The little girl on examination had no idea what she was saying. WTF indeed! The human language, before our very eyes and ears, is being reduced from words to letters as we resort to communicating by little more than high-tech smoke signals. Yet the arch-testers of the Common Core champion the use of the technological elixir that cures all illnesses and heals all wounds without even pausing to warn us of the potential side effects. We are meant to be ecstatic over how technology will enhance the "new" literacy. We are not invited to consider how much technology is compromising the old literacy. Least of all are we supposed to realize that the remedy for our growing twenty-first-century *illiteracy* is traditional, nineteenth-century education.

I could continue to multiply anecdotes on the counterproductive effects of introducing technology into the classroom in all but the most controlled situations. But the burden of proof should be on the technocrats. They have been making promises now for more than two decades. Where are the results? Where have students been taught to read or write or calculate (in the old-fashioned sense) or to reason better because of the computer? Little wonder that reports coming out of Silicon Valley indicate that children of the technology crowd are actually attending intentionally low-tech schools. As a computer programmer in Colorado once told me, "What you could teach my daughter to do on a computer in a semester, I could teach her in a long weekend. But I can't teach her Latin." The reason the new technology has failed to revolutionize the classroom, just as the television failed several decades before, is very simple. Children are not machines. They can be taught. They cannot be programmed. The idea that we can take lots of "information" and input or download or upload it into children's brains, instead of creating a human conversation between the teacher and the students about human beings and the nature of the universe, is pure, utopian cyber-fantasy.

Common sense, however, seldom prevails in public schools. Technology is now all the rage. In the Common Core documents, the arch-testers must be somewhat cool in their rhetoric. They have to try hard to present their testing and curricular regime as the best of the old and the best of the new. Their supporters, however, are not so coy. The State of Washington's Superintendent of Public Instruction applauds the Common Core, on the home page dedicated to the Core, as follows:

> Common Core is a real-world approach to learning and teaching . . . The standards require a practical, real-life application of knowledge that prepares Washington students for college, work, and life.[22]

The front group Stand for Children, responsible for the Get to the Core website, is even more emphatic.

> Do you know if your children are prepared for college and beyond?
>
> WE LIVE IN A DIFFERENT WORLD . . . Globally connected, technologically driven, fast paced—and yet as a country, we haven't changed what our kids are studying or how they think in over thirty years, while other countries around the world have modernized their approach to education.
>
> Our school system is built for the 1950s, NOT THE 21ST CENTURY.
>
> **Let's Get to the Core.**

Those people back in the Fifties, we are led to believe, were *slower-paced*. Therefore, they must have been less globally-

---

[22] Office of the Superintendent of Public Instruction, State of Washington, www.k12.wa.us/corestandards, accessed 20 June 2013.

connected and slower thinkers and readers. We shall forget the fact that many of those fathers living in the Fifties had stormed the beaches at Normandy and at Guadalcanal. "We live in a different world!" say the education radicals. Yet we haven't changed the way kids THINK in THIRTY years.

There are three things offensive about such fantastic claims, other than their revealing a small-souled chronological arrogance. The first is their falsehood. The public schools have been trying to get students to think in "new ways" for the past fifty years. In fact, the Fifties were probably the last time that the majority of children in the country could get a decent education. The schools have experimented with the way children learn to read. They have experimented several times with the way children learn math. They have given up on teaching history and instead teach "social studies." And public schools have been tampering with the quality and amount of literature taught for some time. *Every* experiment has been a disaster. The response on the part of the education establishment has never been to return to the traditional ways of teaching and learning before the failed experiment but always to come up with a new, untested, more outlandish experiment.

The second offense of this attitude is the assumption that the nature of thinking itself changes radically over time. Since many aspects of our lives have improved, our thinking must be different, according to the radicals. Education has always been the reverse, however. True education consists in both discoveries and certain models of thinking that great minds have left to posterity and that we must master in order to understand the world in any age. One and one always equal two. Euclid's geometry is one such model of clear thinking. Not only does Euclid teach us how to think about figures; he also teaches us how to argue rationally in general. Two thousand years after Euclid lived, one of his most diligent pupils, a self-taught man from rural Illinois called Lincoln, used Euclidian-style proofs to teach the rest of the nation why slavery was a moral and political evil. Anyone graduating high school today, in our twenty-first-century global economy, who is able to think like either Euclid or Lincoln, would be a powerful force in the world. The real problem is that hardly any students can think in this way, precisely because of the nonsense promoted by the progressive educrats over the past half-century, and now by their new bedfellows, the progressive technocrats behind the Common Core.

For all their talk of college readiness, they are having students learn geometry without requiring them to study proofs!

The third offensive thing about such an attitude is that it reveals more than an urge to change education every thirty years. It reveals the desire to change *everything*, especially what children think about the world. The people of the Fifties, you see, are the enemies. Far from being the time of wholesome families as portrayed in *Leave It to Beaver*, the Fifties were the height of racism, sexism, narrow-minded patriotism, capitalism, stuffy moralism, and pent-up sexual frustration. The authors of the Common Core would deny that their program is an intentionally radical political effort. As we shall see, political *change* may be its chief objective.

No doubt certain well-meaning people who want to see education improved will balk at what must come across as anti-technological, anti-modern, Ivory-Tower critiques of progressive educators who are "doing the best they can" in this confusing, changing world. Moreover, the workplace has changed in the last thirty years, so why shouldn't the classroom change as well? To answer those objections for the moment, we should simply ponder the claim "we haven't changed . . . what our kids think in the last thirty years." In place of "what our kids think," consider inserting different phrases to weigh whether this statement can apply across the board. We haven't changed *child-rearing* in the last thirty years. We need a new way of raising children. We haven't changed *love* in the last thirty years. We need to find a new way to love. We haven't changed *fatherhood* in the last thirty years. We need a new kind of father for the twenty-first century. We are still stuck in the past in matters of religious *faith*. We need a new way to worship God in our fast-paced global economy. Our *government* is outmoded; the Constitution is a drag on our productivity. We need to find a new way to do politics in the twenty-first century. We haven't updated *friendship* in the last half century. People still want to hang out and talk to each other. Shouldn't we come up with a better way of friending people, starting with using the word *friend* as a verb? (Oops. Facebook beat me to that one.) *Marriage* is hopelessly out of date. Don't we need to come up with a better *platform* for men and women, you know, to be together?

The assumption of the authors of the Common Core is that since the workplace and technology are constantly changing in the "twenty-first-century global economy," schools must also change with the times. One of the assumptions embedded in that argument is that people are also changing along with technology. When we apply that logic to real human institutions, we must pause. Have the "changes" in the family over the last forty years led to greater happiness? Have the recent changes in politics led to more liberty, justice, and prosperity for the nation? Is marriage stronger or weaker now than it was in the Fifties? In the case of church, is that not a place where we go to learn about events that happened not fifty or sixty years ago but two thousand or more years ago? So the obvious question becomes, are schools essentially the future workplace, where we must train children in all the latest techniques and technology? Or does schooling belong to that class of things that does not get "updated" every week: the family, politics, church, friendship—human institutions and relations for which we must be initiated into certain *permanent* ways of thinking lest we be cast adrift on a sea of moral, cultural, and political uncertainty? I get the sneaking suspicion that the authors of the Common Core, who tell us how to shape our critical thinking for a twenty-first-century global economy (without ever having run a school), do not want these human questions to be asked.

Thus, the phrase "twenty-first-century global economy" (or "society") can be used to tout two parts of the Common Core agenda: its technological Utopianism and its political radicalism. Obviously, the authors of the Common Core must be much more careful with their efforts to influence the political views of the nation's young people. Although there are several indications of this mischief being set up in the Common Core documents, not until we look into actual textbooks will we be able to prove our case entirely. Yet even the introduction contains the seeds of the Common Core's progressive aims. These aims are hinted at in the following paragraph:

> Students appreciate that the twenty-first-century classroom and workplace are settings in which people from often widely divergent cultures and who represent diverse experiences and perspectives must learn and work together. Students actively seek to understand other perspectives and cultures through reading and

listening, and they are able to communicate effectively with people of varied backgrounds. . . . Through reading great classic and contemporary works of literature representative of a variety of periods, cultures, and worldviews, students can vicariously inhabit worlds and have experiences much different from their own.[23]

On the one hand, there is a strong element of truth in that statement. Both the American classroom and the American workplace are more "diverse" now than they were decades ago. Obviously, it helps to know someone's background in order to relate to that person. Nonetheless, there is an extremely popular ideology that holds sway on college campuses and among intellectuals nowadays called "multiculturalism" that celebrates "diversity" as the highest good. Rather than drawing on the American traditions of equality under the law, opportunity for all, and judging people by the content of their character rather than by the color of their skin, multiculturalists debunk (overtly when they can, covertly when they must) America, her history, and her unique place in the world as a leader in freedom and justice. The architects of a system of curriculum, testing, and teaching in American public schools cannot come out and say that they are fervent multiculturalists and despise our great American tradition. Nonetheless, they might be able to de-emphasize and subtly undermine the classic works of literature while they celebrate the contemporary ones in such a way that America's youth develop in literature classes a chip on their shoulder about our tradition. Achieving that goal would certainly make students "college ready" in the sense that what passes for higher learning in this country has become a training ground for radicalism. At the moment, we can do no more than point out that the Common Core's most admirable statement about literature ("vicariously inhabit worlds and have experiences") comes in the context of diversity, and that there is no trace in the Common Core documents that its authors wish to create *American* citizens well-rehearsed in *American* traditions of self-government, opportunity, and moral excellence. Quite the reverse.

---

[23] Common Core State Standards for English, etc., Introduction, p. 7.

Anyone who thinks I have travelled too far afield or have jumped to conclusions about the true aims of the Common Core should read one further phrase found on the opening page of the English Standards. That phrase is more alarming and more revealing than all the jargon about a new literacy and college and career readiness.

The Standards are intended to be a living work: as new and better evidence emerges, the Standards will be revised accordingly.

These words are an echo of what progressive politicians and intellectuals have said about "the living Constitution" for the last one-hundred years: a Constitution that they assert is not a fixed touchstone for all law and the government of the nation, but a document that can become most anything in the hands of "experts" and politicians who do not want to be bound by explicit principles and restraints and safeguards for the people's liberty. The authors of the Common Core are forecasting that their program will change over the next ten, twenty, forty years. In other words, what legislators vote on today will be different tomorrow and unrecognizable decades from now. But the same people will be in charge. What will be the new and better "evidence" that emerges? Who will get to decide what constitutes better "evidence"? Who will do the "revising"? If, as is currently the case, schools that adopt a traditional, classical curriculum perform far better *in college* (to say nothing of the Common Core's standardized exams) than students who are subjected this Brave New Core, will that new evidence lead to the Common Core reverting to a more classical curriculum? Don't bet on it.

In accepting the Common Core, which was adopted by state legislatures with very little conversation about either our world or education, we are simply supposed to nod in agreement to certain prescriptions following from questionable assumptions: that we need some new form of education to make young men and women "college and career ready," that we live in a fast-paced "twenty-first-century global economy," that we must accordingly acquire a "twenty-first-century literacy," that we have to gear education towards an increasingly technological world, and that *change* is the order of the day. None of these assumptions is ever explained or proven. If we ask anyone to explain them, we are given blank stares. In short, the proponents of the Common Core do not want us to engage in any "critical thinking." The computers (the *reading machines*, to quote Huxley) and the experts can do the thinking for us.

Chapter Two
Higher Ends of Education
and of Stories

If college and career readiness in a twenty-first-century global economy are flawed and insufficient ends of education and, specifically, of the study of literature, then we must point to the true, complete ends. The old way of discussing these matters would be to speak of the liberal arts and their role in the making of a complete human being. This language is so alien to us now, however, we must do a bit of preliminary explaining just to get to the point where we can invoke the idea of the liberal arts. If we simply observe how ordinary people—real people, not politicians and "career educators"—view the aims of education, and apply a little common sense, we shall find that, so far from true liberal education having become a thing of the past, it is the remedy for most of our modern ills. Let us therefore take a closer look at why we send our children to school, what children themselves are interested in, and how the world really works. If we can do so without a lot of charts and graphs and pseudo-scientific jargon, but rather by employing what real people believe and the powers of our own reasoning, all the better.

When parents first send children to school in the primary grades, they usually do not use the phrase "college and career readiness" or anything close to it. More likely, they say they want their children to learn to read. On the spectrum of subjects, math (really arithmetic) would come in a close second and writing third, slightly adjusting the order of the traditional "three R's." If pressed further, parents might list some other subjects, but such answers would begin to sound like parents rattling off a report card more than their most heartfelt concerns. Beyond reading, writing, and arithmetic, what parents chiefly expect out of school nowadays is expressed by a vague term that is used without a lot of explanation: "socialization." Socialization itself is a problematic term, and it is invoked by the educrats themselves in order to distract parents from the poor job public schools do of educating students. Yet we shall employ it at present in the traditional sense of making friends and getting along with peers. Thus it is important to realize that what concerns parents most about their children's early education is learning to read (and more broadly the acquisition of language) and learning to thrive in the company of others. These two aims are pretty far removed from "college and career readiness."

If you were to observe children themselves in their early years at school, their own concerns would be even further removed from college and career readiness. The phrase "twenty-first-century global economy" means nothing to them. Rather, young children are usually immersed in the things they are reading at the moment, provided that reading is interesting. At this point, we begin to get a distorted view of the child's nature since the things read in school nowadays are so utterly vapid and forgettable. The Accelerated Reader program, for example, requires students to "read" one simple book after another, silently and individually, with no attempt at discussion or grasp of anything beyond a few basic facts. The current books read aloud in schools, to the extent this traditional practice still exists, are not much better. Nonetheless, whenever a child is exposed to truly good literature, or when fortune favors his stumbling upon good stories outside of school, no persuasion is necessary. Children very readily dwell in the land of the imagination. In their own play, they may very well become the characters and act out the story, just as Tom Sawyer acted out *Robin Hood* "by the book," though he found school itself utterly boring. The last thing anyone has to do is tell a child to read a good book because it will make him "college and career ready." In fact, doing so only makes literature seem less desirable in its own right. In fact, asking children what they want to be when they grow up will elicit responses such as superhero, inventor (of jetpacks and time machines à la Calvin), and ballerina. Such lively minds hardly have to be bribed by the lure of a job into reading imaginative literature.

As children advance in age, the concerns about college and career dawn only slowly. What schools and the culture have become distort children's interests. Yet if we were to survey both parents and students up into the high school years, we would find that their most pressing concerns do not depart radically from their early days in school. By that time students are reading, though whether they are reading well is something the jury is still out on until they get to college. Rather, the larger question at this stage is whether school is valuable or challenging. The value of the school is not related immediately to "college or career readiness." Instead, the value means simply whether the student learns anything during the seven hours a day, one-hundred-eighty days a year, he spends there. Expressed in the student's own words, it is a question of whether school is "boring" or not. Whenever a student attends a truly good school, one in which great books are read and discussed, there is no need to invoke the utilitarian ends of an education. At a truly good school, the question "Why do we need to know this?"—whether the *this* is *Crime and Punishment* or the Civil War or the laws of motion—never comes up. Young people have an innate sense that knowledge of the world—both the human world and the natural world—is intrinsically interesting and needs no outside justification. But in most schools in America, students do complain and ask questions about whether the things in front of them (which students are not truly being taught) have any practical application. They do so because schools are boring, not subjects. Students, not unreasonably, want to escape the chronic boredom, and the "real world" seems to be the thing to escape to. Unlike the days of Tom Sawyer, hooky is not usually an option.

Furthermore, young people are always immersed in the social world around them: the world of friends and enemies, of falling in and out of love, of who likes whom and who's no longer going with whom, of who's in and who's out. Although our modern culture exacerbates the worst aspects of hormonal anarchy and adolescent angst, the lively, at times frenetic, activity of young people relating to each other has always been and will always be a part of the human experience. Indeed, the close attachment to one's friends during the teenage years often compensates for the sheer lifelessness of the academic part of schools and often is the only thing that keeps students wanting to go to school.

Today's schools do not see the connection between young people's keen interest in the world around them and the reading of great literature. They contrive utilitarian reasons for the time students spend in school, always dwelling on how this will help you "one day." Whenever the schools make the mistake of interjecting the merely utilitarian aims of reading into older students' minds, it serves to diminish their interest in learning at all. To say "Here, teenager, read this book so that you will get a job some day," can only lead to students' believing that getting a job is the important thing, reading just some kind of preliminary annoyance, like taking medicine in order to get well. Whereas the younger children are perfectly happy to follow the lead of any adult's suggestion, older children begin to learn the ways of adults. They can tell when older people are saying, "Do as I say, not as I do." The message that schools deliver in spades is, "Jobs and the real world are the important thing. Education is just a necessary, unpleasant step that gets you there. Get through it, and you will be successful one day." How often do teenagers encounter adults, even their teachers, reading and quoting Shakespeare for pleasure? Why, then, would they consider reading books indispensable?

As bad as the public schools have been in subordinating great works of literature to the material concerns of landing a job one day, the Common Core goes beyond anything seen before. For example, the first words printed inside the Teacher's Edition of the Prentice Hall high-school Common Core literature books are "Preparing Students for College and Career." We should stop to think about the significance of that message, something unique in the long history of education in this country. Although, as we shall see, these textbooks leave a lot to be desired for their content, there are still remnants of great stories in them. Would an author of the rank of Herman Melville or Mark Twain have ever consented to having the words "college and career readiness" stamped on the inside of his novel? Is that why those authors wrote their compelling stories in the first place, to serve as some kind of bizarre jobs training program? With Twain being an exception (in some cases), the great authors did not write their books primarily for the consumption of children at all. They wrote them for adults—and not so adults could somehow mysteriously improve their job prospects. Such a limited view of education and of stories is akin to coaches lecturing their Little League and Pee Wee teams on how playing baseball and football as children might lead to habits of physical discipline that will keep them from becoming fat old men. While that piece of information may be true, it is hardly the reason young people should play—or would want to play— team sports. Obviously, this message (too often delivered by a coach who is not himself in the best shape) would hardly come across as inspiring. How does "college and career readiness" serve any better as the motivation for reading great literature?

As important as are learning to read and finding school valuable on the one hand and making friends and getting along on the other, much more is happening from the ages of six to eighteen. Beyond the initial learning to read and "fitting in," what parents worry about most during their children's time in school is whether they will turn out to be good people. Parents worry when one of their children gets in trouble at school. They worry about the influences other children may have on their child. (Less often do they consider what influence their child has on the other children!) The worries only increase when a child reaches adolescence. The contemporary school environment itself is a prominent source of concern these days for parents. Having run a classical school and helped set up many more, I can say with some authority that the reasons parents pull their children out of the regular district schools are about half academic and half moral. Anyone who opens up a charter or private middle school is flooded with applicants. Parents regularly refer to the local middle school as "the zoo" and "the jungle," and with apt references to *Lord of the Flies*. Though no one in the current schools wishes to admit it, the rapid growth of homeschooling in America owes far more to worries about the moral decline of public schools over the past thirty years than their academic decline. Perhaps those Founders of America who wrote the Massachusetts School Law of 1789 were onto something when they wrote about the importance of "piety, justice, and a sacred regard to truth, love to their country, humanity, and universal benevolence, sobriety, industry and frugality, chastity, moderation and temperance, and those other virtues which are the ornament of human society, and the basis upon which the Republican Constitution is structured."

Parents worry about their children's moral development as much as their intellectual development for obvious reasons. The Greek philosopher Heraclitus said it long ago. *Character is destiny.* Even the best educated person who exhibits a debilitating vice or who is altogether morally bankrupt will not only be less likely to go far in life, he may be shunned by his fellow man. No decent person wants to send a child out into the world who is not decent. It is surprising, then, that the authors of the Common Core say so little about the moral purposes of education. Do they themselves not have children?

While young people themselves do not talk about their own moral development very much, nonetheless they use unabashed moral language to describe and judge the actions and character of others. "He's a jerk." "Can you believe what she did to him?" "That's so uncool." "He's so stuck up." (Or, nowadays, "He thinks he's so cool.") "That's not fair!" This is the moral language that young people use, unprompted by any adult. True, it is not always the most elevated language and often not about the most important things. But it is a moral language all the same. Human beings judge other human beings by their words and deeds. "Judge not lest ye be judged" is probably the hardest commandment ever put upon man. If you do not believe that, just go to a high school Prom sometime and listen to how girls talk about other girls' dresses. "Can you believe she wore that!" Young people, like all people, are interested in the other human beings around them. Not only are they interested in seeing what happens to other people and seeing what others are "about"; they take their level of interest to the point of moral judgment. We are all moral spectators of the human drama.

Why is it important to know this common, universal feature of humanity? Why is it important to know that young people's interest in school has a lot to do with their intense, unprompted interest in the world of friends and peers? Why is essential to realize that the natural proclivity to judge others is fundamental to the human experience? The answer is really very simple. What today's education "experts" never observe is that no one ever has to tell the young to be interested in the doings of their peers. That phenomenon is no less true of adults. Every person is interested in the lives and actions of the people around him: their virtues, their vices, their decisions, their victories, their defeats, in short, their *stories*. Such curiosity needs no justification and no other end in view. Furthermore, the more interesting the person in question, the more pronounced and dramatic his virtues or vices or victories or defeats, the more interest he generates in others wanting to know his story. Interesting people draw the attention of others. Well, what is great literature other than the telling of the most interesting lives imaginable by the most accomplished storytellers? There is a little more to it than that, certainly. But at its most basic level, literature offers a window into the thoughts and actions of profoundly interesting human beings. As my wife, an astute reader of literature, puts it, reading great literature is like eavesdropping on other people's conversations. It is irresistible.

The careful reading and study of stories enables us to know who human beings are and therefore who we are. Great literature, then, is one major branch of the formal study of humanity. The other major branch is history and the allied disciplines: politics, law, and economics. Literature is the branch of the humanities devoted to storytelling in beautiful language, the branch that draws most heavily upon the human imagination.[24] If literature is the study of humanity through great, imaginative stories, then what do we learn from literature? Well, essentially everything that pertains to humanity. We learn about good taste and manners. We learn all the individual virtues and vices: temperance and intemperance, courage and cowardice, justice and injustice, honesty and dishonesty, industry and sloth, humility and arrogance. We learn about the human emotions: love, hate, fear, ambition, melancholy, resentment, contentment, grief, mirth, rage, and so many more. By reading great literature we learn both to understand human beings and to sympathize with them. Through this vicarious activity, we are compelled to examine ourselves and thereby attain what used to be called self-government, the ability to discipline oneself so as to achieve the good in life. What Lord Bolingbroke said of history is equally true of literature. It is philosophy teaching by examples. What is a better study of ambition leading to ruin than *Macbeth*? What is a better study of indecision and imprudence than *Hamlet*? What is a better example of adolescent love and passion in their raw state than *Romeo and Juliet*? What is a better model of command than *Henry V*? What is a better narrative of pride and prejudice, self-education and love, than *Pride and Prejudice*? We hang onto these stories through the centuries—we continue to go back to them—for many reasons, but two are foremost. First, they are great and we are drawn to them out of pure interest in the human condition. Second, we need them. Without these great stories, we would be poorer. We would know far less about love and hate, loyalty and treason, hope and despair, faith and faithlessness, heroism and decadence, indeed every aspect of human life, without the unforgettable stories that teach us who we are and who we ought to be.

---

[24] We shall leave aside poetry for the moment, though much of poetry is storytelling, too. The classification of literature as belonging to the powers of the imagination is Lord Bacon's. History belongs to the powers of memory and philosophy to reason. Philosophy, you might say, is the discipline that reasons from these other humanities in order to achieve wisdom.

The study of human character through great literature, then, teaches us how to live. There is one overriding virtue that studying humanity through stories inculcates. It is a virtue that many people try to talk about these days but never very successfully. We hear a lot about the capacity for "decision-making": a talent we are told must be among the qualities people have in a "twenty-first-century global economy." It is never explained. We should stop to ask what is this high art called "decision-making," and how is it best taught? The old way of describing this art or talent was by means of the cardinal virtue called *prudence*. As it is often used today, prudence means simply caution and often implies a fear of risk. Throughout history, though, prudence has been the lead virtue that governs all the others. It is the practical wisdom or the "perfected ability of making right decisions" needed to ensure all the other virtues achieve their ends.[25] Prudence is a kind of common sense made stronger by study and experience. Well, if that is the case, then the question becomes, what should one study?

Though it is hardly obvious to people nowadays, the old adage remains true that the proper study of man is man. At least that is the case with regard to acquiring the virtue of prudence, of expert decision-making. How does one study man, then? Does one just go to the mall or the market and watch people? That helps a little: observing people as we find them in their daily lives. Yet to derive insights into the complex human world, one must do far more than "people-watch." One must hit the books and see what the wisest students of human nature throughout the ages have thought and said about human beings. History is a large part of that study, certainly. Yet literature—great literature—is equally necessary. That is because literature offers us insights that history cannot. While history must always stick to the facts, literature, through the powers of the imagination, can tell us things about our nature that history has no license to do. Even if no one ever killed a pawnbroker while following a false philosophy of power and later suffered for it, as did Raskolnikov, we can learn far more about the moral constitution of man by reading such a story that never happened than we could from an actual murder that did. Even if no sea captain ever pursued a white while across the wide seas, we can learn more about the fine line between persistence and obsession through Captain Ahab than through any textbook in

---

[25] From Josef Pieper, *The Cardinal Virtues*, "Prudence."

psychology. Great stories with great characters, then, teach us how to read people. A keen student of Jane Austen can spot a Wickham from a mile away. Let's hope she can also recognize a Mr. Darcy if she has the good fortune to meet one.

One of the things it is easy to forget in our "twenty-first-century global economy" is how much of the world remains *human*. Virtually all of the discussion about education these days points to technology, and the Common Core (with its accompanying testing programs that will have children behind computers much of the day) will not be the last attempt to make the school resemble the workplace (or what we are being told today's workplace is). No one wants to discuss the extent to which the modern office (as well as the economy at large) remains a human place. Consider how companies work. Are the biggest problems in companies big and small usually the result of employees' inability to use technology? Or are the biggest problems those issues that involve "personnel"? The "human element," as the General in *Dr. Strangelove* called it, remains with us no matter what "systems" we put into place in an effort to make companies run like machines. At the upper end of corporate America, businesses are constantly in search of good leaders and find them hard to come by. At the entry level of rewarding occupations, employers are shocked at the dearth of young people coming out of college with the ability to write and to communicate and who have the requisite "people skills." The managers of stores and franchises that hire hourly workers, both teenagers and adults, labor to find people who can get to work on time, think beyond their immediate paycheck, and have enough order in their lives to become valuable employees and advance in the job. These chronic problems of every business in America are not technological. They are human.

Even the most technological of occupations are not immune from the human element. When a software developer comes home at night, what does he (or she) talk about at the dinner table? Would most of the conversation turn upon the particular design of a new product? Or would it be on the fact that the design is flawed because Bob is screwing up, but Bob has the boss's ear, so "I'm gonna have to show them," and so on? Nowadays we tend to forget that a thousand conversations, human conversations, had to take place for human beings to create the machines that we use. The better the conversations are, the better the products and greater profitability of the business. The worse the conversations are, the more waste and mission drift and "rework."

Literature is the study of human conversation. We as a culture have almost entirely forgotten that simple fact. Literature features human conversation—dialogue—as its foremost element. Shakespeare's plays are dialogues. Novels contain more narrative than plays, but the interaction among the characters (unless they are fighting or kissing or looking at each other) is mostly dialogue. No other form of writing specializes in the art of conversation as does literature. Plato's philosophy is written in dialogues, but that is the exception. Boswell's *Life of Johnson* is technically a biography, but it belongs in the category of great literature precisely because of the rich conversations. History, while written about important people who had important conversations, offers too few *complete* conversations because we do not have records of what historical actors said exactly, and historians cannot simply make things up. It is left to literature, then, to teach us how to have worthwhile conversations. Through reading dialogue, we learn to speak, as well as to pay attention to and interpret the things people say. If one of the greatest complaints of today's employers is that their employees are largely incapable of having meaningful and productive conversations, then how sound a move is it to reduce substantially the amount of literature taught in schools and thus the examples of great conversations? And this at a time when children and young people, the next generation of employees, are transforming their discourse from words to letters? OMG!

The study of literature, so far from being irrelevant or only ornamental, answers many of the fundamental reasons for sending children to school in the first place, as it speaks to the child's own mind and soul, too. Parents want their children to read. Children live in the realm of the imagination. No wonder that for centuries children have learned to read, once they have acquired the skill of decoding, through the great tales of the imagination almost every one of us knows by heart: *Cinderella, Little Red Riding Hood, Goldilocks, Jack and the Beanstalk.* Children and young people have an innate interest in others. No wonder that whenever good stories are presented to them, they continue to read literature for the rest of their lives, some books again and again. Reading great literature, besides quenching the thirst of individuals for knowing their fellow human beings, also enables a person to develop sympathy for others, to learn to judge others, to know and to improve oneself, to understand the human condition, and to develop one's own moral sense. This appraisal of literature, which has almost disappeared from the schools, is nothing new. In fact, Thomas Jefferson extolled literature in just such terms when a young man wrote him requesting a list of books every educated person should read. Along with providing such a list, what we might call a true common core, Jefferson had this to say:

> A little attention however to the nature of the human mind evinces that the entertainments of fiction are useful as well as pleasant. . . .
>
> I answer, everything is useful which contributes to fix in the principles and practices of virtue. When any original act of charity or of gratitude, for instance, is presented either to our sight or imagination, we are deeply impressed with its beauty and feel a strong desire in ourselves of doing charitable and grateful acts also. On the contrary when we see or read of any atrocious deed, we are disgusted with its deformity, and conceive an abhorrence of vice. Now every emotion of this kind is an exercise of our virtuous dispositions, and dispositions of the mind, like limbs of the body acquire strength by exercise. But exercise produces habit, and in the instance of which we speak the exercise being of the moral feelings produces a habit of thinking and acting virtuously. We never reflect whether the story we read be truth or fiction. If the painting be lively, and a tolerable picture of nature, we are thrown into a reverie, from which if we awaken it is the fault of the writer. . . . Considering history as a moral exercise, her lessons would be too infrequent if confined to real life. Of those recorded by historians few incidents have been attended with such circumstances as to excite in any high degree this sympathetic emotion of virtue. We are therefore wisely framed to be as warmly interested for a fictitious as for a real personage. The field of imagination is thus laid open to our

use and lessons may be formed to illustrate and carry home to the heart every moral rule of life. Thus a lively and lasting sense of filial duty is more effectually impressed on the mind of a son or daughter by reading King Lear, than by all the dry volumes of ethics, and divinity that were ever written.[26]

Consider how different Jefferson's advice is from the approach taken in the Common Core. Whereas Jefferson regards the moral worth of a text to be its chief virtue, and the works of fiction to be the most valuable in that regard, the authors of the Common Core are cutting back on literature to make room for "informational texts." The other term we hear coming out of the schools is "non-fiction." On the face of it, non-fiction would seem to outweigh mere "fiction," i.e. things that never happened. This is precisely why those terms are being employed today and the term "literature" is being hushed up. Jefferson, though, who knew a little bit about education and literature and reading and writing, who is in fact one of the greatest "non-fiction" writers in our history, preferred literature to non-fiction because of literature's moral value. Where do we see the *moral* value of great literary works being extolled by the Common Core camp?

Let us assume that Thomas Jefferson knew what he was talking about when it came to education in the eighteenth century. In addition to receiving a classical, liberal education in his youth and becoming one of the greatest philosopher-statesmen in American history, he also proposed a system of public schools for Virginia, was the architect (literally and figuratively) of a great university, and collected so many books that his extensive library became the embryo of the Library of Congress. If any American understood education in the eighteenth century, Jefferson did. The question then becomes, particularly in relation to the study of English and literature, whether so much has changed in the much heralded twenty-first-century global economy. In the world of texting (and sexting) and tweeting and other forms of electronic-speak, as well as rap music and reality television, do young people nowadays need to be exposed to *less* or *more* elegant language through poetry and drama and great novels, in short, through what used to be

---

[26] Thomas Jefferson to Robert Skipwith, 3 August 1771.

called *belles lettres* (beautiful letters)? Do the children of today require more or less development of their imagination? Does it make sense to spend *less* time disciplining the emotions of teenagers through the great works of literature? Is it reasonable to devote *less* attention to the cultivation of the child's moral faculties by following the thoughts and actions of heroes and villains and everything in between? Ought we to read only partial accounts of great stories, leaving the students hanging, so that more time can be given to studying for those all-important "assessments" that never require the reading of a complete book? In short, has our age so far advanced in eloquence and civility and self-government and both personal and public morality that we can easily dispense with those old-fashioned concerns of Jefferson and the other Founding Fathers and turn our attention to the inelegant, morally insignificant, mass-produced, and wholly forgettable churnings of the "information age"?

The way the discussion has been set up by the Common Core, very cleverly as it turns out, is actually false. They want us to choose more non-fiction (the realm of the real) and less fiction (the realm of the not real). Instead, we should refashion this decision to show what is really at stake. It is the choice of imaginative literature over prosaic journalism; of morally inspiring stories over morally inconsequential information; of complete narratives over disconnected vignettes; of great, compelling accounts of mankind's foremost sufferings and enterprises and dreams over obvious summaries of marginally interesting episodes. It is the choice between listening in on great conversations and being left to stew in one's own colloquial juice. It is the choice between reading the daily newspaper or the greatest things that have ever been written. It is the unmistakable choice between reading because it is merely necessary and reading because it is our constant guide to happiness in life.

Yes, happiness. That is a word we do not hear coming from the Common Core—at all. What the Common Core promises is getting students into college and into a career. Assuming that the Common Core could actually accomplish that successfully, we are still left with the question, *Then what?* We should stop to observe the difference between the way the Common Core authors discuss the aims of education and the way the Founding Fathers did. Here is Benjamin Franklin's first line from his essay on the formation of an academy for Philadelphia:

> The good Education of Youth has been esteemed by wise Men in all Ages, as the surest Foundation of the Happiness both of private Families and of Common-wealths.

Here is an excerpt from the preamble of Thomas Jefferson's Bill for the More General Diffusion of Knowledge.

> And whereas it is generally true that that people will be happiest whose laws are best, and are best administered . . . whence it becomes expedient for promoting the publick happiness that those persons whom nature hath endowed with genius and virtue, should be rendered by liberal education worthy to receive, and able to guard the sacred deposit of the rights and liberties of their fellow citizens . . .[27]

Jefferson, of course, was keenly interested in public happiness. Two years before writing this bill, he had declared "That all men are created equal, that they are endowed by their Creator with certain unalienable Rights, that among these are Life, Liberty, and the pursuit of Happiness." Unsurprisingly, he made happiness the end of public schooling.

The most striking thing about today's impoverished chatter about education is that the supposed experts never talk about the most important things. Happiness is one of those things. In fact, it is the end to which all other ends (freedom, justice, virtue) lead in the mind of the greatest philosopher, Aristotle. Modern educators have not read Aristotle. They have not read Jefferson. Yet you could ask any mother what she wants her children to have more than anything else in life. Would not the final answer be *happiness*? The fact that today's educational establishment and the authors of the Common Core do not know that fundamental truth reveals just how out of touch they are with parents, with the children in their charge, in short, with human beings.

---

[27] Jefferson continues to state that those endowed with genius and virtue whose parents cannot afford their schooling should be educated at the public expense.

The study of literature is the study of human happiness. Every great epic, every great play, every great novel, every great poem offers us a window into the human attempt to secure happiness, the goal we are all striving for, however well or ineptly. Therefore the most outrageous offense of the Common Core is not its removal of great literature from the classroom, nor its dumbing down of serious learning, nor its egregious testing regime, nor its obvious failure to do even what it claims to do. These are awful things. Yet the most egregious and inexcusable offense of the Common Core is its further extinguishing the opportunity of young people "to work out their own greatest happiness," in Thomas Jefferson's phrase, through the study of literature.[28] In our present culture, with children and young people being exposed to so many questionable and morally debilitating images and stories, we need great literature more than ever, not less. Children's souls are hungry for stories and images of the good and the beautiful and the true. And we try to feed their hunger with the U.S. Environmental Protection Agency and U.S. Department of Energy's pamphlet on "Recommended Levels of Insulation."[29] How much insight into children and into the moral constitution of human beings do we have left?

Though college and career readiness are a byproduct of a solid education, they are not the primary motivation. The chief reasons for education are to bring children and young people to an understanding of the human and natural worlds and to teach them virtue and self-government. The end of both knowledge and self-government is happiness. Today's children and young people need to understand human beings and true human happiness no less today than they have in the past. Indeed, given the amount of time they spend on video games and social media on their own, the young people of today may need *more* study in the humanities than ever before. Therefore, they need stories—beautiful and powerful stories that instruct them, that inspire them, that amuse them, and

---

[28] Thomas Jefferson, Notes on the State of Virginia, Query 14, on the Bill for the General Diffusion of Knowledge. This statement is made in the context of studying history, though he may have had literature in mind as well, as we have seen in his letter to Robert Skipwith quoted above.

[29] Readers may complain that I and others have honed in on this one example of an informational text that appears in Appendix B, while ignoring the great works of literature that are recommended throughout the grades. Please be patient; the rest of the argument is coming. We have many miles to go before we sleep.

that make them more human. If you are looking for such stories for your children, if you are hoping that they will develop such a human conversation, if you want them to become moral spectators of the world around them, then do not look to the Common Core.

Chapter Three
The Sub-Standard Standards
of the Standards Game

If you are a parent trying to sort through the argument over the Common Core—and have actually taken a look at the document—you may be a little confused right now. On the one hand, there is a lot of controversy about what the Common Core is going to do or not do to your children's education. Yet when you go to the document itself, you cannot really make heads or tails of it. True, there are a lot of promises in the introductory parts of the *Standards for English Language Arts*, etc. But you know the whole discussion is supposed to be about "standards," whatever those are. So you go to the "standards" part of the *Standards* themselves. Here is where things get confusing. You thought, like any reasonable person, that the "standards" would be about specific books that the children would learn. Yet you do not find anything in the "standards" directly related to a book. The books, or suggested books, do not come in the document until Appendix B: 107 pages into the *Common Core Standards for English, etc.*. Instead, it turns out that the "standards" within the Standards consist in descriptions of students performing different kinds of tasks.[30]

The tasks themselves seem rather non-controversial. For example, the standards say that children by the fifth grade should be able to "1. Quote accurately from a text when explaining what the text says explicitly and when drawing inferences from the text. 2. Determine two or more main ideas of a text and explain how

---

[30] The language itself is confusing: deliberately, as we shall see. In this chapter I shall refer to the descriptive skills called standards in lower case and the document itself in upper case. Thus the standards constitute only a part of the Common Core English Standards.

they are supported by key details; summarize the text." By the eleventh and twelfth grades, the students should be able to "1. Cite strong and thorough textual evidence to support analysis of what the text says explicitly as well as inferences drawn from the text, including where the text leaves matters uncertain. 2. Determine two or more themes or central ideas of a text, including how they interact and build on one another to produce a complex account; provide an objective summary of the text."

Sure, that seems reasonable. Students who are reading "a text" ought to be able to do these things. It is not until you begin to ponder these high-sounding words a bit that you begin to have real questions. The first question we might have is why the fifth-grade and the eleventh-grade standards look so much alike. It could be because the act of reading, whether at eleven-years-old or seventeen-years-old, is much the same. But something in us suspects that what we have here is, as in all bureaucratic documents, a set of stock or boilerplate answers. In other words, the standards themselves are a major cut-and-paste operation. Of course, a few words are added to the high-school standards to make things seem more difficult. In particular, we have the word *analysis*. Wow! *Analysis*. But what is literary analysis? It just so happens that the Common Core English Standards do not really tell us what literary analysis is. They leave it to the reader to "infer" what literary analysis is. The *Common Core Standards for English, etc.* therefore is a text that "leaves matters uncertain." Indeed, the Common Core leaves most matters uncertain.

So what is really going on here in the standards part of the *Standards*? I maintain that there are three games afoot. First, the standards themselves are a diversion. As we shall see in subsequent chapters, the real action, so to speak, is in the books[31] and other readings that are imposed on the schools, in the standardized testing that will dictate what gets read, in the selections—and lessons on those selections—found in the textbooks, and in the slavish following of these prescribed lessons in the actual classrooms. By drawing everyone's attention to the standards—indeed by proclaiming that the Common Core is *only* a set of standards and not a curriculum—everyone can be taken in or reassured. Every criticism can be redirected. "We're just giving

---

[31] I use the term "books" loosely here. As we shall see, the Common Core really does not allow students to read complete books.

the states what they need: better standards. You as a state or a district can figure out how to meet these standards in ways that best suit your local circumstances." It reminds one of the Reagan quip, "We're from the government, and we're here to help." The Standards do impose a curriculum, or at least an ideology that easily becomes a curriculum, and the Common Core's "helping" consists in making sure that that ideology is followed. The second game afoot is the effect of "standards" on the way books and subjects are taught. Standards actually drain the life out of a subject: in the case of literature, a story. Standards place an emphasis on "skills" over "content." As such, they impose artificial categories on unique creations. This is not unlike what happens when you have to fill out a government form, or now a form at a doctor's office. You may have gone in thinking you were Joe Rogers with a back pain. But you end up becoming, "male, white, sexually active, middle-income, no criminal history." In other words, you become a demographic classification to put in somebody's (or many somebodies') files for safekeeping. So-called standards do the same things to great stories that should be looked at as unique worlds into which the reader is being invited. The third game results from the first two. When everyone is taken in by these standards, when no one goes into the classroom to see how literature (or any other subject) is studied, when no one looks to the past to see how we used to learn reading and grammar and literature and history and mathematics, then we all end up congratulating ourselves on "raising the bar," and "adopting higher standards" and preparing our children for a "twenty-first-century global economy," and a host of other platitudes. Politicians can campaign on the issue. School superintendents can waste years talking about the trials of implementation and all the extra money they need. Publishing companies can run through three or four editions of official Common Core textbooks, making millions on each edition, each time claiming to get closer to the model of the standards, while in fact gutting what learning is left in schools. And no child will show up to the parade to state simply that "the emperor has no clothes." Why not? Well, because no one has read *the story.* No one has read *The Emperor's New Clothes* or *The Ugly Duckling* or *The Little Mermaid* or any Hans Christian Anderson at all. They are not to be found in the Common Core English Standards. But we will all learn to salute the Standards because the children in public schools will have read "*complex* texts" *like The Emperor's New Clothes*. In short, all the talk in schools about standards is really just a game: a game played with words in order to make us think that children are learning something important when they are really not. And since public schools are ultimately accountable to the public, this game gets played out in the realm of politics.

To figure out how the standards game works, we have to make a brief foray into the mind-numbing world of standards production. Then we shall see how standards work in practice with literature. Let us look at an example of a state standard for "social studies," or what used to be called history. This standard comes from the state of Wisconsin and is intended for the fourth grade:

> Examine biographies, stories, narratives, and folk tales to understand the lives of ordinary and extraordinary people, place them in time and context, and explain their relationship to important historical events. (WI.B.4.3.)

To the uninitiated, this "standard" probably sounds pretty good. Fourth-graders will be learning about ordinary and *extraordinary* people. They will see how these people fit into their time period and how they were involved in important historical events. Most likely the reader's mind immediately goes to the American Revolution—with George Washington, Benjamin Franklin, and "Light Horse" Harry Lee being the extraordinary people, and perhaps Betsy Ross and some hitherto unknown soldier being the ordinary people. Good guess—in a rational world.

What happens in practice is that all the emphasis is put on *biographies* as a genre of writing, not on actual historical figures or events. Furthermore, under the progressive imperative of student-centered learning, the lessons become the scene of educational democracy run amok. Ergo, the students get to choose their own extraordinary people to study and, after extensive *research*, write their own biographies! They will begin by writing a biography of their "neighbor" sitting next to them in class. Later they will choose their own hero. They will spend days drawing pictures, pasting in newspaper clippings, and writing a few meager sentences underneath their art work. That work will decorate a wall of the school and later be sent home, where it will occupy the customary spot on the refrigerator until it is replaced by another, similar "research project." And who will be these extraordinary people intimately connected to important historical events? I saw just such a display of biographies created by fourth-graders in a suburban school in Indiana, which I toured about a year and a half ago. The historical luminaries put forth included Miley Cyrus, Tebow, Beyonce, Elvis, and Albert Einstein (there's one cerebral kid in every crowd!). I urge you to tour the public schools where you live to see if you come up with anything different—*if you are let in*. The principal and all the teachers will pass by such a display, no doubt ecstatic that the children in this school are so clever, so gifted and talented, and having so much fun. And if you were to ask any of them what lesson was learned in history (or social studies), they would each point you to the appropriate state standard for biography and historical events. No one bothers to ask the common-sense questions. In the case of the "neighbor's" biography: How much has a nine-year old really lived? In the cases of Miley Cyrus and Tebow: Are these popular figures really worth investing time on in school? Since those nine-year-old Plutarchs wrote their narratives, Tebow has been cut by two teams and Miley Cyrus has taken up dirty, dirty dancing.

The other social studies standards for Wisconsin are equally worthless. Here are two more that we should ponder briefly:

> Describe examples of cooperation and interdependence among individuals, groups, and nations. (WI.B.4.9)

> Locate, organize, and use relevant information to understand an issue in the classroom or school while taking into account the viewpoints and interests of different groups and individuals. (WI.C.4.6)

The first standard sounds like a great thing. Of course, we are not given any clue as to which individuals, groups, and nations will be studied. It really does not matter to the writers of the standards. They would be just as happy with fourth-graders learning about ancestral peoples in New Guinea as the Founding Fathers. In fact, the standards writers would likely question whether studying the Founders in the fourth grade would be "age appropriate." Hidden in this state social studies standard is a discrete political objective.

The operative word in the standard is "cooperation." That is the concept that the standards-makers (bureaucrats) want to be emphasized in the classroom. The human experience they do *not* want studied is war, presumably the opposite of *cooperation*. Because the standards do not specify actual historical events, there is no suggestion that war will ever be studied. Therefore, what will *not* be studied in elementary school? Practically every war you can think of, starting with the Persian Wars through World War II. That is a lot of history to miss. But missing history is not a deficiency, according to the bureaucratic standards-makers. Knowledge of actual events is far less important than acquiring supposed skills and adopting attitudes, in this case the attitude that "cooperation" is the highest good.

Such a penchant for cooperation, as we can see, is supposed to be extended to one's peers. In the second standard above, the students are invited to "locate, organize, and use relevant information," etc. to solve some pressing issue in the school. What nonsense might this entail? The exercise does no more than follow the old progressive myth about learning by doing. The teacher will engineer some project on recycling (duplicating one already in place) that has the appearance of community, er, school organizing. There will be a lot of energy spent and time wasted. And the students will learn nothing from it.

While these social studies standards are being attended to, what will the students not be learning? Essentially everything: the presidents of the United States in order, every state and capital, the major events of the American Revolution, the basic framework of American government, the history of the rise and decline of Rome, the story of Columbus discovering America, in short, virtually anything worth learning and that young children would be delighted to learn if someone would only teach them.

The standards game, then, is a ruse. Standards are not the same thing as a curriculum. A curriculum, at least one that is worth its salt, tells teachers what to teach. Specificity is the hallmark of a genuine curriculum. The so-called standards that states adopt, however, consist in a vague set of "learning objectives" that are either general skills or amorphous concepts surrounding an academic subject. For the purposes of knowing *what* to teach and knowing how great literature ought to be *taught*, the so-called standards adopted by most states are almost entirely worthless. There is only one exception to that general rule: the state standards created by Massachusetts beginning in 1996 under the direction of John Silber, long-time president of Boston University, who was appointed head of the state school board. The Massachusetts exception in fact proves the rule about so-called state standards since those standards did specify curriculum. Traditional literature made up 80 to 90 percent of the English content.[32] Silber actually wanted to go so far as making every student in Massachusetts read *Moby Dick*. To realize what an achievement that would have been, the reader should know that virtually no public high school nowadays has students read the whole of what used to be considered "the great American novel."

There is, admittedly, a malevolent (though perhaps unwitting) genius in the standards mongering that takes place in the state education bureaucracies. The genius consists in two parts. First, the word *standards* itself is a brilliant stroke. Though at best standards do little more than offer some vague suggestions to teachers and at worst actually foul up their teaching, the word *standards* itself sounds high. Who would ever argue against "higher standards" in education? The politicians and pundits and even parents who rally around higher *standards* for schools mean the word in the general sense and likely never bother to read these mind-numbing documents. Second, for those who do read the standards, they are written so ambiguously that "the viewpoints and interests of different groups and individuals" can take them in any direction. Holding up the standards, the chairman of the education committee in a state legislature could point to the "rigor" students will encounter in their new social studies curriculum. Meanwhile, the professors at the teachers colleges will figure out how to dumb down these standards into predictable projects and activities. Everyone will brag about the state's "high standards" (no different from the neighboring states' standards), and the students will continue to learn nothing.

Now that we have a general sense of the standards game, let us look specifically at the standards part of the Common Core English

---

[32] James Stergios, Charles Chieppo, and Jamie Gass, "The Massachusetts Exception," *City Journal*, Summer 2012. Dr. Sandra Stotsky was a key figure in writing the English Standards in Massachusetts. Dr. Stotsky was originally on the validation committee for the Common Core English Standards but refused to sign off on them and has since written, spoken, and testified extensively against the Common Core.

Standards.   Despite all the contrary claims, these standards are nothing new.   They are no different from the English Language Arts (obnoxiously abbreviated ELA these days) standards that already existed in the states since they suffer from the same maladies that all the state standards do. In short, these Brave New Standards sound high but aim low.

On page 11 of the *Standards*, the reader will get a taste of both the absurdity and the nothingness of state standards. Standard RL-2.9. (reading standards for literature, second grade, standard 9) reads as follows:

> By the end of the year, read and comprehend literature, including stories and poetry, in the grades 2-3 complexity band proficiently, with scaffolding as needed at the high end of the range.

What in the world does that mean?   Most parents and citizens would be afraid to ask. Yet it is really quite simple. Let's break it down. "By the end of the year": the second-grade year in the spring. "Read and comprehend literature": students should not only read the words on the page mechanically but understand what they are reading; what they should be reading is *literature* (at least for this standard).   "Including stories and poetry": yes, we generally think of stories and poetry when we think of literature; what other literature did they have in mind for second-graders? "In the grades 2-3 complexity band proficiently": this refers to the levels of difficulty the arch-testers have created with the pseudo-science of "text complexity" that we shall examine in the next chapter; basically, it means that students in the spring of second grade should read harder books than they read in the fall. "With scaffolding as needed at the high end of the range": "scaffolding" is possibly the favorite educational buzzword of our day; it follows the image of constructing a building: the scaffolding is what builders need to erect a structure, and it gets taken down when the structure is finished; in this case, the structure is students' learning; "scaffolding," then, could easily be translated as "help" or "teaching."   So here is the standard accompanied by a common-sense translation:

By the end of the year, read and comprehend literature, including stories and poetry, in the grades 2-3 complexity band proficiently, with scaffolding as needed at the high end of the range.

Students in second grade should read and understand more difficult books at the end of the year than at the beginning. They may need help, though.

Now that is a rigorous standard! I could only hope that all the supposed experts across the country who have made large claims about the wonders of the Common Core would read that standard and say exactly how this painfully obvious truism is going to sweep aside mediocrity and boredom in schools.

What we cannot fail to notice is how much this standard does not tell us. Realize we are not told how we shall know that the students *comprehend* what they read. Will there be a class discussion? If so, what specific questions will be asked? Will the students be tested on what they read? Will they have to write sentences or just answer easy multiple-choice questions from a pre-fab worksheet teachers find online? Further, we are not told in this part of the Standards *what* (other than in a general sense) is considered literature. Parents might be inclined to think it would consist in famous, classic literature, such as *Tales from the Arabian Nights*. That is unfortunately not the case, at least not in the stories category. Peeking into Appendix B, we can see that the students might be reading Janet Stevens's *Tops and Bottoms*, a text selection that appears in the "grades 2-3 complexity band." [33] Yet the book is marketed by the publishers as most suitable for 4-8 year-olds, or Kindergarten through second grade. Therefore, that appears to be a book that is not at the "high end of the range." Perhaps a better selection would be *Cowgirl Kate and Cocoa*, published in 2006, which also makes the list of Common Core recommended texts for second and third grades. Its publishers claim it is for ages 6-9, or first- through fourth-graders. That sounds ideal. Let's look at the first few pages.

---

[33] We shall examine the text selections in Appendix B in greater detail in chapter five.

Page 1:

Chapter 1: A Story for Cocoa

Cowgirl Kate rode her horse, Cocoa,
out to the pasture.
"It's time to herd cows," said Cowgirl Kate.
"I am thirsty," said Cocoa.
He stopped at the creek
and took a drink.

[illustration of a pond with rocks in it]

Page 2:

[whole page illustration of Cocoa drinking water]

Page 3:

"Are you ready, now?" asked Cowgirl Kate.
"No," said Cocoa. "Now I am hungry."
Cowgirl Kate gave him an apple.
He ate it in one bite.
Then he sniffed the saddlebag.

[large illustration of Cowgirl Kate feeding Cocoa an apple]

Page 4:

[large illustration of Cowgirl Kate and Cocoa looking confused]

Cowgirl Kate gave him another apple.
He ate that in one bite, too.
He sniffed the saddlebag again.

Page 5:

[illustration of Cowgirl Kate and Cocoa looking at each other]

"You are a pig," said Cowgirl Kate.
"No," said Cocoa. "I am a horse."
Etc.

So is this the level of dialogue the agents of the Common Core think is at the "high end of the range" of the grades 2-3 complexity band? It seems pretty simplistic to me.

For a little perspective, let's "compare and contrast" a classic work of literature that is read in classical schools at the second- or third-grade level. What follows is the first page of a child's version of *Aladdin and the Magic Lamp* published by Scholastic.[34]

There once lived a boy named Aladdin, who spent his days in the streets of an ancient city. When his father died, Aladdin had no way to support himself or his mother.

At that time a magician came from Africa, looking for a boy he could use to make himself the most powerful man in the world. When the stranger saw Aladdin, he asked about him. Finding that Aladdin had no father, he said to the boy, "Are you the son of Mustapha the tailor?"

"Mustapha was my father," said Aladdin. "But he is no longer living."

To Aladdin's surprise, the man threw his arms around him. "I knew you at once," he lied. Then he began weeping. "To think I have searched the world for my dear brother only to find he is dead."

For another comparison, here is the first page of an un-adapted version of *Aladdin*:

---

[34] Carol Carrick, *Aladdin and the Wonderful Lamp*, illus. Donald Carrick (New York: Scholastic, 1989).

There once lived a poor tailor, who had a son called Aladdin, a careless, idle boy who would do nothing but play all day long in the streets with little idle boys like himself. This so grieved the father that he died; yet, in spite of his mother's tears and prayers, Aladdin did not mend his ways. One day, when he was playing in the streets as usual, a stranger asked him his age, and if he was not the son of Mustapha the tailor. "I am, sir," replied Aladdin; "but he died a long while ago." On this the stranger, who was a famous African magician, fell on his neck and kissed him, saying: "I am your uncle, and knew you from your likeness to my brother. Go to your mother and tell her I am coming." Aladdin ran home and told his mother of his newly found uncle. "Indeed, child," she said, "your father had a brother, but I always thought he was dead." However, she prepared supper, and bade Aladdin seek his uncle, who came laden with wine and fruit.[35]

Though there are clearly differences between the two versions of *Aladdin*, they both are considerably richer and more "complex" than *Cowgirl Kate and Cocoa*. The first version of *Aladdin* features a few words that are not a part of everyday speech, such as "ancient" and "weeping," whereas the most difficult word in *Cowgirl Kate* is "saddlebag." The sheer number of words on the page is telling. *Cowgirl Kate* has 32 words on the first page, 26 of which have just one syllable. The adapted version of *Aladdin* has 135 words, with a much higher percentage being multi-syllabic, including a number of three-syllable words, such as *powerful*, *magician*, *Africa*, and *Aladdin*. The use of participial phrases in the Aladdin story also makes for more mature reading. More important, in *Aladdin* we are given a much more nuanced scenario. The boy's father has died; the boy spends his days in the streets (idly in the original, an idleness that led to the father's death!); a magician from out of town wants to make himself powerful and for some reason needs a boy to help him; the man somehow knows

---

[35] *Aladdin and the Magic Lamp.* No author. Free edition on Kindle.

about the boy, though the boy knows nothing about the man; and the man lies about his relationship to the boy. What should the boy do? He would naturally be eager to meet a long lost uncle. Should he trust the strange man? How will a magician (the reader must wonder) use the *boy* to become powerful? Will Aladdin be hurt? Will he get into trouble or himself become powerful? Compare this rich scenario to the plot of the modern book chosen by the alleged magicians of the Common Core, now busy introducing themselves to our modern Aladdins, who, if they haven't lost their fathers, have certainly lost their fathers' (or grandfathers') education. *It's time to herd cows, Cocoa*, says Cowgirl Kate in monosyllables. *But Cocoa is thirsty.* Oh, no! Now there is a story a second- or third-grade boy can really sink his teeth into.

This, then, is the standards game: big promises, no delivery. We are told in obscure language that students will be reading complex books. When we look at the books, we find that they are not that complex. As we shall see presently and in subsequent chapters, the teaching of the books is also far from rigorous and often downright silly. Few ever bother to think about what the students in public schools could be doing of real value since too few people still know and not many are listening to those who do, certainly no one in state education bureaucracies. The schools I work with all read *Aladdin* in the third grade. If you would like to place the two selections above, I would suggest the adapted version be read in second grade, while the standard version could be read by most third-graders. Either version could be *read to* students in the earlier grades—with "scaffolding," of course, i.e. explaining big words to small students. *Yet Aladdin is not recommended in the Common Core.* In other words, Common Core Standard RL-2.9. looks pretty good until you know what the words mean and start asking questions.

Contrary to what the arch-testers claim about the Common Core being only a set of standards, the Standards most certainly *do* dictate how to teach literature. Worse, they employ the same methods that have drained the life out of great stories over the last half century. All the predictable, formulaic, story-killing ways of reading literature make their way into these standards: "point of view," the "main idea," "structure," "author's choices," and, of course, the old favorite, "compare and contrast." That is not to say that there is nothing new in these standards. The two innovations (which today's parents did not grow up with) are "diversity" and integrating and evaluating "content presented in diverse media and formats." In other words, the arch-testers want a lot more non-white-male authors and non-Western literature and a lot more fiddling around with computers. Notwithstanding these new and indeed radical features, mostly the Common Core simply reproduces bad teaching of literature. We do not have time to dwell on each one of these story-killing standards, but let us look at one: "compare and contrast."

So heavily does the Common Core rely on the technique of "compare and contrast" to analyze literature, that it might be called the *Überstandard*. It occupies its own category in the ten "anchor standards" that are repeated throughout the document. Yet it also acts as a cancer that eats into other (equally worthless) standards. For example, on page 12 we see how "compare and contrast" can colonize other categories:

> Compare and contrast two or more characters, settings, or events in a story or drama, drawing on specific details in the text (e.g., how characters interact). RL-5.3.

> Compare and contrast the point of view from which different stories are narrated, including the difference between first- and third-person narrations. RL-4.6.

> Make connections between the text of a story or drama and a visual or oral presentation of the text, identifying where each version reflects specific descriptions and directions in the text. RL-4.7. [Though the exact words are not used, this is clearly a "compare and contrast" approach.]

> Compare and contrast the themes, settings, and plots of stories written by the same author about the same or similar characters (e.g., in books from a series). RL-3.9.[36]

---

[36] These last three listed do appear in the compare-and-contrast anchor standard.

Compare and contrast the treatment of similar themes and topics (e.g., opposition of good and evil) and patterns of events (e.g., the quest) in stories, myths, and traditional literature from different cultures. RL-4.9.[37]

Compare and contrast stories in the same genre (e.g., mysteries and adventure stories) on their approaches to similar themes and topics. RL-5.9.

One gets the impression that teachers and students will be doing a lot of comparing and contrasting. If we had time, we could compare and contrast what teachers think of such frequent comparing and contrasting versus what students think. We could then further compare and contrast what genuine students and scholars of literature think about such hokey, boilerplate diversions and what the educational establishment thinks about them. There is a wide gulf between the parties in each one of these scenarios.

While the *Überstandard* of "compare and contrast" may sound exciting, it is really not. In the cases above, students would be underwhelmed. Comparing one character to another in a novel is simply common sense. "Why is Jane a more suitable match for Bingley and Elizabeth for Mr. Darcy?"[38] Do we really need a state-mandated standard for that? Such comparisons would come naturally to any sensible reader of literature. (Do "standards" reveal something we would prefer not to know about our teachers?) Then we proceed to comparing and contrasting first- versus third-person narration. That should take about seven seconds. Written versus visual presentations of the text? "Look at the pretty illustrations, children." Stories by the same author or a series? The Common Core does not really give us any of those, so this is an empty promise. Stories from different cultures? This is an instance of using an empty standard as a pretext for diversity

---

[37] One must wonder at some of these phrases, such as "stories, myths, and traditional literature." Are stories and myths not part of traditional literature? Do they mean *folklore*?

[38] Clearly, this would not be a discussion for fourth- and fifth-graders. I am simply using an example from a familiar novel, which, as we shall see, the Common Core bungles badly.

and multiculturalism. Stories of the same genre? "Does this space adventure remind you of any other space adventure we've been on this year, class?" The shell game of the *Überstandard* becomes clear when we compare and contrast the "critical thinking" the standard seems to hold out to us and the simple-minded discussions that take place in classrooms across the land.

To show the hollowness of "compare and contrast," let us follow the Common Core's directions. The inaugural exercise for this standard appears in Kindergarten:

> With prompting and support, compare and contrast the adventures and experiences of characters in familiar stories. [RL-K.9.]

What discussion would we expect to emerge from this exercise? For the "adventures," let's choose *Little Red Riding Hood* and *Jack and the Beanstalk*. Teacher prompting and supporting students: "Okay, class, in *Little Red Riding Hood* the *main character* [this is the way teachers following standards talk] did not do what her mother said, and what happened to her?" Class: "She got eaten by a wolf." Teacher: "Yes. Very good, class. Now in *Jack and the Beanstalk* the main character didn't do what his mother said, and what happened to him?" Class: "He climbed up a beanstalk and got a golden harp and a goose that lays golden eggs and killed a giant." Teacher: "Okay, class, now *compare and contrast*. What do you make of these similarities and differences?" Class, bewildered: "Maybe Little Red Riding Hood should have asked Jack to help her." "Did Jack use the same ax that the woodcutter used to kill the wolf?" "I think Jack and Little Red Riding Hood will get married and live happily ever after." Teacher: "Good ideas, boys and girls. But remember, these are two *different stories*." Class: "Was the wolf really the giant's dog that climbed down the beanstalk?" And so on.

The great eighteenth-century man of letters Samuel Johnson once said that "patriotism is the last refuge of a scoundrel."[39] Similarly, "compare-and-contrast" is the last refuge of a teacher

---

[39] The comment did not mean that Johnson was against patriotism but that a scoundrel would take refuge in it to hide his character. Today, a scoundrel (or politician) might take refuge in some other easily invoked good, like *caring* about society or the environment or the children, "who are our future."

who doesn't know anything—or of a standards-monger who must pretend like he does know something—about literature. The diversion of comparing and contrasting two different literary works takes the heat off the teacher who does not know one work thoroughly. It is easy to get caught up in all the differences between *Little Red Riding Hood* and *Jack and the Beanstalk* because they have nothing in common, other than the prevalence of supernatural phenomena such as great beanstalks and giants and talking wolves. By offering a cursory glance at the story and then resorting to comparing and contrasting, teachers never give students a thorough reading of a discrete story. Consider just one aspect of "Little Red Riding Hood." It is fairly typical to blame Riding Hood for not doing what her mother told her to do. Yet have we really stopped to think about her well-known actions? A little girl is made to go on an errand in all haste. She doesn't. Why not? Because she stops to *pick flowers*. And to *talk* to someone. Imagine that! A little girl who loves flowers (that is, who gets lost in the beauties of nature) and who likes talking to people! Who ever heard of such a thing? Now that is a point that would never come up in a regular public-school classroom precisely because teachers have not been trained to lose themselves in the beauties of stories but rather to lose their students in the ugliness of "standards."

In short, the more we slow down to think about what characters do in stories, and to consider each story as a different world that we are being invited into, the greater insight we have into characters and their actions. The so-called standards, however, impose false skills or cutesy tricks on literature. Teachers, following the leads of these prompts, end up doing drive-bys in the name of "critical thinking," yet without ever understanding a great story in its own terms. Neither they nor their students ever enter into the unique world of a single, beautiful story and take up residence there, learn to live in that world, as it were. If, as Emily Dickinson told us, there is no frigate like a book, we can hardly consider it "critical thinking" to jump back and forth from frigate to frigate. Anyone who has ever lived aboard a ship knows that the vessel becomes your world. You live there. You get to know everyone aboard and every inch of that ship. As much as you want to get home, you are somewhat sad to leave it when you arrive in port. Yet our teachers, following silly standards, never invite students to board these vessels called books.

Parents who recall their own days in school may smile in remembrance of things past. What I call two-bit literary criticism has been going on for some time. We shall visit an example of it at the high-school level in a moment and examine its clear presence in the Common Core in a subsequent chapter. Nonetheless, there is something new and scary in the Brave New World of Standards. Around the country school principals and the many sundry district administrators insist that teachers post both the Common Core and state[40] standards on the walls of their classrooms. Realize that these standards go on for pages. Posting *all* the standards for *all* the subjects could easily take up half a wall. Further still, many principals are now insisting that teachers write the particular standards on the board that they will be using for each given lesson. Presumably, the reason behind this exercise is threefold. First, by having the "standard" on the board, the teacher will have his or her mind on precisely what the lesson will cover in the eyes of the state education bureaucracy. Second, if a principal or other administrator happens to walk by or sit in on a class (a rare event), the administrator will instantly know which standard or standards are being "covered." And, last but not least, the students will have full cognizance of what "standard" they are being treated to at any given moment of the day. How might that play out in a real classroom? "Okay, first graders, today we are going to

1. Participate in collaborative conversations with diverse partners about *grade 1 topics and texts* with peers and adults in small and larger groups.
    a. Follow agreed-upon rules for discussions (e.g. listening to others with care, speaking one at a time about the topics and texts under discussion).
    b. Build on others' talk in conversations by responding to the comments of others through multiple exchanges.
    c. Ask questions to clear up any confusion about the topics and texts under discussion. SL-1.1.

---

[40] For the subjects besides math and English.

Any questions, first graders?" Hand goes up. "Yes, Julia?" Julia: "Are you saying that you're going to read us a book and we're going to talk about it?" "Yes, Julia, that's just what we're going to do."

It is not a stretch to say that the schools are now operating under a cult of standards. *Everything* must be connected to a standard. *Nothing* can be done that is not a standard. Very few people see the utter poverty of the standards, so the language of standards binds all. Teachers must write mind-numbing lesson plans in which everything they mean to teach or assign is cross-referenced to a standard. These documents get turned in to the office, where they go into a file (whether electronic or physical) and remain there until the end of time, never to be looked at again. Of course, much of this "lesson-planning" becomes a cut-and-paste operation, just as the Common Core Standards themselves have the feel of that wonderful function of Microsoft Office. Though the word "conversation" appears in the Speaking and Listening (SL) Standards, the actual conversations teachers and students have in schools are artificial, robotic, programmed. To realize how absurd this charade is, imagine your professors in college writing up a "standard" on the board, then forcing the entire discussion into that "standard." Yet this is the way students are being made "college ready." Simply put, the public schools are places where common sense is an uncommon virtue. If the way young people learn to read, understand, and talk about "texts" is a preview of how they will read, understand, and talk about the world, we have dark, bureaucratic, nonsensical days ahead of us.

Of course, if you are tricked or intimidated by the phony language of standards you will not think so. If you bother to read the standards (and that is a big *if*) you could well be taken in by the smoke and mirrors. To get a little more training, let's compare and contrast the speaking and listening standard number one for first grade quoted above to speaking and listening standard number one for eleventh and twelfth grades.

1.   Initiate and participate effectively in a range of collaborative discussions (one-on-one, in groups, and teacher-led) with diverse partners on grades 11-12 topics, texts, and issues, building

on others' ideas and expressing their own clearly and persuasively.

 a. Come to discussions prepared, having read and researched material under study; explicitly draw on that preparation by referring to evidence from texts and other research on the topic or issue to stimulate a thoughtful, well-reasoned exchange of ideas.

 b. Work with peers to promote civil, democratic discussions and decision-making, set clear goals and deadlines, and establish individual roles as needed.

 c. Propel conversations by posing and responding to questions that probe reasoning and evidence; ensure a hearing for a full range of positions on a topic or issue; clarify, verify, or challenge ideas and conclusions; and promote divergent and creative perspectives.

 d. Respond thoughtfully to diverse perspectives; synthesize comments, claims, and evidence made on all sides of an issue; resolve contradictions when possible; and determine what additional information or research is required to deepen the investigation or complete the task. SL-11-12.1.

This onslaught of verbiage leads us to believe that high-level "critical thinking" will be going on in these classrooms. We need to translate this standard into what it really means. "Initiate": Are students really going to come into the class and begin discussing literature unprompted? Hah! "Collaborative": what other kinds of discussions are there? "One-on-one, in groups": "So who are you going to Homecoming with?" "And teacher-led": notice this comes *last* in the order. What will the teacher be doing during the one-on-one and group discussion time? (Hint: Teachers spend a lot of time at their computers in a twenty-first-century classroom.) "Diverse partners": the word should be "different"? But the arch-testers want us to love the word *diverse* and use it constantly and promiscuously. Or perhaps they really mean that the groups should represent different sexes, colors, and socio-economic backgrounds. Sub-point a): Do you mean students will actually have to do homework? Wow! "Research": i.e. the Internet, i.e. Wikipedia. Besides, why should students be doing "research" in their literature classes rather than just reading books carefully? Sub-point b): "Decisions, deadlines, roles": "I know, let's, like, do a puppet show on *Macbeth.*" "Oh, that would be totally cool." "Leslie, you do Lady Macbeth, and make your puppet look, like, really mean." Sub-point c): "Divergent and creative perspectives": "*Divergent* (definition 2): departing from convention, deviant." Do the authors of the Common Core want *different* or a *variety* of opinions, or do they actually want *deviant* opinions? My guess is they are after radical, non-traditional opinions that run counter to what the majority of parents still hold as self-evident truths. Shouldn't schools promote sensible opinions rather than divergent ones? Sub-point d): "Diverse perspectives": In case you have not picked up on this yet, realize *diversity* is the highest good. The exact meaning of diversity is not really given. One implication is that there are really never any right or wrong perspectives or answers, except those that would not meet the approval of the diversity crowd. Notice, too, that this standard is entirely *student-centered.* All the injunctions are aimed at what the students ought to do: "initiate and participate," "come to discussions," "work with peers," "propel conversations," "respond thoughtfully." Will the *teachers* require students make reasonable arguments based upon what the book actually says rather than either pure conjecture or argumentativeness? Will there be any teaching going on at all?

A careful analysis of this "standard" on speaking and listening, then, reveals a three-way crash and a cover-up. The wreck involves the vehicle of Deweyite, Romper-Room progressivism ("in groups," individual roles in what are clearly projects, "tasks") running into the high-tech vehicle of the techno-progressives (research, research, and more research, joined by "multiple sources of information" in the following standard SL-11-12.2.), who are further rear-ended by the political progressives of the Left ("diverse," "full range of positions," "challenge ideas and conclusions," "divergent and creative opinions"). The cover-up of this wreck consists in everybody acting as though this bogus standard either accurately describes, or would result in, a thought-provoking discussion rooted in an actual work of literature. It consists in behaving as though the collision of progressive education never occurred. Someone who really wanted to cultivate a genuine conversation about great books would simply not write in this phony way. In fact, all this claptrap could be easily replaced with one word: *Socratic*. That word or concept, though, would be of no help to the teachers and students in today's public schools. Nor would the Common Core help out. Not a single one of Plato's Socratic dialogues makes the list of Common Core exemplar texts. It is as though the founder of philosophy, education, and "divergent and creative" thinking in the West never existed.

Mind you, the average parent is not supposed to raise any sensible questions. In the deliberately confusing world of public education, standards are meant to work as a kind of magic charm. We are supposed to be so enamored with the standards that we do not think much about how these incredible (or incredibly obscure) feats of pedagogy are to be pulled off. The books themselves are almost irrelevant. We are supposed to skip along down the yellow-brick road to critical thinking. What the standards promise will happen and what will actually happen are two different things entirely. But we are not supposed to perceive the difference. We must realize, then, the full effects of the pseudo-standards on actual works of literature so that we shall know how to fight them. That is, we must "compare and contrast" a standards-based approach and the legitimate ways of studying great literature. In order to understand the real effects of standards, then, we have to take a trip down Memory Lane. We have to go back to high school. Now I realize that there is a great risk in going back to high school, given the sweet associations that time in our lives brings to mind: the pep-rallies, the big games, the music, the dances, falling in love, falling out of love: Great Times. Yet it is another memory we must evoke, a memory of actually being *in class*. I know it will be hard.

So there you were, with a book in your hands: a good book in fact, one whose story is so much a part of our culture that it gets spoofed or imitated in teen movies. The book I mean is *The Scarlet Letter*. Let us take a look at a certain passage from that book, one that should be known by every graduate of an American high school:

It was a circumstance to be noted, on the summer morning when our story begins its course, that the women, of whom there were several in the crowd, appeared to take a peculiar interest in whatever penal infliction might be expected to ensue. The age had not so much refinement that any sense of impropriety restrained the wearers of petticoat and farthingale from stepping forth into the public ways and wedging their not unsubstantial persons, if occasion were, into the throng nearest the scaffold at an execution. . . .

"Goodwives," said a hard-featured dame of fifty, "I'll tell ye a piece of my mind. It would be greatly for the public behoof, if we women, being of mature age and church members in good repute, should have the handling of such malefactresses as this Hester Prynne. What think ye, gossips? If the hussy stood up for judgment before us five, that are now here in a knot together, would she come off with such a sentence as the worshipful magistrates have awarded? Marry, I trow not!"

"People say," said another, "that the Reverend Master Dimmsdale, her godly pastor, takes it very grievously to heart that such a scandal should have come upon his congregation."

"The magistrates are God-fearing gentlemen, but merciful overmuch—that is a truth," added a third autumnal matron. "At the very least, they should have put the brand of a hot iron on Hester Prynne's forehead. Madam Hester would have winced at that, I warrant me. But she—the naughty baggage—little will she care what they put upon the bodice of her gown! Why, look you, she may cover it with a brooch, or suchlike heathenish adornment, and so walk the streets as brave as ever!"

"Ah, but," interposed more softly, a young wife, holding a child by the hand, "let her cover the mark as she will, the pang of it will be always in her heart."

"What do we talk of marks and brands, whether on the bodice of her gown, or the flesh of her forehead?" cried another female, the ugliest as well as the most pitiless of these self-constituted judges. "This woman has brought shame upon us all, and ought to die. Is there not law for it? Truly there is, both in the Scripture and the statute book. Then let the magistrates, who have made it of no effect, thank themselves if their own wives and daughters go astray!"

"Mercy on us, good wife," exclaimed a man in the crowd, "is there no virtue in woman, save what springs from a wholesome fear of the gallows? That is the hardest word yet! Hush, now, gossips! for the lock is turning in the prison door, and here comes Mistress Prynne herself."

. . . When the young woman—the mother of this child—stood fully revealed before the crowd, it seemed to be her first impulse to clasp the infant closely to her bosom; not so much by an impulse of motherly affection, as that she might thereby conceal a certain token, which was wrought or fastened into her dress. In a moment, however, wisely judging that one token of her shame would but poorly serve to hide another, she took the baby on her arm, and, with a burning blush, and yet a haughty smile, and a glance that would not be abashed, looked around at her towns-people and neighbors. On the breast of her gown, in fine red cloth surrounded with an elaborate embroidery and fantastic flourishes of gold thread, appeared the letter "A". . . .

The young woman was tall, with a figure of perfect elegance on a large scale. She had dark and abundant hair, so glossy that it threw off the sunshine with a gleam, and a face which, besides being beautiful from regularity of feature and richness of complexion, had the impressiveness belonging to a marked brow and deep black eyes. She was ladylike, too, after the manner of the feminine gentility of those days. . . . And never had Hester Prynne appeared more ladylike, in the antique interpretation of the term, than as she issued from the prison. Those who had before known her and had expected to behold her dimmed and obscured by a disastrous cloud, were astonished, and even startled, to perceive how her beauty shone out and made a halo of the misfortune and ignominy in which she was enveloped.

Well, what do we make of this scene?

Before saying anything about Hester, we should probably spend a little time getting to know the people in the crowd that has gathered outside this jail. We shall soon learn what the woman's crime was. How do the people talk about it? Specifically, how do the *men* and *women* talk about it? Is there a difference? Do the older women have opinions that differ from the younger? Do the opinions of the less attractive differ from those of the more attractive? By digging into the conversation that actually takes place, we learn in fact that the women are much harsher on Hester than the men and the older women are much harsher than the younger, at least judging by the "young wife." Why?

"Why?" opens up a lot of possibilities—possibilities that should be discussed in class. Are the older women present more removed from the passions of young women, while the "young wife," holding a child by the hand, may better know what could have driven the adulteress to her crime? Is the "ugliest as well as the most pitiless" of these women not so much offended on behalf of Biblical law as she is jealous? How many men have desired *her* in such a way? And is it not true that the men, however righteous they may be, cannot avoid being attracted by Hester's beauty while the women, however just they try to be, find it nearly impossible to refrain from being jealous of it? Aren't women simply harder on women than men are? (If I am not mistaken, several girls in the class, having survived the slings of arrows of adolescent popularity, would say, "Yeah-uh, girls are like *way* harder.")

Once the teacher has pursued this line of questioning (which very much fits in with Hawthorne's description of these unnamed Puritan "gossips"), she might play Puritan's advocate by asking the most obvious question yet one that is probably not brought up in a hundred classrooms across this land. "*Should* the women be upset with Hester? What is, after all, the question that would be on everyone's mind?" The students may not get it at first, but in time it might dawn on one or two. The real question in that crowd would be, simply, *Who is the father?* That question matters. If you were a woman standing in that crowd, what might you be thinking, as hard as you tried not to? Hester's crime was not committed with an unmarried man; otherwise she would have just married the fellow. Puritans, like any other people, did that all the time. Leave aside Dimmsdale; the people have no right to suspect him at this moment (nor should the reader if the teacher stays away from bringing up the literary device known as "foreshadowing," i.e. giving the surprise away). Hester is young; she is beautiful; you are getting older and your beauty is fading. How do you know the father is not *your husband*? Might that possibility help explain, at least in part, why the women in this crowd are harsher than the men?

If you were in a class where such questions were being asked and discussed, a good twenty or thirty minutes would have passed even before getting to Hester's emergence from the prison. And they really would be thirty *good* minutes, because the students would be thinking about the people in this story. They would be getting to know them. Once Hester arrives on the scene, there is much more to talk about, of course. Here are a few possible questions. What sort of woman can stand up to this kind of public scrutiny? Is her composure, even defiance, at this moment a virtue? If so, what virtue? This public demonstration of Hester's punishment is meant to teach a lesson. What is the lesson that is supposed to be taught? Is that the lesson being taught? Playing Puritans' advocate, we might ask: Should Hester, given what we know so far (which is not much), feel more guilt for her actions? Consider her child. How much chance will that child have in this world? Or, if not Hester, should *someone* feel guilt for this crime? Here we have a woman alone with a child being punished for adultery. Where is the lover of that woman? Where is the father of that child? Is he hiding in the crowd? Is that what a man does—hide and let a woman take the fall? Hester is described as being "ladylike." Is that the description we would expect of a woman for this crime? Are Hester's beauty and being ladylike somehow on trial? What kind of person (or woman) is Hester? What does it reveal about her that she has simultaneously a "burning blush" and a "haughty smile" and a "glance that would not be abashed"? Might this aspect of her character explain, at least in part, her crime or misdeed? Looking ahead (yet without giving away the story), we can ask: What kind of character would it take for Hester to repair her relations with her fellow townspeople? Is it likely that she will be able to? At one point, the scarlet letter itself is said to have "the effect of a spell, taking her out of the ordinary relations with humanity and enclosing her in a sphere by herself." What kind of sphere is that? How is it possible for a person both to live among a people and yet live completely apart from them? Is it good for man—or woman—to be alone?

These are by no means the only questions that could be asked of this important scene in American literature. But they are, I warrant, questions that could lead to a discussion about Hester Prynne and her little town that would help students begin to understand the very human story that unfolds in *The Scarlet Letter*. And they would be glad to do so. In fact, you might find that students would not be able to put the book down. The crucial question for the moment, however, is whether this was the kind of discussion you had on *The Scarlet Letter* in high school. Or, were you like most students (I am one of them) utterly bored to death with the following predictable, dreary "analysis"?

"Okay, class" begins the teacher, "what do you think about the setting?" No answer. "Well, is it a dark setting or a light setting?" One diligent student raises her hand. "Yes, Molly?" "It's a dark setting." "That's right. See how the mood is dark, class?" Teacher writes on the overhead "Dark setting." The class, many of whom are also writing notes to their classmates, pause to write down these words: "dark setting." "Okay, class, now do we see any foreshadowing?" No one, not even Molly, perceives any foreshadowing. Uncomfortable silence. Teacher says, "Class, go to where it says 'the Reverend Master Dimmsdale, her godly pastor.' Wherever you see the name Dimmsdale, until the author tells us what is going on, that's foreshadowing." The class,

following the teacher, writes down "Dimmsdale—foreshadowing."
"Okay, class, let's talk about characterization. So, let's start with
all these people that are just there at the beginning of the story,
waiting for the main character to come out of the prison. Would
you say these are flat characters or round characters?" Molly cries
out, "Flat characters!" "Yes, that's right. But remember, Molly,
we're working on our listening skills as well as our speaking skills.
So be sure to raise your hand the next time you have a contribution
to make. Alright, then, I'll just write up here 'flat characters.'"
The teacher writes *flat characters*. "Now, let's see, what kind of
character do we think the main character, or the protagonist, is
going to have? Johnny, we haven't heard from you for a while.
What kind of character do you think this Hester is going to have?"
"I dunno." "Well, let's see, do you think she will be a static or
dynamic character?" "Uh, dynamic?" "Yes, very good. She will
be a *dynamic* character because we will see *change over time* and
character development." "Okay, class, it's too soon to look at the
rising action because we're just looking at the setting in this
chapter, so we'll just skip that for now. But does anybody see *the
main idea* developing?" Molly's hand instantly goes up. "Oh, I
know. It's man, or I guess, *woman* versus society. Yeah, like
everybody's against this main character Hester, so it must be *man
versus society*." "Very good, Molly." Teacher and students write
"(wo)man vs. society." Teacher continues: "Okay, class, let's turn
to the next chapter and see if we can find any rising action." And
for the next twenty-two chapters every student, except for Molly,
will hate this book.

Though I might not get every single detail right, this is pretty
much what the study of literature in high school has been for at
least forty years. It is utterly mechanical. Once the teacher and
students map out the supposed plot structure and assign the
appropriate literary "terms" to the various literary devices "the
author" uses, there is, we are led to believe, nothing left to talk
about. In other words, the students will all "learn" that the "main
idea" is "(wo)man vs. society"; yet they will learn nothing about

either the woman or the society in the story. They will simply learn nothing interesting about the book.[41]

Anyone with any common sense should see that this is not the way to study literature. Literature is about people. Literature may be fiction, but it is still about people. And we do not get to know—least of all figure out—*people* by asking them what their main idea is or whether they are in the middle of a rising action and heading towards a climax or if they could tell us their "setting, characterization, and plot." True, literature is written by an author. But I defy the arch-testers to find one good author in the history of the world who wanted his or her stories to be dissected in such a lifeless, mechanical way. We get to know books in the same way we get to know people. We spend time with them. We observe them. We think about them. We have conversations with them. Above all, we ask them questions. Some stale souls may think it is not possible to ask questions of a book when the book cannot answer back. But the book does answer back! We just have to be paying attention when the answers are given, however discreetly.

Why, then, do schools teach literature in this dry, artificial way rather than in the way great authors meant their stories to be read? Well, there are two main answers. One is bad teaching. The other is standards. In fact, bad teaching and standards are simply one big chicken-and-egg argument about why the schools are bad. So let us look at our two main themes or "central ideas" and "see how they interact and build on one another to produce" school failure.

Reading great literature, as we said, is much like getting to know people. But people are different. The people found in great literature are particularly different—individual. Each story is unique. Mystery shrouds both the characters and the story since the people in stories, like people in real life, do not just come out and tell us why they are acting in a particular way—assuming they know themselves, which they often do not. Therefore, to be a keen reader of literature, one must be an astute interpreter of human beings and the human condition. Well, not many people are.

Teachers have to stand up in front of rooms full of students. The students will not get the ball rolling. They expect the teacher

---

[41] At the risk of redundancy, the present argument will be repeated in chapter six with actual examples taken for the Common Core. Since this artificial and bankrupt way of viewing literature has become so planted in our minds, and must be uprooted for any genuine literary education to flourish, I hope the reader will not mind my reiteration on this theme.

to know something. If the teacher is *not* a keen reader of literature nor an astute interpreter of the human condition (which is exceedingly likely given the monopoly of the ed schools) then he, or she, needs a crutch. In rides the Teacher's Edition to the rescue. The Teacher's Edition to the textbook, augmented by some silly practices concocted in ed schools, offers all kinds of boilerplate plot devices, canned questions, and pseudo-literary jargon that will help the teacher get through the class. The rest of the story is already familiar to us.

What about the STANDARDS: the Common Core Standards or any other standards? Standards are a very obvious byproduct of the progressive philosophy of education. The progressive establishment values skills over knowledge. Deep down, the progressives are not even keen on the idea of amusement, despite what they say about all the "fun" that is supposed to take place in the elementary school. Therefore, they do not like the idea of students just reading, having a conversation about, and enjoying *The Scarlet Letter*. They do not know what such a conversation looks like; nor do they care to participate in one. Rather, they want the students getting some kind of mechanical skill out of books that will supposedly be useful in the workplace. But "skills," though a word the progressives use, does not sound lofty enough. It sounds too much like plumbing or auto repair.[42] So they elevate skills into "standards," a high-sounding word. "We need to have *standards* in education!" say the progressives. According to the educrats, the problem with our schools is not the fact that progressive education has attempted to kill off all remnant of true learning. That would lay the blame at their door. It's that we don't have the right standards! The new arch-testers, who are the new progressives, are even more adamant on the rule of standards because standards are *measurable*. They can be collected into data! You can't measure the depth of a mere conversation, after all. And everything about education must be *measurable*. No one bothers to notice that the best examples of teaching in the history of the world took place in the form of *conversations*, the leaders of those conversations being Jesus and Socrates.

---

[42] Not that I have anything against plumbing or auto repair. But those are *skills*, not arts. Compare the number of different kinds of sink fixtures or transmissions to the number of different personalities.

So where do the makers of standards get their standards? *They* are not teachers. So they have to go to the sources of what takes place in the classrooms already: to the ed schools or to the publishers of classroom-in-a-box Teacher's Editions, both obviously wanting the teachers to go right on doing what they are doing. Everyone who stands to profit, whether financially or politically, is in on the game, though not everyone knows how much it is a game. The people who are the most affected are really those who have the clearest view of the subject. If you ask a student what he learned in English class today, he will say likely say, "I dunno. It was boring." He is not saying that because he is a disaffected teenager. He is saying that because it is true.

Most parents today, as well as most state legislators, were brought up in this way of "studying" literature. If they were not weaned of this nonsense in college, they are likely still under the impression that learning literature consists in armchair literary criticism. Anyone who bothers to look at the standards, which are utterly boring and hardly worth reading, might wonder, as we have said, what the big fuss is over. "Analyze the impact of the author's choices regarding how to develop and relate elements of a story or drama (e.g., where a story is set, how the action is ordered, how the characters are introduced and developed.)" That is cleverly written. It is high-sounding enough to make us think something rigorously academic will take place in the classroom. It is obscure enough to keep us from really knowing *what* will be taking place in the classroom. It is technical enough to make the arch-testers giddy. It is formulaic enough to allow the publishers to package it up nice and tidy in a teacher's edition. It is predictable enough to reassure the teachers they will have a crutch before going into a classroom and having to talk about difficult books like *The Scarlet Letter* and *Billy Budd*. And it sounds serious enough to make parents and taxpayers think that their children's time and their own hard-earned money are not being utterly wasted. "Sure," says the parent, decades after his own battle with boredom. "I remember this stuff in school. What's the big deal?" The big deal is that as soon as you ask a student an important question arising out of a specific work of literature, whether ten years or ten minutes after the class that ought to have discussed such a question, the student crumbles. "Was Dimmsdale a coward?" "What, who, huh?"

To the story-killers, the books themselves, the great stories of Western Civilization, are not real and not important. They want *skills* (the measurable, technical things) to be derived from the books. Therefore they are delighted when certain predictable questions or tasks are imposed on great books that yield pat, predictable, and, above all, measurable answers. They think that the skills derived from bastardizing books in this way will be more useful in the TFCGE[43]—in the "real world"—than the mere human pleasure and insight derived from reading a compelling story. That the teachers don't understand the stories very well makes it easier to pull this scheme off. Game, set, and match.

When standards become the goal of learning, the stories and characters—in all their rich variety and individuality—must be sacrificed to the standards. But something else must be sacrificed, and the cloistered computerati, confined to their cubicles, staring at data for ten hours of every day, cannot for the life of them see what that thing is that they kill off—or delete. It is nothing less than our understanding of our fellow human beings. People who work in *the real world* have to deal with difficult, idiosyncratic, imperfect, and sometimes wonderful human beings—every day. Knowing how to "handle," how to approach, how to get along with, and how to inspire those human beings is the *art*—not the science and not the skill—of human relations. We cannot know and get on with our fellow human beings until we take an interest in them. And we cannot ever get close to understanding them until we take an interest in humanity. Great literature is the study of humanity. Serious readers of great literature—studied on its own terms, not through a plot graph—cannot but be keen judges of their fellow men. By trying to force stories into a formula, the story-killers make them less applicable to the real world of real people.

When you come to know a great work of literature, you may be surprised how much it teaches you about the world. Just take up a book someday that you were supposed to have read in high school and see what mysteries it unveils. For starters, with the opening scene of *The Scarlet Letter* in mind, ask a woman, almost any woman, whether she would prefer to have woman as her boss or a man. You may be surprised at the answer.

---

[43] Twenty-first-century global economy. It is about time this hackneyed phrase gets its own acronym.

Chapter Four
Complexity without Quality

The "standards" themselves are not the worst offense in the Common Core English Standards. Were the arch-testers only trying to force down the nation's throat a set of standards, as worthless as those standards are, we could not accuse them of removing the remnant of good books left in the public schools; of deliberately introducing politically charged "texts" into the curriculum; of promoting biased interpretations of traditional literature that remains; and of blocking the way to genuine school reform. We would simply say that a national set of standards is a nationalization and systemization of bad teaching and reveals a chronic failure to understand stories in their own terms. We would not call the authors of the Common Core radical innovators. But the arch-testers do not stop with standards. They do much, much more.

Reading the *Common Core Standards for English Language Arts*, etc. is an invitation to marvel at how much common sense we have lost in the last half century of progressive control over schools. In the old days, the heads of schools just told the public that they would be teaching the three R's in the primary grades and reading certain books with the students in the upper grades. Everyone knew what that meant. Everyone knew what the three R's were. And everyone knew what reading at the higher levels meant. Moreover, everyone, including the general public, knew what books ought to be read. One teacher might prefer to teach *Othello* over *King Lear* (in addition to other plays of Shakespeare), but it was still Shakespeare being taught. Such was the state of elementary and secondary education in our great-grandparents' day and in our grandparents' day. Had the Common Core been proposed back then, it would have elicited a howl of laughter.

As we have seen, over the course of the twentieth century the schools abandoned the traditional ways of teaching literature and adopted a set of Mickey Mouse "standards" or skills that reduced literature to simplistic formulae. But some of the literature remained. This was not so much the case in the elementary schools which were partly turned into Romper Rooms and whose students were given more "age-appropriate material" to read (i.e. no classics) and saddled with the infamous SRA's. Yet it is true that until almost yesterday, you could still find some good books at least being *assigned* in high schools: *To Kill a Mockingbird*, *Romeo and Juliet*, *Hamlet*, *Huckleberry Finn*, and *The Scarlet Letter*, to name a few. That is important. The monks of the scriptoria who, hour after hour, wrote out the Greek and Roman classics when scarcely anyone in the West could read, who themselves usually did not appreciate the valuable treasures they had in front of them, at least kept books alive in an almost sacred act of transference. Just as Montag in *Fahrenheit 451* saves books, hardly knowing what to make of them, so might the assigning of the right books and stories in high school, however ineptly taught, act as a kind of moral and cultural preservative. The end-game of the Common Core, though, is not just to replace fifty sets of worthless state standards[44] with a national set of worthless standards. The Common Core authors seek to undo our moral and cultural heritage found in the great books, and to do so without letting anyone know what they intend. We must figure out how they are managing to pull this feat off.

The mysteries begin to be solved when we look closely at the manner by which the Common Core orchestrates the selection of "texts" to be read and which students will surely be tested on. The arch-testers promote three criteria of text selection: *complexity*, *quality*, and *range*. For reasons that will become clear, virtually all of their attention is given to *complexity*. To justify this criterion of selection, the arch-testers offer the earth-shattering revelation that students should be required to read and comprehend "literary and informational texts of steadily increasing complexity" over the course of their years in school. To justify this truism that no one ever questioned, the Common Core authors offer a tedious thirty-five-page Appendix A whose purpose is to make people believe that the Common Core is "research-based" and that its effects will

---

[44] Or forty-nine, if you exclude Massachusetts.

be to bring more complex "literary and informational texts" into the schools. A term they are sneaking into their argument is "informational text." They are hoping their emphasis on *complexity*, joined with the aims of preparing students for a scary "twenty-first-century global economy," will allow them to import brave new informational texts into what, once upon a time, had been a literature curriculum.

Complexity is again mentioned at the outset of Appendix B, wherein Appendix A is summarized beginning with the sentence: "Appendix A describes in detail a three-part model of measuring text complexity based on qualitative and quantitative indices of inherent text difficulty balanced with educators' professional judgment in matching readers and texts in light of particular tasks." After this bit of poetry, passing mention is given to "quality" and "range," copyrights are discussed, and then the Common Core authors go on to offer "exemplars" of "literary and informational texts" with desirable complexity, quality, and range.

Not so fast. First, we must ask, is the lack of *complexity* of texts in the schools the fundamental problem with students' reading? Wouldn't it be simpler to say that the schools fail to use the proper methods of teaching reading (i.e. explicit phonics) in the early grades, that the stories students read during and beyond the primary years are insipid, and that when the high schools finally begin to assign the classics the teachers make mush out of them? Furthermore, why are we treated to this mind-numbing argument about text complexity in Appendix A but not given a separate explanation of *quality* and another of *range*? Traditionally, *quality* has been the chief criterion for choosing books for schools, and the category of *range* (as we shall see) is clearly where all the politics is these days. Yet we are given no clear guidelines on what constitutes either the quality or the range of a book, story, or "informational text." Do the arch-testers not know how to explain these criteria? Is this an oversight in their so-called research? Or do they simply hope the unsuspecting public is not thinking too hard about these matters, particularly about *quality*?

We shall look at quality and range in a moment. Let us first see how the authors of the Common Core determine the complexity of a literary or "informational" text. Here is how they describe the process:

Like Dale-Chall, the Lexile Framework for Reading, developed by MetaMetrics, Inc., uses word frequency and sentence length to produce a single measure, called a Lexile, of a text's complexity. The most important difference between the Lexile system and traditional readability formulas is that traditional formulas only assign a score to texts, whereas the Lexile Framework can place both readers and texts on the same scale. Certain reading assessments yield Lexile scores based on student performance on the instrument; some reading programs then use these scores to assign texts to students. Because it too relies on word familiarity and sentence length as proxies for semantic and syntactic complexity, the Lexile Framework, like traditional formulas, may underestimate the difficulty of texts that use simple, familiar language to convey sophisticated ideas, as is true of much high-quality fiction written for adults and appropriate for older students. For this reason and others, it is possible that factors other than word familiarity and sentence length contribute to text difficulty. In response to such concerns, MetaMetrics has indicated that it will release the qualitative ratings it assigns to some of the texts it rates and will actively seek to determine whether one or more additional factors can and should be added to its qualitative measure.[45]

There is a great deal more claptrap like this in Appendix A. What we need is a common-sense translation of this edu-speak, which will summarize the whole argument: "We the authors of the Common Core know that texts must be complex. But we do not know how to talk about literature in its own terms. We do not know how to discuss the interaction among characters. We do not know how to discern the complications of story line. We do not know how to appreciate the beauty of either language or the

---

[45] Appendix A, page 7.

characters' actions. Least of all can we describe the greatness of a work of literature or the sentiments a story cultivates in the reader. We are utterly in a fog about poetry. But we have to come up with some way to describe a text's *complexity*. So we have decided to look around for a computer model of textual complexity. Sure, that is not how the great Samuel Johnson discussed literature in his *Lives of the Poets*. It is not how the great Macaulay wrote on Milton. It bears no resemblance to C. S. Lewis's studies in literature, or Wayne Booth's, or any other respectable, traditional scholar's. But we live in the twenty-first-century global economy, and, by golly, we have to have a computer model! So we've shopped around and found this absurd program called the Lexile Framework. We've chosen that one because the method it uses best guarantees that non-fiction works will rank with or even above the classics (though we don't call them classics). But even MetaMetrics admits that its methodology is flawed because *The Grapes of Wrath* would register as a 2nd-3rd grade book[46] while some nameless hack journalist would score at the high-school level with every forgettable article. But we are determined to have a computer model, so our friends at MetaMetrics have promised they will come up with a computer formula for *quality*. And it will be out soon. And it will work and make perfect sense. Honest."

Perhaps I am an outlier in this discussion, but I find the illiberal scheme of evaluating a text's complexity based on a computer or mathematical model ridiculous. Once again, it is a case of allowing the computers to do our thinking for us. It is no different from judging an algebra problem based on whether it has the same level of humor found in a passage of Mark Twain or the same level of *pathos* found in a Shakespearean scene. If there were ever a case of apples and oranges, this is it. Nonetheless, a genuine expert on this sort of thing, Dr. Sandra Stotsky, who largely crafted Massachusetts' famous state standards, has been testifying around the country that the measurements being employed by the Common Core do not account for the true complexity of works of literature based on other, better models of complexity that are out

---

[46] I am not making this up. *The Grapes of Wrath* scores at the 2nd-3rd-grade level, and the authors of the Common Core are forced to admit it on page 8 of Appendix A. Wouldn't such hard facts cause a sensible person to abandon the computer model of assessing literature?

there. Therefore, the Common Core is giving us a false scale of the difficulty of informational texts *vis à vis* literature.

Common sense compels us to present a simple scenario. Which would score higher in its level of textual complexity on the Lexile Framework for Reading scale, developed by MetaMetrics, Inc.: Appendix A of the *Common Core State Standards for English Language Arts & Literacy in History/Social Studies, Science, and Technical Subjects* or anything ever written by Mark Twain? Well, having survived the jargon of Appendix A, I can definitely say, without even using the Lexile index, that the Common Core authors have written a more *complex* text. They simply have not written a readable one. So which "literary or informational text" should we have our students reading, Appendix A or *Huckleberry Finn*? That should be an easy question to answer. Which one would be more likely to appear on a Common Core standardized test or in a Common Core textbook? Well, we don't know; the "standards" do not tell us. A little research will reveal that there is a lot of jargon from the Common Core documents that has made its way into students' textbooks, while *Huckleberry Finn* is not a recommended text of the Common Core English Standards.

The reader may think that I am exaggerating. Let us enter exhibit A into the record: "The Evolution of the Grocery Bag," by Henry Petoski, published in the Autumn 2003 edition of *The American Scholar*.[47] The short excerpt we are given in Appendix B of the Common Core Standards shows this to be an informative article about how grocery bags in stores have changed over time. I am sure Mr. Petoski is a clever fellow and his article served its purpose. The question is simply whether we want our students to spend their time in school reading a history of the grocery bag while they could be reading Homer or Shakespeare or Dickens. Would Mr. Petoski want his own children reading Dickens or his article on grocery bags?[48] Here is the real evolution taking place. In the old days we used paper bags for groceries. Then we had a choice between "paper or plastic?" Now we just have plastic. How we shopped for groceries did not affect our reading of great literature. In the Brave New Core, however, students are not urged

---

[47] Appendix B, p. 98.

[48] Again, I mean no ill will to Mr. Petoski. I can affirm, as someone who has written several articles that have received some national attention, that I would categorically prefer my own children to spend their time in school reading Homer rather than my articles.

to read Shakespeare in middle school. They are not urged to read any Charles Dickens at all. Yet they may very well read "The Evolution of the Grocery Bag." We are being given the choice not between paper or plastic but Shakespeare or plastic—and the arch-testers of the Common Core want us to choose plastic.

Some might assert, "Well, what does it hurt if the kids read a contemporary article every now and then, on the history of grocery bags or any other modern convenience?" But the issue is not about one article. It is about the introduction of many such readings into the curriculum that could do nothing but supplant genuine literary classics. "But the Common Core does not dictate curriculum," say the Core authors. Obviously, the Core authors think we do not know Standardized Testing Rule #1: *the schools slavishly teach to the tests*. If there will be a high number of modern "informational" texts on the tests, then the schools (with the filthy rich publishing companies leading the way) will spend their time drilling the kids on the separate histories of grocery bags and dental floss and Velcro and skateboards. Students will not be reading more great literature but far less.

The "complexity" of Appendix A is a model of bureaucratic obfuscation, leaving the reader guessing at the authors' character and motives. On a first reading, the technical language appears too daunting for the average concerned parent to unravel. A second reading, though, yields an egregious example of the modern education bureaucracy's losing all common sense. The Common Core authors go to great lengths—using "Lexile indexes" and "qualitative and quantitative measures of text complexity"—in order to prove that students should be taught to read "complex" or challenging books. Furthermore, as they get older, students should read *increasingly* challenging books. Eureka! Was that basic axiom of education ever in doubt? Appendix A reminds one of the long, sententious letter of Mr. Collins in *Pride and Prejudice*, about which Elizabeth asks her father after hearing it, "Can he be a sensible man, sir?" To which Mr. Bennet replies, "No, my dear; I think not. I have great hopes of finding him quite the reverse. There is a mixture of servility and self-importance in this letter which promises well. I am impatient to see him." But a third reading may cause us to suspect a *slightly* cleverer character at work than a modern Mr. Collins, the pompous bumbler.

As absurd as is the discussion of literature in the Common Core, there is at the same time an unseen sleight of hand being employed. This sleight of hand, if it goes unnoticed, will serve to justify the entire Common Core. The purpose of Appendix A is nothing short of establishing a *scientific* basis of text selection. It does so by using new, pseudo-scientific measures of a text's "complexity." Thus, complexity becomes the primary thing we look for in deciding what gets read in literature class. Once *science* becomes the basis of text selection—as opposed to the tradition of a generally accepted canon of great literature, or the old-fashioned notion that mostly *literature* should be read in literature class[49], or just plain ol' common sense—there can be no questioning the Common Core's indirect, yet absolute, dictating of curriculum. How can common sense stand up to science! Who will control the science that determines which "texts" fit the right criteria? Well, the *experts* of the Common Core, of course. And remember, "as new and better evidence emerges," new texts will be found acceptable. In other words, the method of selecting texts based on *complexity* is a way of saying that any document the arch-testers want the students to read will be given the same status as Shakespeare or Dickinson or Melville or Poe.

Of course, the proof will be in the pudding. As it stands now, the arch-testers would point to all the literary selections offered in Appendix B to demonstrate their good faith. They want us to believe that they have no intention of replacing great works of literature with modern dross. Appendix B, which we shall take a look at, is window-dressing. The effects of the bad reasoning and, I believe, deception found in Appendix A will become evident in the textbooks, which, as we shall see, are filled with a deadly combination of culturally worthless and politically-charged tripe.

The nation should resist the erosion of literature in literature class. As we have seen, there are fundamental reasons why great works of literature have so long occupied their own esteemed place in the curriculum. One of those reasons is that the great stories of literature contain subtleties that only the most astute reader can perceive. In fact, it is not rare for English professors, who have read and taught certain works dozens of times, to discover hidden

---

[49] I say "mostly" because there is ample reason to read classic, non-fiction works that have traditionally appeared in literature classes, particularly in American literature. These works, though, consist in great biographies, autobiographies, sermons, speeches, letters, and even works of philosophy, as we shall see. There is a vast chasm between those traditional readings and modern "informational" texts.

gems of wit and wisdom in a classic story upon each new reading. Even using the absurd pronouncements provided by the Common Core we can readily see why the attempt to compare the complexity of literature with the complexity of informational texts is a clear case of apples and oranges. Consider the nature of "complexity" in a literary text. One of the key ingredients is "multiple levels of meaning," in the words of the Core authors. The arch-testers do not explain this ingredient very well, but they use satire as an example (probably because it is the most obvious). Satire operates at two levels (at least): the surface-level meaning and the ironical or derisive meaning. The equivalents to satire for informational texts, we are told, are those with an "implicit, hidden, or obscure purpose." This parallel between the two types of texts actually makes little sense. If the overarching purpose of an *informational* text is to convey information, would not having implicit, hidden, or obscure meanings often be a case of bad writing? As the great writer Flannery O'Connor told us, literature ought to be shrouded in "mystery." Informational writers who shroud their work in mystery would simply leave their readership confused. Equating these two types of writing, then, is misguided if not outright impossible.

If the authors of the Common Core were truly worried about students' inability to read difficult writings—particularly "non-fiction" texts—then they would tell us what the real crisis is. For example, they might say that young people, by the time they reach the age of eighteen, and therefore voting age, ought to be able to read *The Federalist*. Without reading *The Federalist*, a person cannot fully understand the Constitution. Since *The Federalist* is a difficult book, we must prepare young people for it by their reading short selections of philosophy—both political and moral—beginning as early as the eighth grade, as well as classic works of historical writing which the Founding Fathers refer to often. The scenario I just described is a real concern, one that is discussed by people who are truly worried about the liberal arts and young people's political education.

That is not, however, the concern of the authors of the Common Core. If it were, then they would spend time discussing the reading of philosophy and the ancient historians. Philosophical works are necessarily complex because they discuss complex things: how the mind works; how human beings live together; what constitutes good and evil, order and chaos, beauty and ugliness. The great ancient historians—Herodotus, Thucydides, Plutarch, Polybius, Tacitus—also write about complex things: complex men in complex situations having to make hard decisions. You would think the arch-testers, for all their talk of real-world "decision-making," would love this sort of thing. Indeed, the education of the Founding Fathers largely consisted in reading the great historians, Plutarch's *Lives* being a kind of Bible for understanding human nature. But you will not find the story-killers telling us to dust off our Plutarch and open it up to the lives of Lycurgus, Pericles, Cicero, or Caesar. That is the furthest thing from their minds. The new "complex" texts are overwhelmingly of recent origin, mostly forgettable, and often riddled with political and cultural bias.

The numbers also tell the story. As we have seen, the Common Core looks forward to a shift in students' reading from "non-fiction" to their dubious category of "literary non-fiction." The proportion between the two is supposed to be seventy percent informational texts and only thirty percent literature by the senior year in high school. Such a shift can only take place with the pseudo-science of text complexity justifying this radical change.[50] The effects are obvious. Just when students should be reading longer and more difficult works of great literature as they advance in high school, they will be reading fewer and easier texts to make room for all the so-called "literary non-fiction." Thus, they will miss out on the truly intricate human stories that students should read in any demanding high school: particularly stories found in longer novels. Despite the hollow assurances that the other classes will share this load, the bulk of the reading for the English Standards will be housed in the English class. Rather than preparing students for the complex dealings of human life, rather than teaching them to interpret human beings' words and actions,

---

[50] There is actually considerable confusion over this point. The Common Core English Standards leave one with the impression that the 70%-30% ratio will be applied by the time the students reach their senior year in high school. Advocates of the Common Core claim that that number will apply only to the total amount of a student's reading, and since the teaching of reading will be "shared across the curriculum," the English classes will not be unfairly burdened. Nonetheless, efforts to pin down the Common Core authors, notably those of Professor Sandra Stotsky, have yielded no clarification. The best guess now is that there will be at least a 50-50 ratio of literary to informational texts, even in the English class.

the attenuated literature classes will serve up a heaping helping of boredom in the name of "text complexity."

Another, ostensible criterion for text selection, we are told, is quality. Quality does not have its own appendix. Quality does not really get discussed in the Common Core English Standards. The references to "qualitative dimensions of text complexity" in Appendix A belong to the discussion of complexity and cannot be considered an argument for quality. There is a reason for the absence of a serious discussion about the quality of literature to be taught in schools. A strong insistence on quality would eliminate the "'informational" texts the arch-testers are trying to import into the public school curriculum. That articles recently written, unseen and unheard of by the vast majority of the public, unknown even to scholars outside the field in which the articles were written, might not live up to the same standards of importance or literary merit as anything written by, say, Milton, seems not to bother the arch-testers. They assure us, instead, that,

> While it is possible to have high-complexity texts of low inherent quality, the work group solicited only texts of recognized value. From the pool of submissions gathered from outside contributors, the work group selected classic or historically significant texts as well as contemporary works of comparable literary merit, cultural significance, and rich content.[51]

So move over, Milton, and make room for Atul Gawande, "The Cost Conundrum: Health Care Costs in McAllen, Texas." One wonders: does an article on the costs of health care published in *The New Yorker* in June of 2009, just when Obamacare was being debated, fill the prescription of *comparable literary merit, cultural significance,* or *rich content*?
 Several obvious questions emerge. Who is in the work group? Who are the "outside contributors"? Which work group or outside contributors or experts will decide which texts get selected in the future, particularly when "new and better evidence emerges"? What determines cultural significance? How do they define

---

[51] Appendix B, p. 2.

"culture"? Do the Common Core authors mean "high culture"? Should we expect students to start reading essays on the symphonies of Beethoven or selections from Vasari's *Lives of the Artists*? Or do the arch-testers mean "*multi*cultural"? Thus, an unofficial quota system may be put in place that guarantees the approved number of articles written by Latin-Americans, Native-Americans, African-Americans, and so on. The most loaded term in the short paragraph on quality is the innocuous *recognized* in "recognized value." Recognized by whom? If a district or a school chooses not to recognize the value of *The New Yorker* article, and all other such articles imposed by an unnamed, unaccountable agency, could that school opt out of the Common Core Standards? Or must we replace Milton and Melville and Poe with "informational texts" of "recognized value" selected for us by, to quote one former opponent of such bureaucratic action, "a little intellectual elite in a far distant capital"?

The phrase "comparable literary merit" is also worth noticing. This artfully chosen set of words is another one of those Mr. Collins moments: "Can he be a sensible man, sir?" What authority permits these unknown testing hacks to pronounce some obscure modern author or journalist *comparable* to Sophocles? Only hubris could lead them to doing so. It is obviously the case that the canon of literary classics should be open to new arrivals. Yet it takes a long time for a great book to prove itself worthy of such elevation, at least a generation. Historical ages pass through literary fads no less than fads in fashions and art and music. The notion of "comparable literary merit" could lead to two bad habits in the selection of texts: chasing bestsellers to make the school curriculum appear "up to date" and "relevant," or, perhaps worse, the rallying around certain postmodern authors (who are usually obsessed with sex and therefore wholly inappropriate for schools) over whom current university literature departments are giddy. As with all Mr. Collins moments in the Common Core, we must wonder whether that is not the hidden aim: to turn students away from the classics with their timeless lessons and towards the new postmodern authors.

Tellingly, the authors of the Common Core do not define quality. This most flagrant of omissions could be because they have not figured out a way to *quantify* quality. That is, they have yet to generate computer software that can spit out a "quality index rating."[52]   But their failure to define quality could owe to other reasons. If they say too much about quality, it could get sensible people to thinking. Are these new articles really on the same level as Homer and Shakespeare? Moreover, quality itself is a rather tepid term. A better term might have been *great*. If we were to ask the question, "Are these contemporary, informational texts actually *great* writings?" what would be the obvious answer? In that same vein, how about replacing the ambiguous term *recognized* with the more decisive word *permanent*: "only texts of *permanent* value." How would *Geeks: How Two Lost Boys Rode the Internet out of Idaho*[53] stack up in the category of *permanent* value next to, say, *Treasure Island* or *Dr. Jekyll and Mr. Hyde*?

Until the wizards at MetaMetrics come out with a program that tells us how we are supposed to think about the literary quality of great books (which will no doubt announce that great works of literature are not nearly as sophisticated as we thought in comparison to certain modern authors whom the arch-testers will be happy to name for us), the story-killers do not want us thinking too much about the *quality* of readings with the Common Core Standards' seal of approval. The arch-testers have to use that word somewhere in the Standards to keep up the appearance of caring about great literature. But the qualities of *quality* itself must be completely ignored for their plans to come to fruition.

The third criterion that the authors of the Common Core sneak in is that of *range*. It is a criterion even less defined than quality. Here is the explanation found in the Standards:

---

[52] As we have seen, the arch-testers are eager to have computers rather than human beings determine what gets read in schools. Above, we looked at the desire to measure *complexity*. But *quality* is also on the radar, as a thorough reading of Appendix A will reveal. See pages 4 and 5 of Appendix A, including these gems: "The qualitative and quantitative measures of text complexity described below are representative of the best tools presently available. However, each should be considered only provisional; more precise, more accurate, and easier-to-use tools are urgently needed to help make text complexity a vital, everyday part of classroom instruction and curriculum planning." And, "Built on prior research, the four qualitative factors described below are offered here as a first step in the development of robust tools for the qualitative analysis of text complexity." Oh, how those teachers in eighteenth- and nineteenth-century America must have suffered by not having such qualitative and quantitative tools of text complexity, and thus failed to make text complexity a vital, everyday part of their classroom instruction and planning!

[53] An eighth-grade informational text.

After identifying texts of appropriate complexity and quality, the work group applied other criteria to ensure that the sample presented in each band represented as broad a range of sufficiently complex, high-quality texts as possible. Among the factors considered were initial publication date, authorship, and subject matter.[54]

As with much of what is written in the Common Core Standards, the language appears inoffensive enough. A casual reader would conclude that it makes perfect sense to offer students a "broad range" of readings. Why should we confine young people, with their different interests and future prospects, to one or two or three kinds of texts?

As in the case of quality, we are given no sustained argument. We are left in the dark as to the "work group" and their discussions. The rigidly computerized approach of finding "complex" texts found in Appendix A gives way to the cryptic assurance that the Core authors know just what "factors" to consider. What did that discussion look like? Was it a feeling they had, or was it more than a feeling? Why, when the arch-testers are looking for a data-driven way of proving that great literature has sufficient *quality*, is there almost complete silence on how to determine *range*? What do these "factors" (of which we are only given three; hence the word "among") actually mean? Range in "publication date" must mean modern authors. I doubt too many tears were shed on there not being enough medieval authors represented. Authorship? Mmm . . . A range of authors can only mean one thing, as we shall see. And range in *subject matter*? What do the arch-testers want us to believe? "There are just too many books about war and peace, love and romance, sin and redemption, adventure and discovery, politics and ambition, and life and death in traditional literature! *The Iliad*: war. *The Aeneid*: war and romance. Saint Augustine's *Confessions*: sin and redemption. *Lancelot and Guinevere*: love and chivalry. *Macbeth*: ambition and murder. *Romeo and Juliet*: love and death. *Julius*

---

[54] Appendix B, page 2. When the Common Core Standards first appeared, the category was called *breadth*. I cannot explain the change.

Caesar: politics, murder, and ambition. *Paradise Lost*: sin and expulsion. *Persuasion*: love. *Wuthering Heights*: love and death. *Tom Sawyer*: high jinx and adventure. *Huckleberry Finn*: adventure and humanity. *Crime and Punishment*: love and murder and redemption. Ugh! Just the same old stuff over and over again. Why can't the great authors come up with something new or at least original? How confined and narrow is the subject matter of Western literature! What we need are the arch-testers of the Common Core to sweep in and show us how to have more *variety* and *breadth* and *range* in our literary choices." Is that what they are expecting? What could *range* in subject matter possibly mean? We ask for the third time, "Can he be a sensible man, sir?"

Where no explanation exists, watch out. For that is precisely where the most flagrant form of politics will sneak in. *Range* is the most potentially radical criterion for choosing what our children read. To understand why, we must know something about establishing a sensible curriculum in the first place. Choosing what children read in school is an act of selection and therefore of limitation. Two factors should govern the selection of any book to be studied in school. First, there is only so much time in the day and in the year. Not everything we might want to read can be read, at least if we stick to the twin principles of reading complete works of literature and discussing them thoroughly. Second, since time is limited, students should study only the *best* works of literature. Economy and judgment, therefore, are essential in the creation of a curriculum. Complexity and quality, then, *if* they are understood correctly, are legitimate criteria of selection. That is because they both serve to limit the number of books to be read and taught. Let's take a couple of examples.

When children are young they should be encouraged to read a lot of books. Not all of those books should make it into a school curriculum, however. That is the great mistake of the reading program called Accelerated Reader. Students read multitudes of different books at their own pace, most of them utterly forgettable, without ever having a common discussion in class on genuine childhood classics. Rather than boring students with such "programs," students should read and discuss classics together (under the direction of the teacher) in school and be left free to read a lot of books at home. The latter exercise does improve reading, but it is not the same as interpreting a classic. For example, my sons love *The Hardy Boys* books. I often read a chapter to them at night. They remember better than I do what cliffhanger we left off with the night before, and they are pretty good at figuring out the clues in the story. Nonetheless, I would never call *The Hardy Boys* "classics" in the ultimate sense nor put those books into a curriculum. The Common Core, however, is clearly enamored with supposed childhood classics of recent origin (not nearly as exciting as the Hardys) that children do not like nearly as much as their teachers do. Consider this list of stories intended for the second and third grades under the Common Core:

> Ruth Stiles Gannett, *My Father's Dragon*; Esther Averill, *The Fire Cat*; William Steig, *Amos and Boris*; Uri Shulevitz, *The Treasure*; Ann Cameron, *The Stories Julian Tells*; Patricia MacLachlan, *Sarah, Plain and Tall*; Cynthia Rylant, *Henry and Mudge: The First Book of Their Adventures*; Janet Stevens, *Tops and Bottoms*; Jim LaMarche, *The Raft*; Cynthia Rylant, *Poppleton in Winter* and *The Lighthouse Family: The Storm*; and Erica Silverman, *Cowgirl Kate and Cocoa*.[55]

Some of these are fine books as far as they go. No doubt many of these books would be read at home, often even before going to school. Nonetheless, these are not books and stories that warrant the attention given to them in schools and now sanctioned by the Common Core. Rather, the Common Core should be endorsing timeless, tried-and-true classics: Aesop's fables; famous fairy tales such as *Little Red Riding Hood*; Greek and Roman myths such as Pandora, Theseus and the Minotaur, and Perseus and Medusa; tales from *The Arabian Nights*; *Alice in Wonderland*; *Rikki Tikki Tavi*; *Little House in the Big Woods*; and American tall tales, such as Paul Bunyan and Pecos Bill. The Common Core only recommends a couple of these books or stories: *Alice* and *Little House*. Ignoring the other classics means (as it has meant for the last forty years) that they will not be read in schools and therefore not appropriated by the majority of children as a part of their moral and intellectual inheritance. Students will therefore be morally and intellectually poorer for not having read them. *Little Red Riding*

---

[55] Appendix B of the English Standards, p. 5.

Hood is a perfect example. That story is not recommended by the story-killers of the Common Core. Yet they do offer a Red-Riding Hood Story *from China* for kindergarten/first-grade students and a "revolting rhyme" by Ronald Dahl about *Little Red Riding Hood* in the fourth/fifth-grade range. A clever twist perhaps, but should not students read the real *Little Red Riding Hood* before going abroad in their fairy tale adventures or witnessing Red Riding Hood take out a revolver and blow the wolf away?

There are no traditional fairy tales recommended in the Common Core: no *Cinderella*, no *Hansel and Gretel*, no *Jack and the Beanstalk*. There are no tall tales, at least not any American ones. There are no Greek or Roman myths in the elementary school. There is no Hans Christian Anderson whatsoever: no Ugly Duckling, no Little Mermaid, no Little Match Girl. Robert Louis Stevenson also does not appear. The entire Common Core enterprise in the elementary school could be summarized by the question, "Why is there no *Treasure Island*?" Yet the authors of the Common Core bend over backwards to bring in these sundry modern authors whose works have not proven themselves beyond a single generation. Understood properly, then, the *quality* of a book—its status as a classic—is a limiting principle, one the authors of the Common Core do not either understand or agree with. The Common Core demands that your children read the latest, but not the greatest.

At the high school level, there are similar judgments to be made. Who could think of a more thrilling read, what books are a greater part of our cultural heritage, than either *Frankenstein* or *Dracula*? Should they be read in a course devoted to British literature?[56] Well, based upon pure literary quality, we would put *Frankenstein* above *Dracula*. Even then, we must consider what will not get read. Do we wish to sacrifice a play of Shakespeare or a novel of either Austen or Dickens to *Frankenstein*? It is actually not an easy call, but it is one that demonstrates how selective one must be in the creation of a meaningful literature curriculum. The solution I have adopted is to assign *Frankenstein* for summer reading—especially since it is a book students are more likely to read on their own anyway—and then have a discussion at the

---

[56] The kind of course that is rapidly disappearing from public high schools, by the way.

beginning of the year about the book.[57] The essential point to realize is that time is at a premium and different works should not be imported just to offer an ephemeral *variety*. The Western canon itself is a fountain of variety, of both story and character.

Unlike *complexity* and *quality*, properly understood, *range* is a criterion of inclusion. The Common Core authors clearly seek to add things to the curriculum that have never been there before. What might those things be? Well, range in authorship can only mean one thing. The arch-testers want more women, black, Hispanic, and "world" authors in the curriculum. They want them in that order. We have already noticed that the Common Core has no particular commitment to the Western, British, and American traditions in literature. If they would be honest with us, we would find that they actually believe that what used to be called the great books of the Western tradition were all or mostly written by white males, and therefore the truths they have to impart are merely the "values" of (now dead) white males. That the West, Britain, and especially America are the places where the rule of law, political and religious freedom, and natural rights have been realized in their highest degree makes no difference to the authors of the Common Core. They want to impose diversity on the public schools. As the well-known Harvard Professor "Skip" Gates, of the Obama "beer summit" fame, once asked a friend of mine going out into the professorial job market in a mock interview, "How many black and women authors will you have in your courses?" That's the bottom line.

Now the truth is, there is a reason to have black and women authors studied in school. The reason is that they can provide deep insights into what it means to be a human being and an American. *But*—and here is the important distinction—these authors should be chosen because they are *great* authors, not because they are *black* or *women* authors. If you can find an author who tells us more about what love is, and how one must come to know a person before loving that person truly, than Jane Austen, please tell us who that author is. I doubt there is one. If there is a better author for telling us what freedom is, by telling us what life looks like when a person is not free, than Frederick Douglass, then please tell us who that author is. I doubt there is one. The idea of reading

---

[57] For a further discussion on *Frankenstein* see chapter seven below, "The Tyranny of the Textbooks."

Jane Austen and Frederick Douglass in order to satisfy some wholly artificial construct called *range*, and thereby establish a quota system for the Western and American canon, should not only be considered anathema to any standard of literary judgment but also a condescending, officious insult to the memory of those great writers. As soon as you start considering Aristotle as a "white philosopher" or the Brontës as "women novelists" or Frederick Douglass as a "black author," you have given up, for all your clap-trap about a "global society," your claim on a common humanity. If you use those authors politically, in an effort to show how close-minded and prejudiced white males and Americans have long been, then you are actually committing historical fraud.

Range of authorship, then, is the vehicle in the Common Core for bringing in authors of "diverse backgrounds." Need examples? Chinua Achebe, *Things Fall Apart*; Amy Tan, *The Joy Luck Club*; Julia Álvarez, *In the Time of the Butterflies*; Alice Walker, "Women"; Maya Angelou, *I Know Why the Caged Bird Sings*; Jorge Luis Borges, "The Garden of Forking Paths"; Toni Morrison, *The Bluest Eye*; Cristina Garcia, *Dreaming in Cuban*; Jhumpa Lahiri, *The Namesake*; Rudolfo Anaya, "Take the Tortillas Out of Your Poetry," and so on. These novels, stories, and poems may be worth reading. They may, over time, come to be judged as great literature. My wife, an extremely discriminating reader of literature and a former English teacher, likes Amy Tan. But just as even *Frankenstein* may very well not be included in a high-school curriculum, so these literary works should be treated with extreme caution. The fact that so many of them are living authors should give us pause. Have they proven themselves over time? The arch-testers show no such caution. We must read works that demonstrate a "range of authors" in each "age band." Why? Well, because the arch-testers tell us we have to.

The story-killers of the Common Core make the absurd, implicit claim that we can add all these authors, just as we can add so many informational texts of "comparable literary merit," without compromising a traditional literature curriculum. The story-killers assure us that districts and schools will be allowed to make decisions about curriculum on their own, that the Common Core is only a set of *standards*. Hogwash. As we shall see when we look at Appendix B in greater detail, and later the textbooks themselves, the Common Core is strong-arming schools into teaching more women and black and Hispanic authors at the same time they are effecting a diminution in the classic works of Western, British, and American literature. There is no way around it. You cannot say, "Teach more of this new thing, but doing so will not affect the old thing," and be telling the truth. Anybody who has ever taught knows this.

"Initial publication date" as an aspect of "range" can have another effect. It requires literature classes to bring in more modern authors. Doing so will clearly eat into the time spent on the classics. What is the leading difference between modern, twentieth-century (and, soon, twenty-first-century) writers and the great authors of the past? Arguably, it is the anti-heroic element. Not all protagonists prior to the twentieth century were moral or great. Achilles had considerable flaws, as did Odysseus, Aeneas perhaps fewer. All of the well-known protagonists in literature have flaws. It would be pretty boring to read the exploits of a character without some roughness around the edges. Yet in most classic stories up through the nineteenth century there is a distinct longing for something great, whether the longing be for love or power or freedom or revenge. The passions and visions and depth of feeling are on a grand scale. Twentieth-century authors and their characters, however, revel in the anti-heroic. Alienation is the underlying tone. The main characters (we can scarcely call them heroes, nor even protagonists) are alienated from their "environment": family, country, peers (friendship has largely died), work, all forms of duty, and God.

No doubt some of this literature should be read. For my money, I would prefer Kafka. The impossible scenario of *The Metamorphosis*, for example, certainly preserves enough mystery in the story to make it worth reading. But filling up the curriculum with as many modern as classic authors, while subtly undermining the classics at the same time, gives students a false baptism in post-modern ennui. The term of art nowadays seems to be the "literature of protest." How far does the Common Core now carry the literature of protest and how far will they carry it? Consider this hard fact. One of the leading publishers of high-school literature books, Pearson/Prentice Hall, devotes two volumes to the study of American literature in the eleventh grade. The first volume is given to all the literature written in America up to 1914. The second volume begins with 1914 and continues to the present. Should the teachers break this down into equivalent semesters, three hundred years of literature will be studied in the first semester, less than a hundred in the second. Not surprisingly, the first section of the second volume bears the dark title "Disillusion, Defiance, and Discontent." More egregious, the first volume, supposedly reserved for the Puritans, the Founding Fathers, Melville, Hawthorne, Poe, Twain, Emily Dickinson, and other luminaries, repeatedly sneaks in modern authors and "texts."

The Common Core authors wish to force on the public schools multiculturalism and modernity by fiat. That may not be all. The criterion of "subject matter" is delightfully obscure. It is impossible to make out what it means in this phase of the Common Core Standards and what it might come to mean in the future of this "living work." Now it may only mean "race, class, and gender," the lenses through which most of the colleges and universities in America currently judge literature. But what if we were to look into the future based on what is already going on in the present? What if we were to project what will become the leading criteria for literature selection in the high schools based on 1) what the colleges and universities find most interesting beyond the race, class, gender fads of the Nineties, 2) the hottest social issue in the high schools, 3) the obvious trends in teen fiction, 4) the social engineering of the publishing companies, and 5) the complete turnaround of the Democrat Party on the subject of gay marriage in the summer of 2013 following a much-anticipated Supreme Court ruling? What if we place the word "range" in front of "experiences" instead of the perfectly innocuous "subject matter" as a criterion of selecting literature? In short, how long will it take for the Common Core to require the schools to feature literature on the subject of homosexuality and with prominently gay characters? I predict it will not take more than three years. The reader may think I am being deliberately alarmist. If so, he should visit a public high school sometime. One of the most active clubs on campus, the one always most prominently featured in the school newspaper, is the LGBT-Straight Alliance.

I realize that these are politically-charged arguments. But anyone who does not think that the Common Core is a political operation disguised as educational reform is woefully blind to the progressive takeover of the schools that has occurred over the last century in theory and the last fifty years in practice. Remember what John Dewey said: "I believe that—education is the fundamental method of social progress and reform." The word "fundamental" was not carelessly chosen. Fundamental: from the

Latin *fundare*, to lay the foundation of. The progressive Left regards the public schools as the foundation of their own political projects, no matter how remote from the true business of schooling. Ask yourself this question: Do we really think that the progressive Left would put a full-court press on the people of America through the news media, publishing companies, movies, and music, and leave the schools untouched by their efforts at indoctrination? They are, underhandedly and cowardly, avoiding any open argument about what belongs in the school curriculum, the very kind of vigorous argument that characterizes the entire Western canon of great thoughts, great deeds, and great literature, and which particularly distinguishes this nation beyond any others to be found in the "global society." The arch-testers, who are actually arch-activists, do not want to have the argument about whether they can use the school curriculum for the purposes of political and social engineering because they know they would lose. Another way of looking at the issue is this: Once "range" becomes a deciding factor, or maybe *the* deciding factor, in choosing what our children read, and once essentially all of public schooling is controlled by a group of unknown, unaccountable activists and bureaucrats, what part of the progressive agenda will not be brought into the schools?

The Common Core is not an effort to get students reading better literature than they presently are. It is not really an effort to make them more "college and career ready." That is just the cover. The Common Core English Standards are a program to impose on students a particular view of the world. It is not a view that most parents want for their children nor that has characterized the long span of our literary heritage. The literature that the story-killers prefer is clearly the literature that puts forth their anti-heroic, anti-traditional, and largely anti-American view of our history and of the world. The arch-testers of the Common Core are selective in their story-killing, then. As they are taking an ax to the classics, they are planting the seeds of the miserable post-moderns.

The decision that state legislators have to make on whether to repeal the Core or not is really not very *complex*. Do we want our children spending precious time on just any random "complex" text that the Common Core authors decide to slip into a standardized exam, or that the textbook publishing giants dig out of their bottomless bins of mediocre writings? Do we want young minds to be programmed with highly suspect political and cultural propaganda? Do we want our children to be lured into the reading of modern authors whose works revel in a jaded, anti-heroic, and often morally debased view of human life? Or do we want students reading the classics? Which will they get more out of, which will better prepare them for the world, which will they most enjoy, and which will more likely contribute to their own virtue and happiness?

Chapter Five
Superficiality and Bias

A casual glance at Appendix B of the Common Core Standards might lead the reader to believe that the authors of that document really do have the best interest of our students at heart, that they really do want young people reading good literature. After all, we see among the "text exemplars" in grades 9-10 a number of genuinely great authors: Homer, Ovid, Gogol, Voltaire, Turgenev, Kafka, Steinbeck, Bradbury, Harper Lee, Sophocles, Shakespeare, Percy Bysshe Shelley, Poe, Emily Dickinson, and so on. Of course, we also see modern authors mixed into the stew under the principle of "range." And we also are given a large number of "informational texts" to be read alongside the literary works. Yet the appearance of so many good authors could prompt us to be charitable with the agents of the Core by applauding all the "good work they've done so far," by allowing for this to be "a work in progress," and by concluding that from the "implementation phase" we will learn a lot of lessons that will then be incorporated into an even better document. College and career readiness is just around the corner. That, of course, is not my reading. Rather, I think one of two better readings of Appendix B (and, of course, the whole document) is possible. Either the authors of the Common Core are hopelessly naïve, or they think that we are hopelessly naïve. It must be one or the other. The Common Core, as it is written, encourages superficiality in reading and bias in thought. Either there exists no coherent philosophy of education governing the arrangement of texts within the document, or there does exist a coherent philosophy: that of obscuring the high, powerful truths about virtue, freedom, suffering, and happiness found in great works of Western literature. Either way, the shoddy organization of the Common Core leads to both superficiality and bias in the teaching of what used to be called literature.

To understand how the Common Core promotes both superficiality and bias, we need to know the two rules of standardized testing. Standardized Testing Rule Number One: *The schools slavishly teach to the test.* This rule applies not only to what schools read but also to the format in which things are read. Standardized Testing Rule Number Two: *The schools teach nothing beyond the test.* All the money, so to speak, lies in what's on the test. It doesn't pay to teach anything other than the test. As such, any list generated by a testing organization, or any set of readings in a textbook put out by a publishing company somehow linked into a testing organization, is exclusive. The teachers will not go outside the sacrosanct list. The authors of the Common Core must know this. Arne Duncan must know this. They can claim innocently that the Common Core does not dictate curriculum and that the local districts are free to decide their own curriculum. Yet anyone who has ever spent any time around schools knows the sequence of events. The state declares that there will be a standardized exam. Panic. Elaborate "programs" geared to the state tests are put into the hands of teachers, published, of course, by Pearson/Prentice Hall, et alia. Relief. One-hundred-seventy-five days of teaching to the test. Five days of testing. That is the pattern. The Common Core does nothing to change that pattern.

Therefore, Appendix B is not a mere list of exemplary texts that give us a flavor of the Common Core. It is a prescriptive *dictat* on the curriculum. It is Gospel. It will remain Gospel until it is altered or replaced with something else.

Knowing that, we can now figure out what effects the Common Core will have on the schools.[58] The first conclusion we must draw is that students will not, assuming they were already, be reading many complete works of literature. They will not be able to in light of the sheer number of titles offered in the Common Core document. Certainly, the arch-testers tell us that excerpts "serve only as stand-ins for the full text. . . . [C]omplexity is best found in whole texts rather than passages from such texts." But reality (and Testing Rule Number One) requires that everything

---

[58] Again, I must caution the reader that the Common Core will be further debilitating schools that have long been in decline.

appearing on a list must be taught. Not only must the extensive list of literary works be taught. So must the "informational texts" be taught. Now the authors of the Common Core tell us that these informational texts will be taught in other classes, that there must be a shared responsibility for literacy across the academic subjects. Where, though, will these "informational texts" appear, specifically in what book? That is an easy one. They will appear in the bulky English or literature textbooks. Thus, in practice if not in theory, these informational texts will be in every English class. The "social studies" teachers will say they are not English teachers. The science teachers will certainly say that they are not English teachers. The students will complain about having to carry two bulky textbooks to a class, which would be the case for both history and science. The principal will be incapable of making a judgment call having anything to do with curriculum and will simply take the path of least resistance and fewer complaints. So the English teachers will end up teaching *This Land Was Made for You and Me: The Life and Songs of Woody Guthrie* and *Cod: A Biography of the Fish That Changed the World*.

Even if the English teachers do not end up teaching the informational texts (they will, I assure you), there is still quite a lot of literature. For grades 9 and 10, there are sixteen "stories" students are supposed to read. Most of them are novels; one is an epic. There are also six plays and a fair amount of poetry. All told, that amounts to twenty-two major pieces of literature in a two-year period. Now if you simply calculate the time that could be spent on these works evenly, there seems to be no problem. Twenty-two divided by two, divided by another two, results in five or six major pieces of literature being read each semester. Of course, that assumes that no other lists are being generated by the Common Core authors and that the textbook publishers do not add in extra readings to cover all their bases. Even so, here is a question for the arch-testers. How long does it take to teach *The Odyssey* to a class of ninth-graders? How long does it take to teach a novel as long as *The Grapes of Wrath*, another recommended book, to ninth or tenth-graders? We are not told by the authors of the Common Core. The answer is that it could easily take up to two months—if you are really teaching the book. That's half of your semester. Will you be able to squeeze in four or five *other* major literary works, in addition to some poetry and, no doubt, grammar, your own exams, and the week lost in state testing, in the other half of the semester? "Have the arch-testers ever taught a class, sir?" is the question we ought to be asking.

Another indication of superficiality is the way the literature is arranged. We looked at the criterion of "range" for choosing literature in the last chapter. What does range look like in practice? Well, in the 9-10th grade band, the selections range from Homer to Marcus Zusak's *The Book Thief* in the category of "stories" and from Sophocles to Athol Fugard's *"Master Harold"* . . . *and the Boys* (a play about apartheid and racism in South Africa) in the category of drama. On the surface, it appears that the Standards have given us the luxury of two whole years to get all the way from the ancients to books that are essentially hot off the press. That is a ruse. All one has to do is ask the question, "Will the students be tested every year?" to realize that Testing Rule Number One will kick in. The students *will* be tested every year. Hence both classic and modern works of literature will be taught every year.

Now here is the rub. It is one of the most obvious and sensible principles of the lost art of curriculum design that students should follow a single literary tradition for any given year in high school. Furthermore, a literary tradition should complement or "align" with what is taught in history. Thus, while students are reading ancient literature, they should also be studying ancient history. While they are reading American literature, they should be studying American history. There are at least half a dozen solid reasons for organizing a curriculum in this way. Yet the Common Core discourages such a sensible organization. Even if we take them at their word (that schools have to go from the very beginnings of Western literature to recent authors in *two* years) that still discourages a sensible curriculum. For example, why not spend one year on the ancients and one year on either exclusively British or British and pre-modern European authors? That is, why not progress through the literary canon in high school *as it was written*? That would still leave an entire year for American literature and a year for modern authors. No, says the Common Core, you must have modern authors in every "band." As it stands now, there is no way to immerse the students in the ancient authors for an entire year and thus form their literary palates on the true classics. Besides that, the great human themes delivered to us by the ancients—honor, duty, glory, country—are hardly developed before modern books (and modern alienation) is brought in. To use the title of one book in the Core, *Things Fall Apart* in the modern era. Shouldn't we build up the virtues of young people a little more before we allow them to see things fall apart?

As we said, the literature curriculum should speak to, should be "aligned" with, what is going on in history. Therefore, a high school must do one of two things: race all the way from the ancients to the moderns every two years (and I think every year based on Testing Rule Number One) in the study of history or, equally bad, allow the two classes to go their separate ways in terms of sensible chronological ordering. Would it not make more sense in the teaching of history to start with ancient literature in the freshman year, continue with the Middle Ages, Renaissance, and early modern period in the sophomore year, tackle American history beginning in the junior year, and study modern history in the senior year? Literature would then follow the curriculum suggested above. Such an organization is not possible when schools "align" their curricula with the Common Core, which is precisely what they are having to do right now. In history, the Common Core features very few "informational texts" from European history and scatters the American history documents promiscuously and without order throughout the years in high school. While the Common Core ostensibly advocates sharing the responsibilities for teaching literacy throughout the school, in reality it prevents genuine conversations among various disciplines from taking place due to a chaos and superficiality in the curriculum.

Even this account is being very generous with the arch-testers. What I suspect will happen in practice is that the publishing companies and schools will act on the principle of *an exemplar text a day will keep the testing authorities at bay*. Notwithstanding the caveat to study complete works of literature, the Common Core's specious claim of not dictating curriculum will keep everyone guessing as to what will appear on the exams.[59] Therefore, rather than reading longer works intensively, the pattern of reading extremely short selections of literature, as shown in Appendix B itself, will become the norm. The motto of the Common Core should be *everything by littles and nothing long*.

---

[59] This thesis is in fact proven by the arrangement of the Common Core textbooks. See chapters seven and eight on the textbooks below.

The bias of the Common Core is, admittedly, a little harder to detect. Their escape clause of offering Appendix B only in order to provide "text exemplars" and "sample performance tasks" almost gets them off the hook. Almost. We have to think hard about Standardized Testing Rule Number Two and study the document with a view to what has been left out. We must remind ourselves that this is a document that contains so-called informational texts such as the U.S. Environmental Protection Agency/U.S. Department of Energy's *Recommended Levels of Insulation* and stories in the form of "I Stand Here Ironing" and poems along the lines of "The Latin Deli: An Ars Poetica." Indeed, there is certainly a *range* of subject matter! But could anything be missing—anything that any traditional curriculum would include?

Surprise, surprise, there is nothing from what would be considered the Judeo-Christian literary tradition. Let us see how far-reaching this omission is. First, there is no trace of the Creation story found in Genesis. Now if there is a more powerfully written and more influential moment in the history of Western writing, I should like to know what it is. Odysseus's return to Ithaca? Powerful, moving, to be sure, but not so powerful, telling, or influential as the Creation of Man. Plato's Metaphor of the Cave? A great moment in philosophy, instructive in our own day (particularly in relation to the public schools) but still not greater than the Story in the Garden. Hamlet's Soliloquy? Another moving and powerful moment in literature, but would the Bard himself think that he had outdone the Bible? Ivan's tale of "the Grand Inquisitor" in *The Brothers Karamazov*? It is hard to find a more intense or instructive moment in modern literature, but Dostoyevsky makes it pretty clear where he got most of his ideas. What else? Yes! There is one more possible contender: Milton's *Paradise Lost*, book IX. The poem is considered the greatest epic (and it *is* an epic) written in the English language, comparable even to Homer. It is about the very Story of the Creation and Fall we are speaking of. Inexcusably, *Paradise Lost* does not appear in the Common Core English Standards. No Milton appears at all.

Now, that is rather extraordinary. It could just be that *Paradise Lost* is a hard poem and the authors of the Core did not think the students would be up to it. But they do not tell us that. There is no regret or apology indicating that, sadly, Milton will have to wait until college. There is no sense of loss that all of *Paradise Lost* would take too long but that students at least need to read Books IX and X (the Fall and the Consequences of the Fall). Besides, wasn't the Common Core supposed to make students discerning readers of high-quality literary texts? Wouldn't the real test of that promise be Milton? Or it could be that omitting Milton from the list of exemplar texts is just an oversight which will be corrected "as better evidence emerges" and as new people are added to the "work group." It is nonetheless a rather amazing oversight given that anyone who has kept his old copy of Norton's *World Masterpieces* from college would see Milton as the culminating author of volume one. Surely, some member of the work group has a copy of *World Masterpieces* on his shelves and consulted the volume during these intense deliberations.

Is missing Milton merely an oversight or part of a pattern? What other great books do not appear in either the literary or informational side of the Common Core house? One of my favorites that does not appear is Augustine's *Confessions*. Most of us know Saint Augustine as the first great figure (other than the Apostle Paul) who marries the classical and the Christian traditions. Moreover, he wrote the first great autobiography,[60] which is rightly considered both a breathtaking literary work and an historical work. His story of the stealing of the pears as a boy (deliberately reminiscent of the Garden Story) along with the account of his conversion are still considered marvels of ancient literature. Still, they didn't make the cut in the Common Core English Standards. You will find these stories, by the way, in Norton's *World Masterpieces*.

What about American history and letters? Does religion make an appearance in any of the Common Core's lists of American texts? Alas not. That is rather extraordinary. John Winthrop's *A Modell of Christian Charity* (calling upon his fellow migrants to become "as a city upon a hill") is rightly regarded as one of the foundational works (maybe *the* foundational work) in American letters, and yet it does not appear. It also has resonance in American history. Ronald Reagan certainly invoked its memory

---

[60] Assuming that Caesar's works are not considered genuine autobiographies but war memoirs. Augustine's *Confessions* were not the first spiritual autobiography, either, but they could be called the first genuinely self-revelatory one. Thus he, like Franklin, curiously enough, seems far more like our contemporary than a saint from the distant past. See Peter Brown, *Augustine of Hippo: A Biography* (Berkeley: U. of California, 1967), ch. 16.

throughout his career. Even more curiously, Jonathan Edwards's famous Great Awakening sermon, "Sinners in the Hands of an Angry God," does not appear in Appendix B. Now I remember reading that one in my high school. In fact, my English teacher had *me* read it to the class. There was a time when every student in America was expected to study Edwards's sermon in high school. But the Common Core authors overlooked it somehow. Strange that.[61]

Now if we look into the lists casually, we find that certain famous texts in American history do appear: several speeches and addresses by the Founding Fathers, speeches of Lincoln, the obligatory Emerson and Thoreau, and documents on civil rights galore. But there is nothing on religion, although America's literary tradition has long been tied up with its religious tradition. Why might that be? Do the arch-testers wish us to ignore the religious tradition in both Western and American civilization altogether? The shorthand way of explaining our culture has always been to say that we are the children of both Athens and Jerusalem. Apparently the Common Core authors only want to include one of those parents. No doubt they would cite concerns of "church and state." But it is one thing to preach a document; it is quite another to teach it. I have taught books of the Bible to both Christians and non-believers. I have taught Nietzsche to Evangelicals. I have taught the theology of Luther to Catholics and the theology of Aquinas to Protestants. I have taught Marx to political conservatives. I have taught Adam Smith to political liberals. The task of teaching requires a teacher to be, in the first instance, faithful to the text to make sure that the students understand it. Books and poetry that are inspired by religion, as well as sermons and even parts of the Bible itself, ought to be read if they 1) are important parts of our heritage and 2) have unquestioned literary merit. Thus, the arch-testers are either oddly unaware of the religious dimension of our literary tradition or they are deliberately excluding it, probably for a reason. Would not leaving out the Creation Story in Genesis, as well as Augustine and Milton and Jonathan Edwards be a way of preventing students

---

[61] This is not to say that these texts do not still appear in literature textbooks with the Common Core logo. It is to say that the Common Core itself does not require a fair representation of literature and letters inspired by religion, particularly Christianity. When such texts are not required anything can change. We shall look at the treatment of these documents in the chapters on textbooks.

from discussing certain important ideas about the human condition such as, say, sin? There is a sin being committed here. I believe the theologians would call it the sin of omission.

Literature derived from religion is not the only obvious omission in the Common Core English Standards. The best way to see the magnitude of another omission is to ask a few, related questions: What famous figure in American history could be considered the architect of the American character? Who was the first self-consciously *American* author? Who is the all-time favorite personage and personality in American history? I believe all three questions would yield the answer *Benjamin Franklin*. But there is no Benjamin Franklin in the Common Core. How inexcusable is this omission?

To begin with, we must point out that Benjamin Franklin's *Autobiography* is rightly considered not only an important historical work but also a literary masterpiece, one of the two or three greatest autobiographies ever written (along with Augustine's). Like all great autobiographies, it is not only a story about the author. It is a moral tale about the making of a country, particularly the virtues that are required to make that country great and prosperous. Franklin's early self-education and his systematic attempts to arrive at "moral perfection" are unforgettable moments to anyone who has ever read them, models of practicality, hard work, and humor. Insofar as Franklin inspires the reader to attempt his own plans of self-education and self-mastery, you would think that the arch-testers would jump at this chance to impart "college and career readiness." It should likewise be pointed out that there was a time when Franklin's *Autobiography* was required reading in public schools across the country. I still remember discovering my grandfather's well-worn copy of the *Autobiography* in a closet containing all his schoolbooks. I would not hesitate to say that finding that book may have changed my life, particularly my desire to read other books on my own, just as Franklin did. Before that, I read mostly Mad Magazine and Sherlock Holmes. We can also say with some certitude that the Common Core authors do not fail to include this great book because it is "non-fiction." The Common Core wants a greater emphasis on non-fiction. Furthermore, the arch-testers feature Frederick Douglass's *Narrative* prominently in their Standards, making it an "informational text" for "English Language Arts" in grades 6-8 and also using it to illustrate "The Model in Action" in Appendix A. As we have said, Douglass's *Narrative* is a great book not only about one life but about the unfolding of liberty in America. But so is Franklin's *Autobiography*. One appears; the other doesn't, inexplicably.

The *Autobiography* is not the only writing of Franklin that could or should have made an appearance in the Common Core. Indeed, the number of Franklin's works that would be read with profit in high school could easily be over a dozen. Let us stick to four. The Common Core authors claim to recommend complex informational texts with "implicit, hidden, or obscure" meanings and with comparable quality to literary texts. Franklin's whole career was devoted to writing such essays, two which should be read by every American.[62] One is called "An Edict by the King of Prussia," published in September of 1773. In this tract Franklin casts himself as Frederick the Great, who demands that since Britain was settled long ago by Germanic people, restrictive trading policies and high taxes will henceforth be imposed on Great Britain by Prussia. These policies and taxes were, of course, a clear copy of the British impositions on the American colonies. Not only was this satire read at the time; some people in Britain took it seriously and called for a declaration of war against the kingdom of Prussia! Talk about irony! A couple of weeks earlier, Franklin published "Rules by Which a Great Empire May Be Reduced to a Small One." Now this text has for a long time been regarded as a master example of satire, probably the most famous example of satire in American history. This was another work that was still read when I was in high school; though not well explained by the teacher, at least we read it. What is most striking about the absence of either of these well-known writings in the Common Core is that in Appendix A it appears that the arch-testers are making a bid for satire.[63] By the time we get to Appendix B, however, that aim seems to have evaporated since the list of readings is noticeably short on satire. Jonathan Swift, too, is MIA.

Another striking omission is Franklin's "The Way to Wealth," likely his most famous work during his lifetime, which still has resonance today. "The Way to Wealth," written as a speech of

---

[62] Recall this as the "informational text" equivalent to literary satire, albeit a problematic one.
[63] See Appendix A, p. 5, "Levels of Meaning."

Father Abraham, is largely a collection of maxims taken from Franklin's *Poor Richard's Almanac*, maxims mainly dedicated to the ideas of thrift and hard work. We still remember some of these pithy maxims, particularly "A penny saved is a penny earned" and "Early to bed, early to rise . . ." Others that we have forgotten are still worth remembering: "Lost time is never found again"; "What maintains one vice would bring up two children"; and "Creditors have better memories than debtors." Recalling these memorable maxims in light of the Common Core's alleged aims, we must again be struck by the utter obtuseness of its authors. The arch-testers claim to want to produce a certain kind of thinking person: "college and career ready" and prepared for a "global economy." That suggests a practical, hard-working, scientifically-minded, highly literate individual. And yet when we have in our own literary line-up one of the most practical, hard-working, scientifically-minded, highly literate individuals in *the history of the world*—and a global hero and celebrity before there were such things—who frequently gave advice on the way to success and happiness, no one invites him to the game. It is as though we get to coach an all-time, all-star game and forget to invite Babe Ruth. Shouldn't these maxims appear somewhere in the curriculum, at least in the fourth grade if not in the twelfth? Is not a maxim a literary form worth knowing? There was a time when arguing from time-tested maxims paved the way not only to wealth but also to truth.

In light of the foregoing, we should not be surprised to find out that Benjamin Franklin's own account of his experiments with electricity does not appear among the "informational texts for science and technical subjects." Franklin may have been known in his day as the Newton of electricity; the philosopher Immanuel Kant may have called Franklin the "Prometheus of modern time"; the Nobel Prize-winning physicist Robert Millikan may have said that Franklin's law of conservation of charge is "the most fundamental thing ever done in the field of electricity," but that is not good enough for the rigorously scientific minds of the Common Core in their relentless search for high-quality informational texts.

We return to the question of *why*? Is it merely an oversight that America's greatest man of letters in the eighteenth century, one of the three greatest men in the history of this country and by far the most versatile, who himself wrote an autobiography meant, in part, to instruct young people how to be virtuous and happy, should be overlooked by the "work group" and the various, presumably highly-qualified, "outside contributors" to the Common Core English Standards? Or is it instead the case of Franklin's writings being squeezed out, whether consciously or unconsciously, to make room for the African novel *Things Fall Apart* by Chinua Achebe? There is a third possibility, which is more serious than intellectual bankruptcy or flagrant multiculturalism. Maybe the progressive authors of the Common Core do not want your children reading Benjamin Franklin. He may be, in fact, the very last author they want the nation's children reading.

When I call Benjamin Franklin the architect of the American character, I mean that he, above anyone else in our history, both illustrated and promoted America's distinctive can-do attitude and sense of individual responsibility. In fact, the phrase *can-do* could be attributed to him. He once wrote that in America a man is not known by who he *is* (that is, his social class, racial or national background, or who his father was) but for what he *can do*. While such a statement may seem little more than a platitude now, the idea was nothing short of a revolution in Franklin's time. For all of human history, including life among the democratic Greeks, men had been known for who they were—their lineage, their social class, their connections—not for what they could do. Franklin taught his fellow Americans and the world that America is a promise as much as a nation. It is a place where boundless opportunity allows an individual to make as much of himself as he is willing to. If he fails, he has no one to blame but himself. In other words, if Madison and the other Framers (and Franklin was there, too) provided the political structure that allowed freedom to thrive, Franklin articulated the moral message of how the individual might flourish in a free nation.

Just look at Franklin's own life. He was the son (one of seventeen children) of a hard-working candle-maker. Franklin gave himself an impressive education although he had only two years of formal schooling and spent not a day in college. At sixteen he wrote the first series of literary essays in America. In one of those essays he wrote a satire on Harvard College. He established himself as a printer. He was so successful that he could retire in his forties. He was an internationally known writer well before the Revolution (although some of his pieces were printed anonymously, such as "The Speech of Polly Baker," another great literary spoof that is perhaps a little too mature for high school). He became the greatest scientist and inventor of his day.

Contrary to today's progressive stereotype of Franklin, and of the successful man in general, he was not a lone, selfish individualist. Franklin loved and enjoyed people, and most of his great accomplishments were done to help people. He founded a school that turned into the University of Pennsylvania; he created the first fire company in America; he started the first library; he helped found a hospital; his "Junto," a group of young and ambitious working-class men who more or less gave themselves a college education, was the embryo of the American Philosophical Society; he gave away his idea of the Franklin stove by not taking out a patent; he formed a street-sweeping service that would employ the unemployed; he reformed the city watch and made the tax burden more equitable; he wrote at age sixteen on the need for an insurance fund for widows and orphans; he went out of his way to help others. Why wouldn't the authors of the Common Core revel in using Franklin's life and writings to provide lessons of hard work and benevolence for the nation's children?

There is a very simple reason for why the arch-testers may not have jumped at the chance to recommend Franklin to the nation's youth. Benjamin Franklin is the anti-bureaucrat. All of his great accomplishments were done without the help of bureaucracy, and the American Revolution itself was in no small part the overthrow of a bureaucracy. Franklin did not need state "funding" to discover the principles of electricity. Nor did he need the heavy hand of the federal and state governments to create a great school. He did not need the bureaucratic minds of the modern arch-testers to arrive at an extraordinarily good school curriculum. He simply read the best that had been thought and said on the subject, including works by Milton and Locke, and wrote it up himself. Reading Franklin on education today would teach us a lot more about what an education ought to look like than trying to digest all the claptrap found in the Common Core Standards.[64] Above all, a serious look at Franklin's life and writings would teach young

---

[64] See "Proposals Relating to the Education of Youth in Pensilvania" and "Idea of the English School" in Benjamin Franklin, *Writings*, ed. J. A. Leo Lemay (New York: Library of America). This book which used to be one volume has now split into two. These essays are in the first volume.

people and remind the rest of us what it means to be American. For starters, it does not mean being the dependents of an officious, progressive bureaucracy composed of self-appointed experts. The failure to recommend *any* writing of Benjamin Franklin reveals that the authors of the Common Core have no interest in producing virtuous, industrious, self-reliant, inventive, patriotic, benevolent, and happy students, who will soon become citizens in this land.

Of course, I cannot prove this thesis. Perhaps the "work group's" and all the outside experts' forgetting one of the greatest writers and most important people in the American story is just an oversight. As it stands, we just have to wonder whether the work group is getting their suggestions from serious students of literature or from Oprah's Book Club.

Let us turn now to the historical texts. Can we detect superficiality and bias in those documents? We must realize at the outset of this inquiry that the Common Core English Standards are not the history standards. Those will come later, after a few years of our getting used to the Common Core English and Math Standards presumably. Not a small number of people suspect that the agents behind the Common Core learned from previous, unsuccessful attempts to force transparently biased history standards on the nation. Rather than leading with history, the authors of the Common Core adeptly put themselves in a stronger bargaining position by having nearly all the states take the bait in the less controversial subjects of English and math. English may simply be the foot in the door. By the time the history standards come out, you can bet all the pressure will be on the states to work with one "common" generator of standards and tests. The lobbyists will certainly make that case.

At any rate, let's see what the arch-testers have to offer. At first blush, as in the case of the literary works, it appears that the work group has done a wonderful job. We find the Declaration of Independence, references to the Constitution, a letter from John Adams on Thomas Jefferson, Washington's Farewell, and even a selection from Ronald Reagan. Bravo! What a model of comprehensive and non-partisan selection!

Or not. An initial glance suggests that the selections are odd more than anything else. Yet a closer reading reveals the texts have been artfully selected to convey a particular bias against the Founding Fathers. The first oddity is to be found in the way the arch-testers recommend the Constitution. Its first appearance comes in the "informational texts for history/social studies" for grades 6-8. The recommendation reads "United States. Preamble and First Amendment to the United States Constitution (1787, 1791)." Now that is rather curious. The Common Core authors apparently do not think that middle-school students, even eighth-graders, can handle the Constitution as a whole. So they recommend the Preamble, which, of course, could have already been memorized by fourth-graders. And they recommend the First Amendment. Why not the whole Bill of Rights? Is it just too much for eighth-graders? Would it be too much for students at that grade level to learn that, "A well regulated Militia, being necessary to the security of a free State, the right of the people to keep and bear Arms, shall not be infringed"? Is it too much to expect fourteen-year-olds to understand that "The powers not delegated to the United States by the Constitution, nor prohibited by it to the States, are reserved to the States respectively, or to the people"? Realize that these are the same teenagers being told virtually *everything* about sex in their health classes as mandated by state law. They can learn most everything about their sexual constitutions, apparently, but next to nothing about the U. S. Constitution. As a point of comparison, the Core Knowledge Sequence, a well-known K-8 curriculum put out by the Core Knowledge Foundation, requires eighth-graders to study the entire Constitution (including a philosophical background: Founders' view of human nature, concept of popular sovereignty, the rule of law, etc.), the entire Bill of Rights and Amendments 13 and 19, and the *Marbury v. Madison* decision.

While the Preamble and First Amendment are listed at the top of the list of 6th-8th informational texts, a modern book called *Words We Live By: Your Annotated Guide to the Constitution* by Linda R. Monk is listed below. That is curious. Should the students read this entire book? Or will teachers use this as a reference so that they know what to say about the Constitution? Or, more probably, is this a signal to the textbook publishers indicating what modern "scholarship" should be incorporated into the books in order to help "interpret" the Constitution? On page 95 of Appendix B, where a selection is given from Monk's guide, we find what the Common Core authors want the students to think about the Constitution:

The first three words of the Constitution are the most important. They clearly state that the people—not the king, not the legislature, not the courts—are the true rulers in American government. This principle is known as popular sovereignty.

But who are "We the People"? This question troubled the nation for centuries. As Lucy Stone, one of America's first advocates for women's rights, asked in 1853, "'We the People'? Which 'We the People'? The women were not included." Neither were white males who did not own property, American Indians, or African Americans—slave or free. Justice Thurgood Marshall, the first African American on the Supreme Court, described the limitation:

"For a sense of the evolving nature of the Constitution, we need look no further than the first three words of the document's preamble: "We the People." When the Founding Fathers used this phrase in 1787, they did not have in mind the majority of America's citizens . . . The men who gathered in Philadelphia in 1787 could not . . . have imagined, nor would they have accepted, that the document they were drafting would one day be construed by a Supreme court to which had been appointed a woman and the descendant of an African slave."

So there you have it—from the Supreme Court's "first African American" justice. The Founding Fathers were misogynists and racists. Thus, the nature of the Constitution must be "evolving."

In other words, the authors of the Common Core do not trust the schools and teachers to read the Preamble to the Constitution on their own. They need to draw the lesson in, well, black and white. Rather than stressing the amazing achievement it was for a people to declare themselves sovereign, something that had never really been done, and certainly not in modern history, the teachers must show the students what the Founding Fathers did *not* do.

After reading the words "We the People," the iconoclastic teenage students are scarcely allowed to take a breath before being told that the Framers "did not have in mind the majority of America's citizens." Is that the one statement the arch-testers could find on the sheer magnitude on the phrase "We the People"? Not only is this statement made by one of the Supreme Court's most *liberal* justices an obvious stab at the Framers of the Constitution. It simply is not true.

If the teachers and students were urged to read the entire document, and not just the Preamble and First Amendment accompanied by Monk's hatchet job, they might find in Article I, section 2, that "The House of Representatives shall be composed of Members chosen every second Year by the People of the several States, and the Electors in each State shall have the Qualifications requisite for Electors of the most numerous Branch of the State Legislature." Thus the franchise was left up to the states. It was based on the most *democratic* branch of the state legislatures. There were reasons for that. First, the Framers were committed to the principle of federalism, something that is not explained in this selection. Second, the existing franchises in the states were so complex and diverse that there was no guarantee the delegates at the Constitutional Convention could have come to an agreement. Third, had the Framers imposed a single franchise on the states, quite likely the Constitution would not have been ratified at all. Here is an important historical fact. At the time of ratification, some women and free black men were already voting. Had there been a single franchise imposed by the Constitution, you can bet that the delegates from some of the Southern states would not have gone along with blacks being able to vote, so the franchise would have been eliminated for those blacks who were voting, and the chances of women or black men gaining the vote in other states would have disappeared. Further, Linda Monk's careful research apparently does not uncover the fact that during the four decades prior to the election of Jackson, the states systematically did away with property requirements for voting, and the Founders both applauded and were a part of these efforts. Thus, Article I, Section 2 in reality acted as an invitation to expand the franchise, not to limit it. At no place in the Constitution are either women or men of any race prohibited from voting.

In short, this is a case of the arch-testers programming an answer into the curriculum: an extremely politicized, controversial answer resting on a shaky historical foundation whose premises can be disputed by the document itself. Meanwhile, the word "evolving" does not even raise an eyebrow. And that is exactly what the arch-testers want: for young people to think of the Constitution as an "evolving" document, that started out as unfair and therefore as something that can become anything a party in power or the fancy of the moment wants it to be—with an amendment or without. Thus, students' first foray into the study of what might be called America's "Constitutional soul" is nothing more than a superficial, biased, drive-by killing of the Constitution designed to take place as a wholly uninformed discussion over the course of a single class period.

Let's give the authors of the Common Core another crack at the Constitution. That chance comes in the ELA "informational texts" for the 11th-12th grade band. The recommendation reads "United States. The Bill of Rights (Amendments One through Ten of the United States Constitution)." Thus, as eleventh- or twelfth-graders, right as they become eligible to vote, the students will read the whole Bill of Rights! The Common Core says *nothing* else about the rest of the Constitution.

That is not the last word on the Constitution. The arch-testers offer a brief selection from *America's Constitution: A Biography*, by Akhil Reed Amar, a law professor at Yale, on the three-fifths clause. Here is part of that selection:

> These two small problems, centering on the seemingly innocent words "among" and "Persons" quickly spiral out into the most vicious words of the apportionment clause: "adding three fifths of all other persons." Other persons here meant other than free persons—that is, slaves. Thus the more slaves a given state's master class bred or bought, the more seats the state could claim in Congress, for every decade in perpetuity.
>
> The Philadelphia draftsmen camouflaged this ugly point as best they could, euphemistically avoiding the S-word and simultaneously introducing the T-word—taxes—into the equation . . .

Now this is really very curious. The short selection (including the brief parts I have not quoted) cannot be regarded as a complete explanation of the three-fifths clause: how it came into being, how it was debated in the Convention, what it actually meant. A full explanation of the three-fifths clause (invariably misunderstood by students) would take substantially more space than the arch-testers give it. This selection is so chopped up that it could only confuse rather than clarify, particularly insofar as the apportionment clause is not really explained in the excerpt.

The bigger question is, why is the three-fifths clause the *one* part of the Constitution (which the students may not have read, remember) that gets singled out for commentary? The students are not given a selection from *The Federalist* or from Justice Story's famous commentaries on Article I, section 8, for example, which outlines the powers of Congress (and consequently limits them). The students are not offered any learned commentary on the Bill of Rights, pointing out, for example, that the First Amendment begins with the words "Congress shall make no law . . ." and the Tenth Amendment ends with the words "or to the People." In other words, rights were understood by the Founding Fathers as being necessarily protected by a *limitation* on the power of government. Instead, the *one* excerpt we are given indicating how students will study the Constitution in high school—after that *tour de force* in middle school—conspicuously includes the highly charged words "vicious," "master class," "camouflaged," and "ugly." Unquestionably, what the authors of the Common Core are prompting the history or government teacher to do is blast the Founding Fathers for their hypocrisy, deception, and racism. The arch-testers are not in the business of imparting understanding, rather of ginning up hostility.

Readers who are used to this progressive mantra will become offended, no doubt. "But the Founders *were* racist. How could they have allowed slavery to exist beyond the Revolution? How could they have said 'All men are created equal' and continued to hold slaves?" This, in fact, is the simple-minded stereotyping and self-righteous chastening of the Founders that the nation's teachers are currently drilling into their pupils' hopelessly empty heads. Every year when I ask my freshmen just to explain the words "All men are created equal," hands go up. "Well, they said 'all men are created equal,' but what they really meant was 'all white men are created equal.'" Students do not know anything else about the Declaration, but they know to say that. It is a reflex. The only problem is that it is dead wrong. The case against this reading of the Founders' ideas on equality would require a chapter at least as long as the present one. Suffice it to say that the Founders themselves, even as they were debating the three-fifths clause, called slavery an evil. As strange as it may seem, George Mason, the author of the Virginia Declaration of Rights, from whom Jefferson borrowed heavily in writing the Declaration, and who was himself a considerable slaveholder, excoriated slavery from the floor of the Constitutional Convention in terms as fervent as any later abolitionist. The basic historical fact we must realize is that the Founding Fathers *inherited* slavery. Human history had never known a time without slavery. The really interesting question to pose is whether the Founders did anything to remove slavery from the world. A compelling argument could be made that they did.

As the Framers were debating the Constitution, the Congress (under the Articles of Confederation) were drafting the Northwest Ordinance, based largely on an earlier idea of Jefferson, which outlawed slavery in the Northwest Territory, allowing the new states coming into the Union in that substantial territory to be free. Those states became Ohio, Indiana, Michigan, Illinois, and Wisconsin. The Constitution itself put a date on when the slave trade could be abolished. The Founders made good on that promise, signed into law by Jefferson the first moment it could take effect. All states except South Carolina, by the way, had already done away with the slave trade. In 1794 the Congress prohibited slaves from being exported. In 1798 the Congress prohibited slaves from Africa being taken into the Mississippi Territory.[65] The abolition and manumission of slavery in the United States actually has a long and largely unknown history. At the beginning of the Revolution, slavery was permitted in all states. In 1777, the year after the Declaration was signed, Vermont abolished slavery. Over the next three decades several other states followed suit: Massachusetts, New Hampshire, Pennsylvania, Rhode Island, Connecticut, New York, and New Jersey. Many prominent individual Founders, such as Alexander Hamilton and John Jay (the first Chief Justice of the Supreme Court), took part in

---

[65] See Abraham Lincoln, Peoria Speech, 16 October 1854.

these efforts by forming manumission societies in their own states. Meanwhile, there were noteworthy (though often unsuccessful) efforts to curtail slavery or to manumit slaves in the Southern states, including numerous instances of personal manumissions on the part of individual slave owners. By 1810, 76 percent of the blacks living in Delaware and 23 percent of those living in Maryland were free.[66] Nor can we fail to point out important personal examples offered to the nation. Benjamin Franklin became president of the Pennsylvania Society for Promoting the Abolition of Slavery. His last published work, less than a month before his death, was a satire on the slave trade. That document does not appear in the Common Core. George Washington, in a last will that was meant to be a lesson for the nation, manumitted his slaves. That document does not appear in the Common Core. Given these political and personal efforts, it was not unreasonable to think between 1776 and 1808 that slavery was on the wane in America. No part of this story gets told in the Common Core.

This reading of the Founding Fathers on slavery is not simply my reading. I can claim no such originality. It is the reading of Abraham Lincoln. During his famous debates for the U. S. Senate with Stephen Douglas, Lincoln appealed to the words of the Declaration again and again. It was Douglas who introduced the specious claim that what Jefferson really meant was that all white men are created equal. Lincoln threw down the gauntlet by inviting Douglas to prove when the Founders had ever said or written that "all men are created equal" really meant "all white men are created equal."

> I believe the entire records of the world, from the date of the Declaration of Independence up to within three years ago, may be searched in vain for one single affirmation, from one single man, that the Negro was not included in the Declaration of Independence; I think I may defy Judge Douglas to show that he ever said so, that Washington ever said so, that any President ever said so, that any member of Congress ever said so, or that any living man upon the whole earth

---

[66] See Thomas G. West, *Vindicating the Founders: Race, Class, Sex, and Justice in the Origins of America* (Lanham: Rowman and Littlefield, 1997), ch. 1.

ever said so, until the necessities of the present policy of the Democratic party, in regard to slavery, had to invent that affirmation.[67]

No proof was ever produced. Further, Lincoln pointed out many of the significant marks of disapproval that the Founding Fathers placed upon slavery in their lifetime. As for the word "persons" that our modern Constitutional scholar takes offense at, here is Lincoln's accounting for it:

> In all three of these places, being the only allusions to slavery in the instrument [the Constitution], covert language is used. . . . And I understand the contemporaneous history of those times to be that covert language was used with a purpose, and that purpose was that in our Constitution, which it was hoped and is still hoped will endure forever—when it should be read by intelligent and patriotic men, after the institution of slavery had passed from among us—there should be nothing on the face of the great charter of liberty suggesting that such a thing as Negro slavery had ever existed among us.

So there is the difference. The modern scholar claims (or we are led to believe so by the irresponsibly edited selection in the Common Core) that the use of "persons" rather than slaves was a "vicious" cover-up. What Abraham Lincoln said is that the Framers of the Constitution "expected and intended the institution of slavery to come to an end. They expected and intended that it should be in the course of ultimate extinction."[68] Therefore they did not want to desecrate the Constitution with the taint of the word *slavery*. Whom are we to trust in our reading of the Constitution, Akhil Reed Amar or Abraham Lincoln? The authors of the Common Core fail to show us the courtesy of giving us that choice.

---

[67] Abraham Lincoln, The Lincoln-Douglas Debates, Galesburgh, 7 October 1858.
[68] Abraham Lincoln, The Lincoln-Douglas Debates, Alton, 15 October 1858. Not surprisingly, the Lincoln-Douglas debates to not appear in the Common Core.

No doubt the challenge of an inherited institution of slavery was difficult for the Founding Fathers. They, more than we shall ever know, knew just how difficult, perhaps insoluble, it was in their own time. That challenge was one that generations before us solved *for us*, spilling their own blood to do so. Our carping self-righteousness is that of a spoiled, misbehaving child. If we are to judge the Founders, we should use the one criterion that ought to apply to any human being or society: Did they leave the world a better place than they found it? That question could specifically be asked of their response to slavery: Did the Founders place slavery on the path of ultimate extinction, as Lincoln said they did? Before we (a "we" that includes the nation's teachers and self-proclaimed school reformers) rush to judgment, we should realize that posterity will judge us by the same *standard*. How will we measure up on the task of educating our children, for example? The question of the Founding Fathers on slavery, more than anything else in our history, ought to be treated with the utmost caution and responsible scholarship. The way the history of slavery is now taught in schools is simply irresponsible. Among other things, the point is never made that there was a vast chasm between the philosophy of the Founding Fathers and the philosophy of John C. Calhoun and later apologists in the 1850s who called slavery "a positive good." To the superficial, biased mind, it is all one big lump called history.

Nothing that Abraham Lincoln said about the Founding Fathers or the Constitution is to be found in the Common Core. And it never will be. Allowing Lincoln to vindicate the Founders,[69] or allowing the Founders to speak for themselves, an even more sensible idea, would spoil the designs of these progressive (i.e. liberal) activists cleverly disguised as education reformers. Those designs include discrediting the Founding Fathers and ensuring that the Constitution (like the Common Core English Standards) remains an "evolving" document wholly removed from its original purpose of protecting the liberties of the people from the perils of an unaccountable government run by ambitious, officious men unchecked by the rule of law. We might turn Justice Thurgood Marshall's comment on its head: what would surprise the Founders most about this country would not be that women or black people can vote and hold public office and serve on the Supreme Court.

---

[69] This phrase is borrowed from Tom West.

What would surprise them would be how hopelessly ignorant almost all Americans are of their own history and of the Constitution that protects their inalienable rights. They would be incensed to find out that the men and women ultimately in charge of the nation's schools should want it to be that way.

We could offer other instances of bias, superficiality, and omission in the Common Core. Why, for example, is no Mark Twain recommended for the high school, leaving *Huckleberry Finn* conspicuously absent? Why is George Orwell's essay "Politics and the English" listed but neither *Animal Farm* nor *1984*? Why is Ronald Reagan's Address to the Students at Moscow University included rather than his First Inaugural or speech at the Brandenburg Gate? Given time, I could answer these questions, but it might try the reader's patience. Suffice it to say that once you have eliminated one of the two great historical forces in the Western tradition, once you have completely forgotten one of America's great Founders and the architect of the American character, once you have painted all the Founders as racist hypocrites, and once you have made the Constitution an evolving document without students ever having read it, while at the same time you have gotten the nation to accept that authors of unproven value should be read as equivalents of the classics—and you have enforced these practices through standardized testing with the force of law and public funding behind it—the rest is pretty much mop-up. You can turn young minds most anyway you want to.

Chapter Six
Two-Bit Literary Criticism

As we have seen, the story-killers of the Common Core commit a variety of crimes in their so-far successful attempt to dictate to the students of America what they should read and should not read. They substitute so-called "informational" texts, typically articles by modern writers or even tedious policy documents, for great literature. They squeeze out the classics further by forcing schools to offer a "range" of literary works written by both recent and lesser-known authors. Though they deny it, their injunctions to adopt quantity over quality will result in the failure to read complete works of literature and thus deprive students of both the pleasure and intellectual exercise of seeing a single story through to its conclusion. In addition, they continue the practice of forcing questionable "standards" onto literature rather than deriving insights into the human condition unique to each work of literature, thereby encouraging in students a cookie-cutter approach to complex stories and rendering young people utterly bored as a result. This last crime against our literary heritage warrants further investigation. Although we have already encountered the bad teaching of literature in the public schools in our discussion of "standards," we must see how these standards turn out when applied to real works of literature. As such, we must realize that the Common Core is adding nothing new to the mix except expense, further dependency on mind-numbing textbooks, and a nationalization that will be much harder to reverse than the current, progressive (though relatively localized) stranglehold on the schools. The lesson to take home is that even when the authors of the Common Core recommend (or seem to recommend) great works of literature, their superficial, limited, and silly means of studying these books only ends up killing great stories.

Whenever I ask my college freshmen, who come from around the nation, what they have learned or remember about some of the great works of literature, I find that they know very little. Though *smart*, they are not well-educated. They can vaguely recall that Hester Prynne "had to, like, wear that red letter or whatever." They certainly know that *To Kill a Mockingbird* has something to do with racism, though they know precious little else about the story. And they *may* know that Tom Sawyer tricked a bunch of kids into painting a fence, though whether they glean that information from their studies or the general culture is never quite clear. As for having a discussion about any of these great American classics, they are unable to. Viewed from one angle, this is all very funny and subject to a parody along the lines of Leno's "Jaywalking." Yet this is the real picture of the graduates of our public schools—who have spent over *twelve thousand hours* in those publicly-funded schools. In other words, the students graduating from public high school throughout the nation, even the brightest, cannot have a thoughtful conversation about *a single book.* Why not? It is still the case that at least *a few* good books are put into the hands of students, even today. The students who cannot say anything meaningful about those books remember them being assigned. They remember class time being devoted to them. They just cannot remember learning anything that is in the books—and for a very simple reason. They didn't. The reason owes primarily to the intellectually bankrupt methods of teaching literature in this country.

The Common Core English Standards, so far from providing a remedy to our national semi-literacy, actually institutionalize it. To explain why requires a foray into the nature of teaching literature. The basic reason our students do not understand or even like good literature is that stories are presented to them through the lens of what might be called *two-bit literary criticism.* The teacher does not invite students to read a literary work and understand it on its own terms: through the lives of the characters, their virtues and vices, their longings and heartbreaks, their attempts to find happiness in the confusing arena we call life. Rather, the teacher requires the student to dissect the story *indirectly* through speculation about how the author created the story. False categories are imposed upon the story such as "author's point of view," "main themes," "main idea," and so on. Much attention is placed on literary devices. Plot structure is a big component of this approach (rising action, falling action, climax, etc.). Students do not get to know the characters but rather "characterization," that is, how the author created the characters. When these false categories are exhausted, the teacher can always bring in the old favorite, "compare and contrast." It is essential that as much time as possible be spent on these diversions so that the story itself is not discussed. That is for a very simple reason. Talking about stories—trying to figure out why characters do things (just as why *real people* do things)—is hard. It requires patience and study and thinking. Just reflect for a moment on the few people you know who have what is called "a good judge of character." Or, conversely, consider the many people you know who have a bad judge of character. Think about the number of people who have been hired where you work (or whom you have hired yourself) who have not "turned out well." Think about the number of women who have "ended up with the wrong guy." Reading character, then, getting at the root of another person's soul, is hard. Therefore reading literature is hard. There is no way around it. But it is a simple matter to force a story into a contrived plot graph. *The Little Mermaid*? Rising action, climax, falling action. *War and Peace*? Rising action, climax, falling action. It's easy!

So ingrained in our minds is this manner of treating literature that it must seem highly irregular to consider that there might be another way, a better way. Yet the proof is in the failure. Today's children and young people do not understand literature. Two-bit literary criticism is the reason. The absurdity can be easily exposed. Do we really think that the great Mark Twain, who made fun of most everything, would have written his great novels so that a century later students in somnolent high schools could trace meaningless plot graphs? What about foreshadowing? That is a favorite "literary device" to impose upon stories artificially. The problem with foreshadowing is that pointing it out gives away the ending to the story! Presumably *suspense* and *surprise* are also elements that authors use to keep readers reading. But there is never any *surprise* in a public high school class. If an amateur reviewer on Netflix does such a thing, a "spoiler alert" sign is posted. There is no spoiler alert to warn students of bad teaching techniques. Finally, what are we to make of the contrived thematic categories: man vs. man, man vs. society, etc.? We never see the common words of everyday life, the words that truly describe human thought and behavior—education, courage, love, lust, hope, despair, self-delusion, misunderstanding, strife, and so on. The words that describe human life are innumerable. Therefore, the *true reading* of literature leads to an endless probing of the complex human psyche and of the English language. That sort of probing is assuredly not taking place in our public schools. Every book comes as a pre-fab, easy-to-assemble exercise in contrived jargon.

The easiest way to see the difference between how books are currently taught and how they ought to be taught is to observe how people talk about good movies. After viewing a good movie or television program, people do not say, "Wow, the screenwriters of *Jaws* really did a good job with that rising action," or, "The theme of *Rocky* was definitely man vs. man," or "The *main idea* of *The Godfather* is . . ." Instead, they discuss the characters and the actions *directly*, sometimes at the very basic level of "I liked so-and-so" or "Boy, I hated that guy." That direct discussion of movies and shows that even young children are capable of having is precisely the discussion that ought to be taking place about great literature in all our public schools across the nation. Obviously, the discussion should go beyond "I liked him" or "I didn't like her." But that is what education is for: to discover the deeper meaning and motives of human beings by improving the conversation about them. The similarity of movies and great literature is not a stretch. Shakespeare's plays were performed before a public audience. Many, if not most, movies began as books. If *fictional* movies and television shows can have such a hold on the American mind, then why don't great works of literature have a similar hold? Are the writers of *The Big Bang Theory*, though clever, better authors than Homer? The reason is simple; we never really read and discuss literature. Our so-called teachers get in the way.

Those who read closely the "Sample Performance Tasks" contained in Appendix B will find that the Common Core English Standards simply reproduce the failed methods of teaching literature that have largely divorced Americans from their literary tradition and have rendered them less able to understand any complex human phenomenon. On this account, the Common Core Standards offer nothing new and nothing improved. The bureaucratic story-killers serve up the same contrived questions we have come to expect in the utterly barren landscape we now call "English language arts" in the public schools. As such, we can only conclude that the arch-testers do not really know the stories, do not understand them, and certainly do not love them. We might easily see this to be the case by looking at how the arch-testers treat a couple of truly great, classic stories. Further, we should also look at how these same techniques turn out when applied to an historical document. As we go through these texts I would urge the reader to put himself in the position of being in a public-school classroom for hours every week and also having to take standardized exams. I would urge him to try to add up the untold hours of boredom that millions of children are put through every day. Further, I would ask the reader to see the difference between the current teaching of literature and how books ought to be read, simply by picking up these books and reading them anew without the intrusive, unhelpful prompts of the arch-testers. To encourage the reader in this endeavor, I shall add my own alternatives to the "sample performance tasks" provided by the Common Core.

First we encounter *The Adventures of Tom Sawyer*. The text is recommended for the 6-8 grade range. That makes sense. Of course, it could also be read in the fifth grade, as is the case in the Core Knowledge curriculum. That is part of the problem of prescribing grades for the reading of certain books, even when, as in this case, a broad, sensible range of ages is offered. Would all the Core Knowledge schools out there, some that have been in existence for two decades, have to alter their curriculum in order to accommodate the testing of the Common Core?[70] At any rate, let's look into what the arch-testers make of this great book, one of the classic American stories that every person should know and love.

The selection offered in Appendix B of the Standards is taken from chapter two. It is a part of the famous fence-paining scene. The text reads "From Chapter 2: The Glorious Whitewasher." This is actually a piece of careless editing. The authoritative editions of *Tom Sawyer* contain no chapter titles.[71] Over the years, different publishers have added them. For example, The Weekly

---

[70] Obviously, the thing to do would be not to alter the school's curriculum and rather count on the students to recall what they had learned about *Tom Sawyer* the year before (assuming it appeared on a sixth-grade Common Core exam). But that is not how schools act; they are slavish to the test.

[71] In the table of contents, one does find humorous chapter summaries or descriptions, but those are not the same as chapter titles, and "the glorious whitewasher" is not among them.

Reader Classics offers this same heading for chapter 2, but the Norton Critical Edition and The Library of America do not. If Twain did not want chapter titles, should the authors of the Common Core add them? This point may seem too subtle for some, but it does suggest a sloppiness on the part of the arch-testers, as well as a lack of familiarity with the book. Moreover, since one of the prescribed techniques of story-killing is to spend an inordinate amount of time discussing the title, it is very likely that teachers could ask their students what they think "the author" meant by the title "The Glorious Whitewasher," in this case a title he did not write. Finally, we have already made the point that the reality of standardized testing is that schools are increasingly teaching only selections of great literature rather than entire works. That the arch-testers offer as a sample the exact passage we would expect them to reveals that they have no intention of sending opposite signals. Aside from these cautionary notes, we do agree that this is passage of great literature worth knowing. The real question is whether the authors of the Common Core understand it.

Here is the "Sample Performance Task" we are given:

> Students summarize the development of the morality of Tom Sawyer in Mark Twain's novel of the same name and analyze its connection to themes of accountability and authenticity by noting how it is conveyed through characters, setting, and plot.[72]

This "performance task" is drawn from Reading Standards for Literature 6-12, RL.8.2, in case you are interested, which reads "Determine a theme or central idea of a text and analyze its development over the course of the text, including its relationship to the characters, setting, and plot; provide an objective summary of the text." In other words, this is boilerplate. No real thinking went into the making of this question. It does not have *Tom Sawyer* specifically in mind and could have been asked of *The Ugly Duckling* or *The Brothers Karamazov*. As such, it offers little help in understanding one of the greatest scenes in American literature.

---

[72] Appendix B, p. 89.

Let us begin by noticing what the "performance task" (what is a *performance task*, by the way?) does not take into account. Nothing is said about the obvious humor contained in the passage. One of the funniest scenes in all of literature does not even crack a smile in the arch-testers. We are not invited to laugh about what boys find valuable, what Tom considers his "worldly wealth": bits of toys, marbles, and trash; and what he accumulates: a kite, in good repair, a dead rat and a string to swing it with, a piece of blue bottle glass to look through, a key that wouldn't unlock anything, a kitten with only one eye, a dog-collar, but no dog, and so on. Nor is our attention called to the rich, humorous lines in the passage: "At this dark and hopeless moment an inspiration burst upon him! Nothing less than a great, magnificent inspiration"; or "boys happened along every little while; they came to jeer, but remained to whitewash." What great lines, wholly unappreciated by the new architects of the nation's standardized testing! Nor is any mention made of the mock lesson—or what could be a real lesson; you can never be too sure with Twain—of the passage:

> Tom said to himself that it was not such a hollow world, after all. He had discovered a great law of human action, without knowing it—namely, that in order to make a man or a boy covet a thing, it is only necessary to make the thing difficult to attain. If he had been a great and wise philosopher, like the writer of this book, he would now have comprehended that Work consists of whatever a body is *obliged* to do and that Play consists of whatever a body is not obliged to do. And this would help him to understand why constructing artificial flowers or performing on a tread-mill is work, while rolling ten-pins or climbing Mont Blanc is only amusement. . . .

We could add other laws of human action to our understanding brought about by this passage. What, for example, do we learn about *boys*, which Twain suggests is true of men as well? Of course, the arch-testers would never allow such a "gendered" question to enter into the study of a literary work. The modern university is obsessed with gender, but if the study of gender casts boys in a positive light, or if it imparts a "stereotype" that some feminist scholar somewhere might construe as being unfavorable to girls, then that reading will not be allowed to stand. We cannot prove that the arch-testers subscribe to this bias, but we cannot fail to notice that probably the best novel about boys *ever written* does not have the word "boy" in the "sample performance task."

One other oddity strikes us about what the arch-testers' "performance task" does not contain. We are not asked to identify the leading character traits in Tom. That would be an easy and sensible question to ask: What do we learn about Tom in this passage? More to the point, what seems to be Tom's leading character trait? Presumably, that question would lead to a discussion about Tom's *cleverness*. The question could also bring up other, perhaps less desirable (and yet still endearing) aspects of Tom's character such as his hatred of work and chores. At the same time, the discussion could lead to knowing what Tom likes to do (and why) as well as the not insignificant fact that Tom's cunning gets the fence painted far better than he could have painted it himself. Thus, the obvious initial questions to ask students about this passage, particularly in advance, are, "What do we learn about *Tom* in this passage? What do we learn about *boys* in this passage? What do we learn about *work* in this passage?" Had the arch-testers asked these three sensible questions, we would know that they had at least read and understood the story. And they would have set the table for any competent teacher to foster a lively and enlightening discussion with any class of adolescents in the country.

In contrast, what do the arch-testers want us to hone in on? The first word that strikes us is *morality*. No doubt, morality is an important part of literature since it is a vital part of the human condition. The world would be in a state of nature—solitary, poor, nasty, brutish, and short—without morality. Mark Twain, in his own way, is a moral author. But—and this is a big *but*—morality, as that term is understood by everyone—is the last thing either Mark Twain or his great character Tom Sawyer is after in this adventure. A boy who wins a Bible in church by trading his "wealth" gotten by the fence-painting trick for tickets awarded for memorizing Bible verses, when he himself knows not one verse, and who plays with a pinch-bug during a boring sermon in church, is not the protagonist of a straightforward morality tale. In fact, Twain offers a classic line on Tom Sawyer's regard for *morality*:

"He was not the Model Boy of the village. He knew the model boy very well though—and loathed him." If we were to do a little research into our literary history, we would find that Twain himself loathed straightforward, saccharine morality tales written for children. Of all the words that could have been used to offer a key to Tom Sawyer's character, *morality* must be among the two or three worst.

What is the answer the arch-testers are looking for? That Tom did not show much in the way of *morality* in the fence-painting scene, but over time his morality will "develop" through some magic called the author's "characterization"? That's boring. It is also not true. Certainly, Tom's character does develop over the course of the story, but it would be a crucial mistake to think that this or any other of his doings are meant to expose some fatal flaw that must be worked out. Tom is a boy. He is a spirited boy. His *adventures* (as in The *Adventures* of Tom Sawyer) are the undertakings truly spirited boys pursue. We could list them all here, but the reader should go back to that book (or read it for the first time) and revel in Tom's exploits, unhampered by officious advice that tells us to summarize the development of Tom's morality.

Two similarly absurd terms are *accountability* and *authenticity*. The former goes hand-in-hand with *morality*. We are presumably supposed to assert that Tom is not being very *accountable* in not painting the fence himself. Here is a question for the arch-testers: does the fence get painted? Does it get painted better by a multitude of boys or by Tom's doing it alone? 'Nuff said. *Authenticity* is the real howler, however. Authenticity is a term used to diagnose depressed, alienated characters in modern literature. The various existential whiners produced by Camus and Jean-Paul Sartre and Fitzgerald are vexed over their "authenticity," but Tom isn't. Do the arch-testers really mean *honesty* and use a more sophisticated term to impress us? If they did, they goofed. They have Tom dead wrong. Even when Tom is lying through his teeth, he is perfectly authentic. He is not alienated from his world. True, he is often bored with adult society and nonsense. So he turns every part of the dull, adult world into a game or an adventure. There is hardly a character in literature more *authentic* than Tom Sawyer. What you see is what you get. Besides that, how are we going to talk about *authenticity* with twelve- through fourteen-year-olds? They, like Tom, are refreshingly authentic. It is only when students reach the high school that they begin to play the games of deception about who they are. I would love to see one of the arch-testers go into a real classroom—where the rubber hits the road—and have a discussion about *authenticity* with thirteen-year-olds. Such a thing should be put on youtube. Then we would be able to see the *authenticity* of these people as teachers of literature and school reformers.

The senselessness does not end with *morality* and *authenticity*. The arch-testers want us to talk about Tom's morality via the "themes" of accountability and authenticity so as to figure out *its* (morality's) connection to "characters, setting, and plot." Or something like that. Now we have already met Tom: the protagonist, the hero. So are we supposed to figure out Tom's morality in relation to other characters? The wording is so unclear it is hard to say. The reading of the question I just offered may be generous. I actually do not think they know what they meant. If, however, this is what they meant, why did the arch-testers not just ask the simple question, "How does Tom treat other people?" That question would bring out Tom's character a lot better than "summarize the development of the morality of Tom Sawyer in Mark Twain's novel of the same name and analyze its connection to themes of accountability and authenticity by noting how it is conveyed through characters." You can try this yourself if you have a twelve- or thirteen-year-old at hand. Ask my question and then assign the Common Core's "performance task," and see which one elicits an answer.

Moving right along, what are we to make of setting and plot? Are we being asked to summarize Tom's morality in relation to the setting? That is very strange. How might Tom's morality have anything to do with the setting? Tom and Sid are being brought up in the very same house, Aunt Polly's, and yet their *moralities* (their characters?) are very different. Now if the arch-testers had asked how Tom's sense of adventure relates to the setting, we could actually get somewhere with that question. We could show how Tom's spirited character thrives in a small town. There are plenty of places to go a-swimming when he is playing hooky. He can find hollow tree stumps containing "spunk-water" so necessary for ridding himself of warts. And every small town has a spooky graveyard nearby to go exploring at night. If I were teaching the class, I would not dilate on the setting *per se*, because doing so drains the sense of reality out of the story ("Oh, class, look at how the author gives us such a good setting here!"). But we could at least agree that *some* of the story-killers in our schools know *something* about the stories they kill. The story-killers of the Common Core plainly do not. If they do, I wish they would offer us their version of a "sample performance task" answered satisfactorily. We await with bated breath. And plot? How is the development of Tom's morality, which is somehow connected to accountability and authenticity, conveyed through plot? Who knows or cares? I suspect this is the moment when the teacher will whip out her handy, portable plot graph and kill off what is left of the students' interest.

Let us restore this story to life simply by reading it. Tom Sawyer is a boy's boy. He lives in pursuit of adventure. True, he is a mischievous boy, an unruly boy, but that is just another way of saying that he is a spirited boy. We are being invited to participate in Tom's adventures (vicariously) and to admire his spiritedness. If we need proof, we must look no further than the preface to see this to be the case:

> Most of the adventures recorded in this book really occurred; one or two were experiences of my own, the rest those of boys who were schoolmates of mine. Huck Finn is drawn from life; Tom Sawyer also, but not from an individual . . .
>
> Although my book is intended mainly for the entertainment of boys and girls, I hope it will not be shunned by men and women on that account, for part of my plan has been to try to pleasantly remind adults of what they once were themselves, and of how they felt and thought and talked, and what queer enterprises they sometimes engaged in.

"Intended mainly for the entertainment of boys and girls": Do you really think Twain wanted boys and girls puzzling over "authenticity" and morality's relation to "characters, setting, and plot" or rather being "entertained" by adventures and lively characters, that is, by stories of interesting and funny boys and girls?

The word *adventure*, which appears in the title, also puts a nail in the coffin of the arch-tester's question. By adult standards, Tom's half-brother Sid is moral. Would we want to read a story called *The Adventures of Sid*? Sid is to be found behind his aunt's skirts most of the day. The adults in the story, by the way, who are responsible for the common standards of *morality*, are portrayed as boring, pompous, unreliable, and wholly in a fog about real boys. If anything, there is a strong suggestion that the natural ethics of children are superior to the contrived, respectable, and often false ethics of adults. But we should not have to prove such things to students. They would have an intuitive grasp of the book if they were just invited to read it, really read it, perhaps with a few questions to guide their way.

Now it is true that Tom's character could be said to develop over the course of the story; that is, his sense of adventure pulls him into situations that test both his mettle and his goodness. But the way to get at that question is not to begin by asking about morality in relation to the fence-painting scene and how morality "develops" over the course of the novel. Rather, the question to ask is whether Tom has the makings of a hero, or qualities of the heroic. In the fence-painting scene we are invited to laugh, no doubt, at both Tom and at boys in general. But we are also invited to marvel at Tom's cleverness. His sense of adventure and his unruliness had gotten him into trouble for playing hooky (which he did with some justification given how boring school was, as we learn later). So he found himself in a bind. He had to paint a fence. He would miss the adventures of the day and, worse, be made fun of by other boys. He had to find a way out of his plight. He did so in the cleverest way imaginable. Cleverness, cunning, quickness of mind is, or can be, a quality of the hero. Tom Sawyer lives by his wits. There have been other great heroes in Western literature who have lived by their wits, the most famous one being a man from Ithaca named Odysseus.

The fence-painting scene can be read and enjoyed in its own right. But if we must try to connect it to the rest of the story, we should think about how Tom's cleverness is being honed by these boyish tricks so that one day he may be able to do something great. Here are the questions I would ask to enlist such thought about the scene.

> Did Tom prove that there is more than one way
> to skin a cat—or to paint a fence? Which is
> better—Aunt Polly's way or Tom's way? Why?
> What talents are necessary to get a fence painted
> Tom's way? Does Tom reveal any qualities that
> could be considered heroic? Use the text to
> support your answers.

Would you prefer answering (in writing) and having a discussion about those questions or the ones provided by the authors of the Common Core? How about at age thirteen?

I have seen both approaches used, and I can assure you that the difference in students' interest and what they learn is like night and day. The arch-testers fail miserably to grasp this, one of the most famous scenes in American literature. What is more, they serve up to the teachers of the nation canned questions that drain the life out of this great story and that in practice will only bore a class of teenagers to death. Any boys of spirit *should* be tempted to play hooky if that is all our schools have to offer. The irony of this dry-as-dust, cookie-cutter approach to studying literature is that it fails to impart an important aim of education the arch-testers tell us they wish to ACHIEVE. The arch-testers tell us that we are living in a twenty-first-century global economy. Today's young people will have to be great problem-solvers and decision-makers! I prefer the terms *judgment* and *prudence*, but we'll go with the flow for a moment. What is the fence-painting scene but a classic case of problem-solving? Tom is forced to paint a fence. He doesn't want to paint a fence. He knows the other boys will laugh and jeer at him. This memorable scene takes place in the days long before www.stopbullying.gov ended all the world's bullying problems. Moreover, he is poor in terms of what boys consider wealth. He wants to be rich. So what does he do? He uses his wits to solve his problems! Should we not at least stop a moment to applaud his rapid decision-making before pedantically criticizing his lack of authenticity? Should the arch-testers not be delighted to have such a brilliant decision-maker in such a young hero? These ostensible education reformers really cannot see the forest for the trees. In their efforts to reduce this wonderful adventure to a formulaic "standard," they have failed to appreciate what is unique and great. They have missed Tom Sawyer by a country mile.

If the arch-testers cannot understand boys, let's see if they understand young women any better. If there was ever a classic novel from the past that girls and young women in the present have adopted as their own—despite the differences in social conditions and mores and manners between our age and the story's—that novel is clearly *Pride and Prejudice.* It continues to sell in the tens of thousands every year, yet without it being required reading in schools. It is not surprising that there are two films based on the book that remain popular.[73] Nor is it insignificant that, though we are a nation of mostly poor readers owing to the failure of our schools, this is one book that the students who have read it more or less "get."[74] Thus, if there were ever an opportunity to seize upon a book that is already a part of our cultural consciousness and to teach it well, *Pride and Prejudice* is that opportunity. What will the Common Core do with it?

The authors of the Common Core recommend the book as an eleventh- or twelfth-grade reading. Great. I still think that the Common Core should not be telling schools which books should be read in which grades, but at least they are recommending the book.[75] The question, then, lies in how they think this great story ought to be studied. Here is their "sample performance task":

> Students *analyze* the first impressions given of Mr. and Mrs. Bennet in the opening chapter of *Pride and Prejudice* based on *the setting* and how the *characters are introduced.* By comparing these first impressions with their later understanding based on how the *action is ordered* and the *characters develop* over the course of the novel, students understand *the impact* of Jane Austen's choices in *relating elements of a story.* [Emphasis in the original.]

---

[73] The six-hour A & E version with Colin Firth is clearly the superior, the Hollywood version featuring a ridiculous emo-Darcy who appears ludicrous to anyone who has read the book.

[74] This statement does not invalidate my previous comment that there is not one book that professors can count on students knowing. The reading of *Pride and Prejudice* remains largely a female phenomenon, and, though many young women have read the book, that does not mean they have thoroughly studied it.

[75] Or, they are recommending a portion of the book . . . or, maybe no part of the book will be read at all. See chapter seven.

First, we must state that our *first impression* of these two sentences is that they are a big jumble. If we are to take off points for style, as any responsible composition or English teacher would, we must state emphatically that virtually every sentence written by the standards-mongers would be marked down. Beyond that, we shall try to understand this present, inelegant couplet.

The principal, though unstated, assignment is to place oneself in the dubious position of armchair novelist. All the emphasis is placed on "Jane Austen's choices" in creating aspects of the story (such as how characters are introduced) instead of who the characters are and how they behave. That is, we are not being invited to treat the characters as real people. The problem with this approach is that the mind will not invest itself in things that are not real or that seem artificial, contrived, and constructed. Now the skeptical reader will say, "But wait, this is fiction. We know already that the characters are not real, that they never lived." Though true in one sense, that objection is manifestly untrue in a larger sense. Yes, we know we are reading fiction whenever we pick up a novel. At the same time, our minds allow us to enter into a state of suspended disbelief. We do not think about the characters not being real as we read. On the contrary, we read the book as though the characters *are real*. If, however, some officious interloper tells us at every juncture that "the author" is doing this or that with the characters, then we lose interest. We think we are being played. Or we just get tired of being interrupted every time really interesting things begin to happen.

This is not only true of fiction. All books have authors. Historians have to craft their stories no less than novelists theirs. If, for example, you were reading an account of that cold Christmas night in 1776 when Washington was taking his men across the Delaware, and some historiographical critic kept jumping in, saying, "Now look how Flexner here uses the element of *suspense* in order to make you interested in Washington's fate," what would you think? You would think, "Back off, you annoying intruder, and let me find out what happened to Washington and his men!" After reading the account, you would want to talk about *Washington*'s determination, the *army*'s suffering and bravery, the miracle of such a thing ever coming to pass, the effects it had on boosting morale, and a host of other things affecting the historical actors themselves. You would not be nearly so interested in how

James Thomas Flexner crafted his account, though, truly, Flexner is one of the great biographers of Washington. Readers are naturally invested in characters, whether real or fictional, more than in authors.

One of the ironies of literature is that the great authors write stories about characters who are greater (or more interesting) than they are. Shakespeare could not have been greater than Julius Caesar or Henry V. He never commanded armies and defeated entire peoples in battles. Jane Austen, for her part, never got married. Rousseau did not bring up his own children. Dostoyevsky never killed a pawnbroker just to show he could. And yet these people wrote incredible stories about those things happening. Though we can certainly admire them as authors—by saying, for example, "I love Jane Austen"—the more attention we place upon the authors *as we are reading the stories* they crafted, the less their stories end up meaning to us. The more we speculate on how a character was created, they less we think of him as real and the less we want to know him. Would the great authors themselves have wanted their readers admiring various tricks of the craft of writing or rather completely invested in the stories as they are reading them? If the first time we read or hear the lines, "Friends, Romans, countrymen, lend me your ears," we think "What a great line from William Shakespeare!" we are already a step removed from caring about Antony's fate. Is that really what the great playwright of the Globe Theatre wanted out of his packed audiences? Two-bit literary criticism, the artificial requirement of adolescents to play armchair novelists and playwrights, is killing off the great stories of this country and of Western Civilization. Who killed Homer?[76] It turns out to be the teachers of the classics themselves.

To test our thesis, let us move on and see whether the Common Core brand of two-bit literary criticism actually helps us understand *Pride and Prejudice*. "Students analyze." As we have seen, the word *analyze* is a very important one for the arch-testers, although they never define it. What are we analyzing? "The first impressions given." Now this is very interesting. Students of Jane Austen know that *First Impressions* was her initial idea for the

---

[76] This is the title of a book by Victor Davis Hanson and John Heath, who argue that modern classicists, with their own forms of literary criticism, have killed our interest in the classics.

154

novel's title. Of course, the first impressions Austen originally meant were those that both Elizabeth and Mr. Darcy formed of each other at the ball in the assembly-room where they first met, impressions that are not easily removed. "First impressions" here in the Common Core, though, has been changed to the "first impressions *given*." Given by whom? Well, despite the passive voice we see that the interest has been shifted from the first impressions the *characters* have of each other to the first impressions given by the *author* about her characters. Here, then, is a clear instance of an author wanting to draw attention to the *characters* through a title (as she did even better with the words *Pride and Prejudice*) while the two-bit literary critics want to draw attention to the author. Thus, the arch-testers want to take us out of the story that the author herself wants us very much to be in. Worse, about whom have we been given these first impressions? Mr. and Mrs. Bennet, say the arch-testers. What? You would think that if there must be one sample performance task for the entire book, it would be about Elizabeth and Darcy. You would think that if the words "first impressions" would be invoked, attention would be drawn to Elizabeth and Darcy. But, no, we are supposed to think about the first impressions given by the author of Mr. and Mrs. Bennet. As much as two-bit literary criticism, this question is beginning to have the feel of a Wikipedia-generated "performance task." We must ask, in the spirit of Elizabeth, "Could they have read the novel, sir?"

But we shall continue to indulge this question. Once again, we see that *setting* is a big deal. We are not asked just to describe the setting, though, but to explain how it affects our first impressions of the characters. Well, this is boilerplate standards lingo. It is not really meant to make any sense, and those who are asking the question have not really thought about it. That is obvious if we just simplify or clarify the question by asking how the *setting* might have anything to do with the *character* (virtues, vices) of the characters. Lydia Bennet and Elizabeth Bennet are two characters as different as any who appear in literature. And yet they are found in the same setting! In fact, the same family! Mr. and Mrs. Bennet are also utterly different. And yet they are found in the same setting! But the arch-testers want us to explore our first impressions (of character, presumably) based upon the setting of the story. The whole thing falls apart when you look at it closely.

There is a lot more claptrap in this question that we shall not waste time in attempting to unravel. The second sentence is worth considering only to show how utterly confused and clueless these people are about literature: "By comparing these first impressions with their later understanding based on how the action is ordered and the characters develop over the course of the novel, students understand the impact of Jane Austen's choices in relating elements of a story." I maintain that this is simply nonsense. This is the result of running great books through the standards mill. It will be left to the textbook companies (for a pretty penny) to chop this up into some really dry and processed literature-food, as opposed to being happy with just publishing the novel. For argument's sake, though, we should see what happens when we do attempt what the arch-testers tell us to do. Does the performance task correspond to the novel? Absolutely not.

The arch-testers picked the words "first impressions." They further told us to look at Mr. and Mrs. Bennet in light of first impressions. "First impressions" implies that our opinions will change or that those impressions are deceiving. In this second question, we are being invited to compare our first impressions with our later understanding. Further, a very important word is used: *develop*. "How the . . . characters develop over the course of the novel" is the wording, dissected from the other parts of the question. So, basically, we are being asked to observe how our first impressions of Mr. and Mrs. Bennet are off or just plain wrong, and how their characters *develop* over the course of the novel. Any true lover of *Pride and Prejudice* will laugh at this suggestion. Mr. and Mrs. Bennet are two characters who categorically do not *develop* over the course of the novel. They do not improve, they do not change, they do not learn a lesson, they do not know any more at the end of the story than they do at the beginning. Mrs. Bennet is simply hopeless. She is a comical figure throughout the novel. She has next to no self-awareness. Though tied up in the fortunes of her daughters, she really has no sympathy for them; it is rather her "nerves" that are always her foremost concern when things go badly. Mrs. Bennet does not develop and is not capable of developing. *Mr.* Bennet is a lot smarter. It is from her father that Elizabeth gains her intelligence and humor. But he does not develop either. Because of his bad parenting, he puts Lydia at risk. He *does* go out looking for her, and seems to sense the severity of his other daughters being put at risk due to her frivolity (which he has allowed in his home). But he is delivered of the family's ruin by Darcy's actions, not his own. He does not recognize Darcy's greatness. Moreover, the line that shows that he has not developed (improved, gained insight) as a character—"For what do we live, but to make sport for our neighbours, and laugh at them in our turn?"—reveals that Darcy was right, at least in principle, in his rejoinder to Elizabeth in the famous drawing-room scene:

> The wisest and best of men,—nay, the wisest and best of their actions,—may be rendered ridiculous by a person whose first object in life is a joke.

Mr. Bennet, clever though he is, views life, including his own marriage and family, as a kind of joke. Elizabeth deserves better.

In fact, looking at the story as a whole, it is remarkable how Elizabeth and Darcy are the only characters who develop, improve, or change. Mr. Collins doesn't. Lydia most certainly doesn't. Mr. Wickham doesn't. Charlotte Lucas, later Collins, recognizes that her marriage is not ideal, but she does not recant her earlier, utilitarian philosophy about marriage. Jane and Mr. Bingley are perfectly nice people, but they are not terribly thoughtful in the way Elizabeth and Mr. Darcy are. They remain as genuine and innocent and good-natured as they begin the story. In fact, the *lack of development* (of change or education) is what marks *all* the other characters. This is by no means a deficiency of Jane Austen. Rather, her insight into human nature seems to be that most people *don't change*. This is a case where the canned "development" question completely contradicts the author's own story. Just as *morality* is one of the least appropriate words to use of Tom Sawyer, so the word *develop* in relation to Mr. and Mrs. Bennet is wholly out of place. That the authors of the Common Core English Standards, which will govern the teaching of literature throughout the nation, would ask this question of a book that is so well known is astonishing. It suggests that they either have not read the book or do not understand the book, and, either way, do not care about the book. Our greatest stories are being entrusted to the care of the people least able to preserve them.

What would a legitimate question or series of questions look like in relation to *Pride and Prejudice*? Here are some that I have used in class with students, at both the high school and college levels. Obviously, they are not exhaustive. A few people who really knew the book should be able to sit down in a room and come up with dozens.

> Other than love and procreation (which are no doubt essential) are there other reasons for marriage? Consider the relationship between Elizabeth and Mr. Darcy. Do they gain anything from each other over the course of their acquaintance? What is each person without the other? What virtues attract them to each other? What vices repel them? What will their marriage be built on? Could their courtship be called an education? In light of the relationship that emerges between Mr. Darcy and Elizabeth, what do you make of Mr. and Mrs. Bennet's marriage? What is this marriage based on? Are there lessons to be learned from it, even negative ones? Develop an overarching thesis that answers all these questions.[77]

Now the clever reader will see exactly what I am doing with these questions. I am asking students to consider how the strange courtship between Elizabeth and Mr. Darcy is itself a kind of education. They each have impressive virtues, but they each have considerable flaws. Each also lacks an element of self-awareness. Over the course of the story, each teaches the other something important. Their coming together improves them. Further, we can extrapolate from this experience that the purpose of marriage itself is to improve two limited people by making them into a whole. Love and marriage, then, constitute a kind of education—a very important education. By looking at Mr. and Mrs. Bennet's marriage, we can see what happens when this education does not take place. The education (proper rearing) of the children is in jeopardy. It takes place only by happenstance. Judging from the daughters, the Bennets are two for five, and they are extremely

---

[77] Not wanting to give away the ending, I would only ask this question *after* students had read the book. I would use other, less leading questions, while reading the book. This question might appear on an exam.

lucky in those two. In short, my questions are all geared towards *development* of character and the lack thereof, just as the arch-testers' question is supposed to be. The difference is, I am really looking at the characters and not drawing upon a contrived, cookie-cutter standard concocted by standards-pimps who sell out good literature to bureaucracies and publishing companies. I am worried about the characters in this book—I treat them as real human beings—just as we must assume that Jane Austen wanted us to do.

One thing the reader should notice about the difference between my questions and the Common Core "performance task" is that mine are written exclusively with the book in mind. It is one of the cardinal rules of good teachers of literature that all questions have to emerge out of the actual story at hand. One way to test whether a Socratic literature question will prove thought-provoking and answerable—indeed to test the *authenticity* of it—is to see whether it addresses that story and that story alone. In general, if you could substitute any other proper names into the question, then it is boilerplate and really does not have the exact story in mind. Boilerplate questions on the part of the teacher elicit uninspired, canned, boilerplate answers from students. We can test whether a question or assignment is legitimate by seeing whether we could apply it to another, completely different literary work. Let's try that exercise, first with the Common Core's performance task for *Pride and Prejudice*:

> Students *analyze* the first impressions given of Tom and Aunt Polly in the opening chapter of *The Adventures of Tom Sawyer* based on *the setting* and how the *characters are introduced*. By comparing these first impressions with their later understanding based on how the *action is ordered* and the *characters develop* over the course of the novel, students understand *the impact* of Mark Twain's choices in *relating elements of a story*.

Nothing has changed. The performance task is equally boilerplate and equally vanilla, and the students would be just as bored in trying to read the book in this way. Now let's look at my questions.

Other than love and procreation (which are no doubt essential) are there other reasons for marriage? Consider the relationship between Tom and Aunt Polly. Do they gain anything from each other over the course of their acquaintance? What is each person without the other? What virtues attract them to each other? What vices repel them? What will their marriage be built on? Could their courtship be called an education? In light of the relationship that emerges between Tom and Aunt Polly, what do you make of Huck and Injun Joe's marriage? What is this marriage based on? Are there lessons to be learned from it, even negative ones? Develop an overarching thesis that answers all these questions.

It doesn't work, does it? My questions have a specific story in mind. The performance task of the Common Core has absolutely no story in mind. Still don't believe that the Common Core is in large part a cut-and-paste operation bearing no resemblance to reality?

Here is another irony. Even if we admitted that having two-bit literary criticism take us out of the story is a legitimate exercise, would we want that to be the function of high schools? Would we not leave literary criticism to college or even graduate school and let teenagers just enjoy reading a book for the first time? Is there not enough labor involved in simply understanding the book at the level of figuring out why the characters do the things they do? Better still, which approach better prepares young people for the future? Very few of them will go on to become literary critics. How many of them will get married? How many of them, then, will need to know what marriage really means so that one day they might have an Elizabeth-Darcy marriage and family rather than a Bennet marriage and family, in which, among other things, the husband does not respect his wife? How many of them need to know these things so that their marriages and homes will not turn out worse than the Bennets'? Much of the students' future happiness is tied up in their understanding what the characters learn in this story, not how the novel was supposedly crafted. Are the progressive authors of the Common Core not so worried about the state of love and marriage and the family these days as most ordinary people are?

The authors of the Common Core have disappointed us so far in their treatment of two of the most memorable works of literature ever written. You would think the arch-testers would bring their A-game to the discussion of *Tom Sawyer* and *Pride and Prejudice*. Not so. Now we must see how they do with what they ineptly label *informational texts*. To figure out whether the new educational regime will be any better at "non-fiction" than fiction, we should simply take the historical document that every American should know the best, the Declaration of Independence. The arch-testers recommend this reading for the eleventh or twelfth grade. Here is the sample performance task.

> "Students *analyze* Thomas Jefferson's Declaration of Independence, identifying its *purpose* and evaluating *rhetorical features* such as the listing of grievances. Students compare and contrast the *themes* and argument found there to those of other *U. S. documents of historical and literary significance*, such as the Olive Branch Petition." [Emphasis in the original.]

That's it? Such guidance should strike any careful reader as pretty thin. Moreover, we should notice the same pattern that we have seen with the literary works. There is no indication that the arch-testers had any single work in mind when generating the question, with the exception of the phrase "list of grievances." Otherwise, students could analyze the "purpose" and "rhetorical features" of any public document or speech in U. S. history. In fact, one could analyze the purpose and rhetorical features of a television commercial. The terms "themes" and "argument" bring us no closer. And, as we have said, "compare and contrast" is the last refuge of a desperate, clueless teacher. But we cannot leave it at that. We must *analyze* the Declaration according to Common Core Standard RH.11-12.2.

The Declaration is to be *analyzed* in light of what? Its *purpose*. Now that could be as simple as saying the colonies were declaring independence, a Grant's tomb question that the teacher poses to the class. "What is the purpose of the Declaration, class?" The class answers, "To declare independence." There is no indication in the question itself that the arch-testers might wish students to go beyond that. If they wanted the students to state a larger aim, such as providing a philosophical foundation for revolution, liberty, and self-government, presumably they would have alluded to the *philosophical* argument of the document. As it stands, the arch-testers do something very different. They draw our attention to the list of grievances or charges against the king.

Now that is a little surprising. When most of us think of the Declaration, what first comes to mind are the transcendent words "We hold these truths" or "all men are created equal" or "Life, Liberty, and the pursuit of Happiness." It is not that the indictments are not important. Indeed, they act as evidence in a legal case, an indictment of the "He": the king who had oppressed the colonies and was now being identified and blamed. That the grievances refer to a particular historical moment, though, unavoidably means that they have less permanent relevance to either contemporary Americans or to a "global society" that has often looked to America's Declaration when it needs a model and an inspiration for freedom. (Admittedly, the lines "He has erected a multitude of New Offices, and sent hither swarms of Officers to harass our people, and eat out their substance" never seems to grow old and bears a striking resemblance to the legions of officialdom the Common Core will no doubt bring into existence.)

What instructions are being conveyed to the teachers by the arch-testers' highlighting the grievances rather than the philosophical parts of the Declaration? Is the teacher just supposed to say, "Look, class, at that long list of grievances—now that's how you make a rhetorically strong argument!"? Is that the ideal discussion that should be taking place on the Declaration? Shouldn't the students—juniors or seniors in high school—be *analyzing* the *complex* philosophical arguments, especially since *complexity* is the Common Core's principal criterion for choosing texts in the first place? Is not *complexity* the bugaboo of the twenty-first-century global economy? Apparently, the complexity of this *eighteenth-century* public document is too much for the authors of the *twenty-first-century* Common Core since they avoid the truly *complex* parts of the Declaration like the plague!

That the authors of the Common Core are foundering can best be seen in the lifeless direction to "compare and contrast." Thus we meet our old friend, the *Überstandard*, again. Applied in this setting, we see the hoax in that educational talisman. Why would teachers "compare and contrast" the Declaration of Independence with other document*s* (plural) of historical and literary significance? The Declaration *is* the foundational rock of principle in American history. The Declaration defines the first principles of being American. It is the place to start whenever we want to understand ourselves. Almost any speech of Lincoln would tell you that. Therefore the Declaration must be understood first and foremost—*on its own terms*—before we can hope to understand or judge any other writings in American history. "Comparing and contrasting," before students know the Declaration itself, would serve to create a hodgepodge, a miscellany, and—what is likely being aimed at—a diversion that keeps the teachers' and students' attention off the Founding philosophy of this nation as expressed in the Declaration of Independence.

What are the possible causes of this blatant mishandling of the Declaration? There are at least three possible causes, so the reader can take his pick. The first is that the authors of the Common Core have no confidence in teachers being able to have a conversation about the philosophical basis of American liberty. So the arch-testers and the textbook authors will make sure that the teachers are only required to make the most commonplace observations (Wow, look at all the grievances!). The second possibility is that the arch-testers themselves do not understand the Declaration and are held prisoner by their own intellectual claptrap. The third possibility is that the present assignment is just a ruse and perhaps even a temporary one. The arch-testers know that they must include the Declaration lest they be criticized for leaving out America's birth certificate. At the same time, they are adamantly opposed to the Founding of the country being portrayed in a positive light. Accordingly, they wish to divert attention from the truly remarkable aspects of the Declaration. Worse, the present assignment is simply a temporary placeholder. When the public is no longer looking, the arch-testers will replace this innocuous performance task with one fingering the alleged *hypocrisy* of Jefferson's writing that "all men" are created equal despite his having slaves as well as the *oversight* of "women" apparently being left out. The philosophical foundation of the document will not be looked at, therefore, unless the students get to *analyze* the supposed inadequacies of the Declaration. Such will be the discussion when they get to the much beloved Seneca Falls Declaration of Sentiments:

> We hold these truths to be self-evident: that all men and women are created equal . . . The history of mankind is a history of repeated injuries and usurpations on the part of man toward woman, having in direct object the establishment of an absolute tyranny over her.[78]

In short, the object will be to do a hatchet-job on the Declaration just as we have already seen done on the Constitution. To explain the mishandling of the Declaration by the arch-testers, we must wonder: was it incompetence, ignorance, or ideology? Of course, these three explanations are not mutually exclusive.

If the reader needs further proof of the incompetence or duplicity of the arch-testers, he need only look at the document that is mentioned: the Olive Branch Petition. Why would that be chosen? That's easy. Because it has a completely different purpose from the Declaration: to appeal to George III's better sentiments by swearing continued loyalty. In other words, the "performance task" is throwing teachers a softball: "Look at how the Olive Branch Petition is trying to patch things up with the King, class, and then contrast that with how the Declaration goes after the King. What do you think about that?" If not wholly unimportant, this is about the *least significant* thing the authors of this assignment could have come up with. It is looking backwards. In a history class, it would be fitting to trace the progress in the American mind *from* loyalty *to* revolution but not the reverse. In an English class, you would never go backwards in this way, either, unless you were wholly incapable of having a discussion about both the meaning of the Declaration and the art of arguing from first principles. The compare-and-contrast "standard" is simply a shell game designed for, we must assume, teachers who cannot take their classes through a single document and must consequently keep shifting back and forth from one to another.

---

[78] Appendix B, p. 13 and p. 172.

164

Now if the teacher wanted to bring in another document to *understand* the Declaration better, that might be a legitimate exercise. No one with any knowledge of the American Revolution would choose the Olive Branch Petition, however. The obvious thing to do would be to refer back to selections of John Locke's *Second Treatise of Government*, the source of the Founding Fathers' thinking on natural rights. It would also make sense to look at the Virginia Declaration of Rights written only weeks before by George Mason (with a little help from James Madison as well).[79] The Virginia Declaration most closely resembles the Declaration of Independence. The purpose of the comparison would not be to show that Jefferson was not particularly original (both documents borrow heavily from Locke) but rather to understand better those statements in the Declaration that are tightly compressed, in part for literary (I would say poetic) reasons. For example, the Virginia Declaration of Rights states, "That all men are by nature equally free and independent and have certain inherent rights . . . namely, the enjoyment of life and liberty, with the means of acquiring and possessing property, and pursuing and obtaining happiness and safety." Though less rhetorically powerful, that account of rights spells out some aspects of the Declaration that we now find hard to understand, particularly the idea of equality. Indeed, you might say that equality is the founding principle that trips people up most since they often confuse equality of rights and of opportunity with equality of conditions, or what we now call "social equality." That is, equality is a right, not an entitlement. The Virginia Declaration, as authoritative as the Declaration of Independence for signaling what the Founders meant by the term equality, helps clarify our nation's first principles. Not surprisingly, we do not find the progressive bureaucrats of the Common Core seeking to clarify those first principles for the nation's young people.

Thus, it is precisely the tough questions about liberty, equality, rights, and happiness that are not elicited in this "sample performance task." Nothing about this "task" indicates that the authors of the Common Core understand the significance or the philosophical meaning of the Declaration of Independence. They treat the entire document as just another vehicle for an exercise in rhetoric, and not a particularly challenging one. They do not seem

---

[79] Specifically on the topic of religious toleration.

165

to care in the least about the principles on which this nation was founded. They do not have the common sense to include the words *self-evident* or *liberty* or *equality* or *consent* in their "task." Nor do they offer even a passing reference to "the Laws of Nature and of Nature's God."[80] Do we really imagine that our young people, following the amorphous, Mickey-Mouse "standards" of the Common Core, will emerge from the nation's public schools better citizens, better workers, and better men and women?

What would a real "sample performance task," i.e. a meaningful series of questions, on the Declaration of Independence look like? Here are a few to get us started.

> What is a self-evident truth? Can you give an example of an obvious self-evident truth by which you live? What is the significance of being "created"? What is meant by "equal"? What does "unalienable" mean? What is a "right"? How is a right different from a duty? Does a right imply a duty? Where do rights come from? Where do they not come from? What is liberty? What is happiness? Is happiness a passing mood or a permanent condition? What is the significance of "the pursuit" of happiness being a right but not happiness itself? With regard to rights, what is the role of government? What is "consent"?

These are not easy questions. I spend two full days with my college students on these questions, and that is not nearly enough time. We never make it to the "grievances," which in Jefferson's masterful language are better called, "a long train of abuses and usurpations." Before coming into my class, my students, graduates of the public schools—though bright and studious and full of energy—cannot offer a single, coherent sentence to explain what a right is. That is certainly not what Jefferson would have wanted

---

[80] This is an instance when we see that the arch-testers are not serious about either legitimate comparisons or genuine science. Why is there no question about the connection between Newton's views of the universe and the Founders' views of civil society?

out of public schools. The Common Core will not help this great nation one iota in eradicating our widespread civic illiteracy. It will likely make things worse.

The fundamental lesson we learn from the revealing "sample performance tasks" in the Common Core English Standards is that the people who wrote them do not truly understand the classics of literature and history. They do not understand *The Adventures of Tom Sawyer* or *Pride and Prejudice* or The Declaration of Independence, three great texts that would be contained in any legitimate core curriculum and that *anyone* claiming to be a teacher in the liberal arts should know thoroughly. Those who will be in charge of the testing—which nowadays drives the teaching—do not know these great works, and, what is more, they do not love them. At least that is one explanation. The other, far more disturbing in my mind but equally plausible, is that the progressive story-killers know very well what these books and documents mean. What better way is there to keep boys ignorant and wholly disillusioned with school than by making a mess of *Tom Sawyer*? What better way is there of discouraging young women from having traditional ideas of love and marriage—and from waiting for Mr. Right—than making a mess of *Pride and Prejudice*? And what better way exists for keeping America's future voters and citizens wholly ignorant of what their rights are and where those right come from—and government's limited though important role in securing those rights—than making a mess of the Declaration of Independence? If progressive ideologues would have wanted to undermine our traditional ideas of boyhood, of womanhood and family, and of liberty, yet without raising too many suspicions, could they have done a better job? The authors of the Common Core understand the power of boredom.

What young people need, and deep down what they are hoping for, is a conversation. They need a conversation about the "real world" alright. But the Common Core, for all its promises of "college and career readiness," does not offer any insights into the world, whether the human world or the natural world. The authors of the Common Core project the same false images on the walls of our intellectual cave that progressive education has projected for decades. What young people need and want is not a contrived conversation about "characterization" but a real conversation about character. What young men and women need and want is not a lot of hokum about "setting" but a genuine discussion of families and friendships and moral and civic duty and love and happiness. What interests every student I have ever met is not some artificial commentary on "plot" but the close study of actions and their consequences. These conversations are the result of the genuine reading of the great books and the great events—the great stories—of our tradition. If we kill off those stories by replacing them bit by bit with insignificant drivel, and by chopping up those stories that remain into a lot of two-bit literary jargon, we will lose those books, and in so doing we may very well lose the minds and hearts of our children.

Chapter Seven
The Tyranny of the Textbooks

If the proof is always in the pudding, then the truth about the Common Core English Standards must be in the textbooks. Whatever the discourse surrounding the adoption of the Common Core—the promises, the arguments, the hoopla—what matters in the end is the actual instruction that takes place in the classrooms across the nation. And instruction these days is largely dictated by the textbooks that are put into the teachers' and students' hands. If schools and districts are slavish in following standardized exams, the teachers themselves are slavish in following exactly what appears in the textbooks they are given to teach from, obviously hoping that the material therein will prepare their students for standardized exams. No inquiry into the Common Core could be complete, then, without a close look at some of the Common Core textbooks supplied by the willing accomplices at Pearson/Prentice Hall.

Before looking at some of these textbooks, however, we must fully understand the role textbooks have come to play in the teaching of literature in this country. As it turns out, the close examination of a contemporary literature textbook offers a window into school decline. Such was the case before the Common Core, whose senseless requirements will simply make an already bad situation worse. Let us then recognize the absurdities of our children's literature books in order to find some remedy for our present ills and our future ones even if we abandon the madness of the Common Core. We shall find that the once and future progressive tyranny over the schools owes a great deal to schools' blind following of bad textbooks. In fact, that tyranny may be impossible to achieve without such books.

The first thing we must do is separate in our minds good *literature* from a literature *textbook* as customarily assigned in a high school. Good literature does exist in a book. But it originates in a single book in the case of a novel or play, and in a collection by the same author in the case of short stories and shorter poetry. No great author has written a book so that it would one day appear in a student's anthology. When we think of reading literature in school, then, we should have in mind individual books and individual stories, such as Mark Twain's *Huckleberry Finn* or George Orwell's *1984* or Shakespeare's *King Lear*. We should not have in mind a big clunky thing called "the book."

There are several reasons behemoth textbooks actually *discourage* the sound reading and study of great literature. The first and most obvious is size. To realize this, all we have to do is weigh and measure a textbook. The Prentice Hall Common Core literature textbook for the tenth grade weighs eight pounds. It measures 9 ½" x 11". The Folger edition of Shakespeare's *Romeo and Juliet* weighs six ounces and measures 4 ¼" x 6 ¾". The Penguin edition of Fagles's translation of *The Iliad*, possibly the largest work of literature a student could read in high school (or in college) weighs under two pounds. It measures 5 ¾" x 8 ½". Now which is a student more likely to carry around with him voluntarily? If a student had to wait, say, in a doctor's office for an unknown length of time, would he be more inclined to take a copy of a Shakespeare play or an eight-pound literature anthology? Which, by the way, would make him look smarter, "cooler" even: *Julius Caesar* or a hulking textbook that signifies his subordinate station in life? Further, would even the most avid reader of books look forward to "curling up" at night with Prentice Hall's eight-pound LITERATURE, *Grade Ten*? Of course not. What Ambrose Bierce once said of a book he was reviewing—that its covers are too far apart—is true of every literature textbook in our public high schools.

A further hindrance is the "care" taken of these textbooks. The school district buys a few thousand of these bulky things and distributes them to the schools. The schools in turn give them to the appropriate teachers. The teachers pass out these books to their students at the beginning of the year, making sure to note that the textbook is in "good" condition. The students lug these things around all year long: not marking them in any way and not making notes in the margins. At the end of the year, the students turn in the books. This is exactly what has gone on in high schools for thirty or forty years. Custom makes this seem entirely normal until we realize what does *not* take place. Students are not allowed to write in the book. How, then, do they underline important passages? How do they write question marks next to parts of the story they do not understand? How do they take notes in the margins? How do they mark up the book during a class discussion? The answer is, they don't. The book is to remain blank—as though the students had never read it, as blank as their minds about the book. Of course, any true reader knows what a crime this is against literature. "Reading" a book without marking it up—or annotating it, if you prefer—is tantamount to failing to have a conversation with a genius sitting next to you because you do not want to seem rude and disturb him. Every year graduates of public schools go off to college and are horrified when their professors tell them that they must *write in their books*—and if they fail to do so, they will never understand those books.

Worse than not being allowed to write in their books, students cannot keep them. The thought is a wholly foreign idea. I remember when I was in high school I once offered to buy my literature book. The teacher did not know what to say. She had never in all her years had a student make such a request. So she sent me to the office. They didn't know what to do, either. I got to know one of the assistant principals, though, who had the key to a large closet that turned out to be a burial ground for textbooks that had been taken out of circulation. He said I could have whatever I wanted, so I took several books. This little event I found strange at the time, but it strikes me as even stranger now. We make students read books in school. But then we take the books back, as if to say, "It might be important (or simply necessary) for you to read Dryden and Defoe and Dickens in high school, but you would never want to look back at those authors' works when you are an adult. They'll have nothing to say to you then." Should it not be the case that we first *introduce* students to great literature in school, but the students, when they have become men and women, continue to look back on the great books they have read: for amusement, for fond memories, and for wisdom? I invite any student to ask this question in a public high school to see what strange looks he will receive. A further question remains. What happens to all those textbooks that school districts purchase, that are used for a few years until they are pronounced "outdated" or "worn out," then replaced by newer, "updated" textbooks? How many hidden closets or forgotten storage bins remain filled with books that no one ever reads while students graduate high school with no books on their shelves or in their minds?

These vices of school literature books are nothing compared to what the books *do* to literature. School textbooks balkanize, sterilize, and abridge great writing. They do so by pulling small pieces of great stories out of their larger narratives, by asking simple-minded and specious questions of these mere pieces, and by jamming so many authors together, none of whom is to be studied in any depth, that students have trouble knowing one from another. To realize the effects of the textbook approach to literature, just ask yourself this question if you went to a public high school: How much of Homer did you actually read? Chances are high that you were told about the Trojan Horse and maybe a little about Odysseus on Calypso's island.[81] You might have read the encounter with the Cyclops. It is unlikely you read the whole account of Odysseus' return to Ithaca. Today Telemachus is virtually unknown. Odysseus' other exploits you likely know nothing about.[82] And, of course, you are a stranger to the whole of *The Iliad*. (Even if you did read these things, as we have seen, there is no guarantee you understood them, owing to the application of two-bit literary criticism in so-called class discussions.) The reason for this patchy knowledge of the Western world's two greatest epics is that you never had copies of either *The Iliad* or *The Odyssey* in your hands. You had merely what the editors of the textbook and/or your school district and/or your teacher thought you could handle or what the class had "time" for. If you were now pressed to recall how the remainder of your time in freshman English was spent, you would have a hard time coming up with any fruitful encounters with great books.

The question we must ask ourselves is *why?* Why would we give students, under the guise of studying literature, giant textbooks that they have to lug around and cannot take notes in, which we take back at the end of the year, as though the sentiments and scenes therein have no permanent value, and whose contents

---

[81] The episode of the Trojan Horse takes place after the action of *The Iliad* and is only alluded to in *The Odyssey*. Vergil gives an account in *The Aeneid*, which is one among several reasons to read the great Roman epic that has been lost in public schools for half a century.

[82] Appendix B features only the opening lines of *The Odyssey*.

are the merest whisper of learning and of stories? The overarching reason is, of course, that schools do not know and value these great stories. To be more specific, though, we must consider what literature books have been, what they are now, and what they are becoming. We might call these three styles of textbook the ghost of literature past, the ghost of literature present, and, yes, the ghost of literature future. Thereby we shall get to the root of the problem, just as Scrooge discovered his own fatal shortcoming.

The ghost of literature past is the kind of textbook *we* carried around in school. The pages contained mostly the writings of famous authors. There were several illustrations, mainly portraits of the artists or paintings inspired by the period under review. A short biography of the author and a little information about the context of the writing appeared at the beginning of each selection, and several review questions (usually factual in nature) appeared at the end. That was about it. The book did commit the crime of ripping short selections out of longer works of literature. This practice made it easier for teachers to perform their two-bit-lit-crit incantations on the stories. In the case of freshman English, the point was never to read complete works of literature written in beautiful language that speak straight to the soul. That is, the reason for serving up a smattering of *The Odyssey* was not to give young people a view of the heroic and of the passions of men, but rather to introduce the students to an *epic*. The reason for having them read *Romeo and Juliet* was not to unveil to hormonal adolescents the heights and dangers of love and passion and invite them to sympathize with the star-cross'd lovers but to get them to recognize a *tragedy*. The motto for this genre-based literature spattering ought to be the line from the theme song of *Rawhide*: "Don't try to understand 'em/ just rope, throw, and brand 'em."

The textbooks of old did not offend the eye upon opening them. They were closer to the Norton anthologies used in college classes, meaning that they placed a premium on the written word. Things have changed considerably in the last twenty years—and not for the better. School textbooks have been recast in order to cater (we are led to believe) to the MTV generation. The margins, the increasingly long sections before and after the actual selections, and even the background space on which the selections are printed, are cluttered with modern gadgetry and razzmatazz. Not only does this razzmatazz distract even the conscientious reader from the actual story or play or poem at hand, but its steady growth has reduced the amount of the book devoted to actual literature. The ghost of literature present, then, consists in half literature (with most of that in short extracts) and half razzmatazz and claptrap.

The ghost of literature future consists in . . . no literature. The publishing houses were already cutting back on the amount of genuine literature. The Common Core gives them license to replace literary texts with "informational texts." The unnecessary, distracting, and often misleading commentary continues to increase. Often it now takes three or four pages of preliminaries to get to an author's writing in a section ostensibly devoted to his or her works. Illustrations of various sorts have proliferated. Officious updates proving how "relevant" an author still is (clearly pandering to contemporary culture) have become a regular feature. And the formerly non-intrusive questions at the end of selections have bloomed into boring multi-page assignments drilling students in the worst two-bit literary criticism. If this trend continues—and it will—we shall soon have literature books with no literature.

I wish I were exaggerating. Let us take a look into an actual Common Core textbook. Seventeen pages of Prentice Hall's *The British Tradition*, volume 2, that bears the logo of the Common Core, are supposedly devoted to Mary Shelley's *Frankenstein*. What do the clever editors at Prentice Hall do with those pages? The first two pages are taken up by modern author Elizabeth McCracken telling us about a scary nightmare she had as a child, inspired from watching movies such as *Frankenstein*, *Bride of Frankenstein*, and *Abbott and Costello Meet Frankenstein*. She spends most of these two pages dilating upon this dream. She also writes about her reading "awful books—ghost stories . . . then true crime books about murderers, cannibals, disasters at sea . . ." She does not go on to tell us that she later read Mary Shelley's novel and that it left all those other writings in the dust, or that *Frankenstein*, being true literature, did more than frighten: it captured an important aspect of the human condition. In fact, contemporary author Elizabeth McCracken does not tell us anything about Mary Shelley's *Frankenstein*. It is not even clear that she has read it. The Critical Reading box that bears the image of the Common Core asks probing questions such as, "What types of frightening movies and books did McCracken enjoy as a child?" Now that is exactly the sort of thing someone picking up a copy of *The British Tradition* would want to know! But that is not all. A silly image taken presumably from a horror movie circa 1955, is accompanied by the searching "Critical Viewing" question, "Which details in this image of Frankenstein's monster convey terror?"

On the following page (the third so far) of this wind-up to Mary Shelley, students are informed of different literary terms such as "Gothic" and "Romantic." They are likewise introduced to the "reading strategy" of making predictions (a favorite game of the two-bit literary critics that almost always results either in irrelevant and absurd chit-chat or in giving the story away). Let us apply this reading strategy to the Common Core edition of *The British Tradition*, volume 2. I *predict*, based on the three pages we have encountered so far, that Pearson/Prentice Hall will squander an opportunity of having students read one of the most remembered philosophical novels of the nineteenth century.

The next page introduces Mary Shelley. That seems reasonable to me. There is even a nice portrait of her as a young woman. The haunting blue background (they are really playing up the Gothic theme) I could do without. On the next page we are presented with another warm-up to Shelley's text: mostly a photograph of a small castle situated near the Alps and a modicum of information about the myth of Prometheus. Finally, we reach the objective of Mary Shelley's actual words on page 761, on the *sixth* page of our endeavor. These words turn out not to be *Frankenstein* or even a short selection from *Frankenstein*. Rather, they are an *introduction* Shelley wrote about writing *Frankenstein*. Okay. So does this introduction serve as some kind of inspiration to go off and read the real novel? Apparently not. There is no invitation to read the book in the students' edition. No study questions are provided that might guide their reading of that story. Only on page 763 of the Teacher's Edition is there the barest hint that *some* of the students ought to read *some* of the book:

> **Enrichment for Advanced Readers**: Have interested students read a segment of Mary Shelley's *Frankenstein*. Then, ask them to prepare book reviews comparing the Frankenstein monster to Shelley's description in her introduction to the work. Ask them to discuss how the book compares with similar novels they have read.

What we learn from this prompt is that the central focus of this literature book is not the reading of *Frankenstein*. Teachers may (or may not) ask interested students (two, four, or half a dozen?) to read a *segment* of the book (presumably a brief one only describing the monster) that will lead to two silly compare-and contrast-assignments, one involving "similar novels they have read." (Have they read any? They haven't read *Frankenstein* yet.) What about the students who are not "advanced readers"? What is being done to help them become better readers? And why should even the advanced readers read only a few pages out of this classic?

What should students be doing if not reading *Frankenstein*? According to the notes in the margins of the Teacher's Edition, they should begin by offering to the class "classic examples of urban myths, tales of alien abductions, or ghost stories. (Examples include stories of alligators in the sewers, a man abducted for his kidneys, and aliens landing in Roswell, New Mexico)." (The word "classic" is being used very loosely.) To reinforce the findings of this "brainstorming activity," students should also "write a paragraph based on one of these modern urban myths." The class will also discuss Mary Shelley's introduction in various ways. Helping out, Elizabeth McCracken offers several more "scholar's insights," including one informing us of another ghost story about a man who buried his murder victim at the base of a tree "only to find that the next year's apples all had a clot of blood at the center of them." On the following page, we learn that Elizabeth McCracken did read the book, which she found better than the movie because, she tells us, in the book the monster can actually talk. Teachers are prompted to ask students why they think the film version would choose to keep the monster silent. Since the class will not be diverted enough with all this talk of movies, the Teacher's Edition also recommends that talented and gifted students "illustrate one aspect of Shelley's imaginings that is especially Gothic in its mood" and "display their Gothic art to the rest of the class." Do the editors realize that all this extraneous discussion of monsters and ghosts only serves to preserve the silly Halloween caricature of *Frankenstein*?

Apparently this caricature is what they want. On page 766, students are encouraged to "write a brief autobiography of a monster." The editors point out that monster stories are usually told from the perspective of "the humans confronting the monster."

The editors of *The British Tradition* want to turn the tables and have students ask themselves "what monsters think about their treatment." Now there's a great exercise in multiculturalism! Those poor, misunderstood monsters. Thus, students are being asked to write a monster story. What good could come from this? Without reading the novel *Frankenstein* itself (which does in fact tell much of the story from the monster's perspective), students have no way of knowing how *human* this Gothic tale really is.

After a mere three and a half pages of Mary Shelley's introduction, the book offers a series of questions under various headings: Critical Reading, Literary Analysis, and so forth. Some of these questions are steeped in two-bit literary criticism. Others require students to delve into the moral realms of science and creation. One is a question asking students to interpret a modern cartoon about Frankenstein—funny, but out of place in this literature book. Notwithstanding whether the questions are good or bad, the enterprise is as false as the worst Hollywood versions of *Frankenstein*. The questions offer the façade of learning without genuine learning having taken place. That is for a very simple reason. My wife, the former English teacher who recognizes pretense when she sees it, took one look at these pages and put it very simply: "They (the editors) are requiring students to have opinions on something they know nothing about." Who needs to read and learn from *Frankenstein*, or any other book for that matter, when a person can just spout off in pseudo-intellectual jargon—and never be called to account because no one else has read the book? The production of such opinions in uninformed young people leads to *hubris* and intellectual dishonesty. Perhaps such practices are simply sloppy education at work. Yet there is another possibility. What if unfounded opinions in young people are in fact what the authors of the Common Core are after? Keep that question in mind for when we get to the Common Core textbooks' treatment of the Constitution.

The section allegedly devoted to *Frankenstein* does not end there. The editors of *The British Tradition* bring you "live from New York . . . it's Saturday Night!" That's right. Under the heading "contemporary connection," this literature textbook apportions five pages to a script of a *Saturday Night Live* parody on Frankenstein and information on the show itself. Students are asked "to share their impressions of the long-running comedy show." **Possible response**: "Students may report amazement that the lively comedy show has been on the air for more than 33 years, or they may mention its many talented comedy artists or talk about sketches that they found most memorable." (When we were in high school did we have to be told by our English teachers to watch *Saturday Night Live*?) Again the talents of the talented and gifted students are called to the fore while the un-talented and non-gifted kids get to sit on the sidelines. The former are invited to "take roles and do a dramatic reading of the SNL 'Curse of Frankenstein' transcript" printed in this book. "Encourage them to rehearse in small groups; obtain simple props, makeup, or costumes; and present their interpretive reading to the class."

Although only the talented and gifted kids will get to act it out, the class as a whole will read and interpret this skit, accompanied by the teacher's insights handily provided in the margins of the Teacher's Edition:

> Villager #1: [to Head Villager] Well, maybe you're the monster!
>
> Head Villager: [shakes his head] I'm not the monster! [points to Frankenstein's monster] Look at 'im! He's got a square head and green skin!
>
> Frankenstein's Monster: Oh, great—now it's a racial thing! You know what? You guys are a bunch of fascists! [villager with a lit torch again steps too close] *Seriously*, du-ude! Get that fire away from me! . . .
>
> [Instructions in the margin of the Teacher's Edition]
> Point out the use of the term *fascist*. Explain its traditional political meaning and how it has been extended to refer to any right-wing extremist group.

"Has been extended": The passive voice is a curious thing. Who has done the extending? Do the editors of *The British Tradition* approve of that extending? What constitutes "any right-wing extremist group"? Would that include the Tea Party?

The editors of the Common Core version of *The British Tradition* encourage readers to make predictions. I predicted that the editors would waste an opportunity for reading Mary Shelley's *Frankenstein*. As it turns out, those editors encourage teachers to have students talk about monsters (and perhaps their dreams about monsters), draw pictures of monsters, write an autobiography of a monster, dress up as monsters, talk about *Saturday Night Live* and share their favorite skits from that program, and act out a *Saturday Night Live* script. According to the "time and resource manager" provided next to a Common Core logo in the teacher's edition, these various discussions, activities, or whatever you want to call them, would take four days. I know that the things described would easily exhaust a week or more. At no point during that week would the students have read and discussed the actual book called *Frankenstein*. Instead, they would have spent an entire week and seventeen pages (only three and a half which have any of Shelley's own words on them) in fumbling around and about *Frankenstein*. Any college professor who would later want to have a discussion about this novel with students would be perplexed by their not knowing anything. They would not be able to answer the simplest factual questions. Where did the story take place? What led Dr. Frankenstein to create a living being? Was the monster bad from his "birth"? Did he kill anyone? If so, who and why? Bigger questions are obviously off the map. What do we learn about humanity from this tale about a monster? Do we learn anything about education? Does *Frankenstein* reveal anything about God or creation? Students would get nowhere close to such questions. They are too busy exchanging ghost stories.

Any guess as to the grade level at which all this "critical thinking" would take place? The senior year in high school. The second semester of the senior year in high school. That's right, seniors in high school are supposed to dress up as monsters and write their own autobiographies of monsters. Editors at Pearson/Prentice Hall, I ask you, as a real (not imaginary) college professor: How in the world will such superficial reading and Mickey Mouse assignments make students more *college ready*?

My larger, overarching prediction is that high-school literature books will continue to follow this trend of replacing literature with junk until there is no literature in them, just bread and circuses for the millions of young men and women who are apparently thought to be incapable of reading a great story. The educational treason being committed here is the fact that a good teacher (or simply a good reader) could sit down with any group of high-school students in the country and have them hooked on the story of Frankenstein in ten minutes by doing no more than reading the actual book. And those students would not let go of that book until they had read it to the end. Nor do I mean just the "talented and gifted" students.

So far from taking this sensible approach, the textbooks are designed to *get in the way* of students' reading. This becomes clear when we look closely at the sections of the new Prentice Hall Common Core textbooks called "independent reading." In both *The British Tradition* and *The American Experience* we find a couple of pages following the major sections advising students of books they should read "on your own." In *The British Tradition* at the end of the chapter called "Rebels and Dreamers" we find recommendations for Jane Austen's *Pride and Prejudice* and Mary Shelley's *Frankenstein*—at last!—as well as works by William Blake, Percy Bysshe Shelley, and Walter Scott. There are at least four problems with this way of recommending literature to high school students. The first is obviously the dim chance that students will notice this section of the textbook and act upon it. The second is the reality that students' valuable time is already being wasted in class (and presumably with homework in the form of these mindless activities that are assigned) with things other than these great works of literature. Therefore a student who *does* want to read these literary classics must make extra time in his day outside the time given to the regular English class and its silly homework! The third flaw in this mirage of independent reading is the difficulty students will have in trying to understand these books. The simplistic readings in the regular class do not prepare students to grapple with harder works on their own. Finally, we must ask the obvious question. Why is *Pride and Prejudice* included among the independent reading titles? That great novel, you will recall, is one of the *exemplar texts* for the Common Core. That elevated status led us to believe that every high-school student in the nation might be reading it. Not so. There is clearly a bait-and-switch being perpetrated here. So far from encouraging the reading of great literature, the set-up put forth in these textbooks actually inhibits young people's discovering and enjoying the great books.

Just when you think things are bad, they end up being worse. Although there is no *Pride and Prejudice*, a selection of Jane Austen does appear in *The British Tradition*, volume 2. It is a letter Austen wrote to a niece concerning a marriage proposal the latter had received. This letter is coupled with an excerpt from *A Vindication of the Rights of Woman* by Mary Wollstonecraft (the mother of Mary Shelley). The assignment planned for these two readings is introduced in the margins of the Teacher's Edition:

> Tell students they will be writing an article for a women's magazine at the end of the eighteenth century in England. They should speculate on the rights women did or did not have at that time. Students should use conjecture to discuss women's feelings about careers, education, and marriage.

The letter from Austen to her niece, as you might expect, is not a proto-feminist tract. In fact, Austen described her niece's suitor in terms that would honor even Mr. Darcy:

> His situation in life, family, friends, & above all his Character—his uncommonly amiable mind, strict principles, just notions, good habits—all that you know so well how to value. . . . Oh! My dear Fanny, the more I write about him the warmer my feelings become, the more strongly I feel the sterling worth of such a young Man & the desirableness of your growing in love with him again.

What do the textbook editors do with such warm commentary on the virtues of a man? Under the heading of "social commentary," they emphasize the class basis of Austen's account, drawing attention to the criterion of "social status." Though Austen herself wrote "& above all his Character," then listed several aspects of his *character* in detail, the Teachers' Edition does not employ that word. The closest they get is "respectability," a word Austen does not use in this passage. The Teacher's Edition further coaches the teachers to distinguish between "conscious and unconscious social commentary" in order to get students to recognize "this letter as unconscious social commentary." Translation: Jane Austen, one of the greatest story-tellers of all time, particularly on the theme of love, was not clever enough to figure out that her novels were really protest literature against all the plights and indignities women suffered in those dark days. In this letter, she was writing *unconscious social commentary* rather than telling her niece that this gentleman was a real catch, but that Fanny should only marry a man she loved.

Lest young women be too caught up in illusions of romantic love, the treatise by Mary Wollstonecraft, incongruously juxtaposed with Jane Austen's letter, will ignite the appropriate indignation.

About the Selection

Wollstonecraft sadly reflects on the fact that women's poor educational opportunities, coupled with society's expectations about feminine beauty, have rendered women silly and vain. In what begins as a sad voice and gradually becomes a more strident one, Wollstonecraft attacks this degradation of women.

Now we see the point of joining these two authors. The radicals of the Common Core have to figure out how to take an ax to Jane Austen's traditional ideas of love, marriage, and womanhood. So they neglect to read her novels, misread a letter that she wrote, and then couple that letter with the most radical woman author of the period. Their hope must be that the students will not go on to read Austen (at least not until college, where the liberal professors will deconstruct her works), or, tainted by this exercise, they will begin such a deconstruction on their own. The new Austen? A man in the nineteenth century who, like Mr. Darcy, might marry a woman in part because of her "fine eyes" would actually be degrading her. And all that commentary on Anne Elliot's "bloom" in *Persuasion* was really unconscious social criticism against the injustices of "society's expectations about feminine beauty." Any guesses as to what the students' articles for the women's magazine will look like? The lesson: Not only will Jane Austen's novels not be read in the Brave New Core; but Jane Austen herself will be misread in order to indoctrinate young women in the tenets of modern feminism.

The absurdity of the situation brings us to the obvious question: Why should there be literature textbooks in the first place? If students would be better off reading their own books, marking them, and keeping them for the rest of their lives; if having those books would better assure that they would read complete stories rather than meager selections of great works; if having serious discussions about novels and plays would make students more college ready (which was part of the original goal, was it not?), then why would the high schools at the very least (and the middle and upper elementary schools, too) not do the obvious thing: give students real books to read? No doubt this question would lead to a number of answers: the lack of a commitment to great stories on the part of the schools, the general decline of education, the decline of the culture, and the simple fact that no one is really paying much attention to what the nation's children are doing in schools. These are all plausible explanations, but they are not the root cause. If Scrooge's greed is the root cause of the decline of his happiness, there must be an analogous cause for the decline of literature in literature textbooks over the last fifty years. That root cause is discovered easily enough if we ask another question. For whom are the textbooks really produced? The dirty little secret is that the textbooks are not produced for the students.

The literature textbooks used in the nation's schools are not for the students; they are for the teachers. This truth becomes self-evident if we just look closely at a Teacher's Edition of one these textbooks. Why do such things even exist? I shall never forget my discovery of their existence. I was in middle school. Once I went up to ask my teacher a question just as the class was finishing up. I noticed that the book she had been reading from was not the same as the students'. That came as a surprise. Why would her book be different from ours? The words Teacher's Edition struck me as odd. Did the teacher get a better book? The next time I got to see a Teacher's Edition, the book was open. I realized that answers to the questions the teacher had been asking us (questions I found boring) appeared in the margins of the book. Why did *the teacher* need answers to those easy questions? Couldn't she figure out such softballs on her own? I felt betrayed—or ripped off. No wonder, as I later found out in high school, our so-called class discussions were so predictable, so halting, so unnatural. No wonder every time I or another curious student tried to ask a question that emerged from the story itself the teacher would try to get us back to what she wanted to talk about. She—all my literature teachers, in fact—had a script to follow. When I got to college, that nonsense stopped. The professors did not have the Teacher's Edition of the textbook; they did not have us read from textbooks. They had the same books we had, though theirs were much older. There was, to be sure, plenty of writing in the margins of their books: *their own notes*. Sometimes a professor would bring in two copies of the book because he had completely exhausted the margins in the first one. Others had to tape their books together or put rubber bands around them since the bindings had failed after decades of serious reading. And the discussions were different, too. The professors just came into class and started talking about the books—they knew them backwards and forwards. The discussions were natural. They did not try to drive the students' answers into some preconceived category or plot design. It is an altogether different story in high schools across the land. Sadly, when we look closely at the Teacher's Edition of an English textbook, we know precisely how ninety percent of the public-school teachers are teaching that book. If you do not believe me, you are free to go observe a literature class in a public high school—if the school will let you in.

So it is to the textbooks—and particularly to the Teachers' Editions—we must go to understand what is now taking place in the nation's schools and how the Common Core will be "implemented." In fact, it would be only a slight exaggeration to say that without the unquestioned, absolute, and unnecessary dominance of the publishing industry over the nation's public schools, the Common Core could hardly be imposed on those schools. By sending out clear signals to textbook publishers, the authors of the Common Core can determine what gets read in class and how the things that are read get taught. That nine-tenths of the nation's teachers are wholly dependent on textbooks for their interpretation of literature, various assignments, and decision of what gets read or omitted in the first place, makes the whole enterprise of high-jacking the nation's schools that much easier. Thus has a real tyranny gained control of the nation's schools. The links of the chain are easy to follow. The authors of the Common Core, through the *dictat* handed down in the Common Core documents and through mandatory testing, tell the publishers what to put in the textbooks. The textbooks in turn tell the teachers what to teach and how to teach. The teachers tell the students what to think—and not just about literature. If the Common Core is a lamentable and hostile *coup d'école*, it should be in the literature textbooks that we find how the superficiality and bias and plain bad reading manifested in the Standards themselves makes its way into the classrooms.

In the next chapter we shall treat systematically one of these textbooks to expose most of their flaws. For the moment, we shall consider three broad patterns that are at work in these books. The first and perhaps the most egregious we have already seen. A textbook, particularly the Teacher's Edition, can become a manual in wasting time. If a teacher and her students were simply given twenty-five copies of *Frankenstein* and told to "read it," it would be much harder to talk *around* the book for a whole week. Even if the teacher just asked a student to start reading the first few pages, simple questions about the meaning of the words and story would start to generate discussion. The Teacher's Edition, as well as a good portion of the students' books, diverts the class's attention away from what ought to be read and discussed. Another vice of literature textbooks we have also begun to see: the combining of the most unrelated readings imaginable. No one in his right mind, who really wanted to read *Frankenstein*, would walk into a bookstore and choose a copy of the book that also had a script from a *Saturday Night Live* skit in the back. That would be the mark of a publisher, a bookseller, and a reader who were not serious about the real story. Modern school textbooks do this sort of thing all the time. This practice makes possible the strange brew that is the Common Core.

The final thing we must be on the alert for is bias: political, cultural, and moral bias. This is a little harder to detect. The editors do not just come out and say, "We want to make all students believe that all *right-wing extremist groups* are *fascists*." Yet they can subtly arrange selections of literature as well as images, and encourage assignments and classroom discussions in such a way, that the troops in the field (the teachers) can get the message. Many of the teachers may not even suspect that they are being sent a message, or that they are instruments in this noxious system. Yet the message is there, hiding in plain sight.

The authors of the Common Core know that in order to maintain a tyranny over the nation's classrooms they have to control the textbooks. The day I testified before the Indiana state legislature, one of the authors of the Common Core, who had written part of the math standards, kept saying that it would be a bad idea for Indiana to hold out against the Common Core. His reason was that Indiana occupies only about 2% of the textbook market and therefore is not a large enough state to drive the production of textbooks in the country. I found that an extraordinary argument in many respects. First, the young man appeared to understand nothing about markets and free enterprise. Virtually every one of the biggest companies around today started out in small markets and moved into larger ones as the demand for their products grew. Second, the young man, intentionally or not, was issuing a barely concealed threat, essentially to an entire state: conform or die. You must either become a part of the national-wide Common Core, and feed at the common trough of textbooks, or go the way of the dinosaurs. So much for federalism—our basic principle of government—and choice—our basic principle of economics. The third thing that struck me, however, which I noted in my own testimony, was this unthinking awe and reverence for textbooks. Admittedly, this young gentleman might have had math more on his mind, and a math teacher probably does need a textbook, although not one emanating from the Common Core Math Standards. Yet he offered no escape clause for English, and my mind immediately went to the monstrous textbooks created in the name of efficiency or ease. This is the heart of the problem. In the pursuit of teaching of great literature, we should be *abandoning* textbooks. In fact, that would be a great new English *standard* to adopt: getting rid of literature textbooks. We should be calling out Montag and his fellow firemen from *Fahrenheit 451* and saying, "Please, burn these textbooks and give us something real to read." Or, to draw on another work of the imagination: if we do not destroy the monster we have created, he may destroy the children we love.

Chapter Eight
Absurdities, Bias, and Lost Opportunities

Convinced, I hope, that studying literature through big, bulky textbooks is not the way to endear great stories to young people, we should proceed to examine an actual Common Core textbook in action. What we shall find is that this textbook, following the methods and the spirit of the Common Core, kills good literature, the enjoyment of reading, and, more broadly, sound learning. We shall also find that the editors of this textbook are both incompetent and biased. That is, they both fail to understand the selections of literature they offer us while they force us into slanted, politicized interpretations that do not derive from the literature itself. The combined effect of this incompetence and bias on the part the textbook editors, following the direction of the Common Core, is a giant, inexcusable lost opportunity in the lives of the young people of this nation.

I have before me a book whose title is not entirely clear. On the front cover and the title page the words that appear are

PRENTICE HALL
LITERATURE
TEACHER'S EDITION—*THE AMERICAN EXPERIENCE*, VOLUME 1
COMMON CORE EDITION

This is rather odd. If the title is *The American Experience*, those would be the largest and the first words to appear. Maybe the students have to be reminded that this book is their LITERATURE textbook lest they should confuse it with their HISTORY textbook when they are at their lockers. Though amused, we should sympathize with the students. The title *The American Experience* could easily be given to a history book. Moreover, as we shall see, there is more jumbled-up history in this LITERATURE book than there ought to be. It is ironic, though, that just as English teachers increasingly call the subject they teach ELA, and as the Common Core is scaling back literature in favor of non-fiction informational texts, the word LITERATURE is growing on the cover of the textbooks.

Predictably, the textbook does not start off with the bang of good literature but with a series of preliminaries. In the students' edition, beyond the unnecessarily long table of contents, the preliminaries consist in some pretty basic material on writing, vocabulary, and the editors' description of "close reading" (i.e. not really close reading) that would be more appropriate in a grammar and composition book for middle-school students rather than in a literature book for juniors in high school. In addition, several pages explain "how to use this book" and introduce "the essential questions." The latter will supply much of the two-bit literary criticism that pervades the supposed "analysis" students are plagued with throughout this book. For the moment, these "essential questions" dwell in the realm of Big Promises. It should be pointed out, though, that the editors actually stumble into a legitimate essential question. They quote the French observer Crèvecoeur, who famously asked, "What then is the American, this new man?" Our question is, what will the textbook editors do with this question? Will they capture the American as he has been? Or will they recast the American, this new man, according to the questionable, revisionist, and radical opinions now found in the modern academy? In short, will we get the real story of America?

The preliminaries in the Teacher's Edition make for far more revealing and migraine-inducing reading. It would be easy for us to get bogged down in everything that is wrong in these preliminary instructions to the teachers. Suffice it to say that 128 pages are given to a printed version of the Common Core standards, to an explanation of text complexity, to introducing the panel of experts who will supposedly advise teachers throughout this book, to the material that is also contained in the students' edition, and, most important, to promoting the various "resources" and products put out by Pearson/Prentice Hall.

The first image the students see for Unit 1—A Gathering of Voices: Literature of Early America, Beginnings to 1800—is a painting of a group of Europeans and Native Americans floating down a river on a canoe with the words of an Iroquois hymn printed on this scene. The painting is Frederic Remington's 1905 *Radisson and Groseilliers*. Were the editors not to say anything about this painting, we would not dwell on it. I like Remington, a truly American artist who is famous for his paintings and sculptures of, well, cowboys and Indians. If it occurred to me, I might find the painting a little out of place. In the section "Beginnings to 1800," particularly in a literature book, would not Benjamin Franklin's portrait be the obvious choice? He was by far the most celebrated and original writer of the period, and there is a mountain of great images available of Franklin reading, writing, and printing. Otherwise, I might expect the Puritans, as the first *literary* Americans, to be given the nod. But, as I say, I would probably not give the matter much thought. Yet the editors of the brave new textbooks, as we saw in the case of *Frankenstein*, are dedicated to what they call the "critical viewing" of images. So let us gain some insight into their version of critical viewing.

In the margins of the Teacher's Edition, teachers are enlisted to ask "What does the quotation [the Iroquois hymn] suggest about the attitudes of the period?" Teachers are fed the **Possible response:** "The quotation suggests that the Iroquois acknowledged and honored their heritage, an appropriate introduction to a unit that explores the beginnings of American literature." Just below that question, teachers are invited to ask, "How does the painting suggest cooperative effort?" and given the possible answer, "The painting shows both Europeans and Native Americans engaged in a creative enterprise." A final question elicits a similar answer: "The literature of the period may focus on cross-cultural engagement and wilderness encounters." A wonderful beginning, we are led to believe, characterized by such a wonderful word: *engagement.*

Now we are obliged to ask our own critical questions. Why in a book of American *literature* are there no English "voices" present in this initial image? (Radisson and his brother-in-law were French explorers and fur traders, working sometimes for the French and at other times for the English). Did the Iroquois—and the Native Americans more broadly—know that they were contributing to *American* literature? Were other Europeans also contributing to that literature? At this juncture, particularly since the editors like to put so much weight on literature's "historical background," it might be helpful to bring in a few facts. The period this painting represents was one of perpetual hostilities between rival imperial powers: the English, the French, and, to a lesser extent, the Spanish. It would be too tedious to list all the wars that took place during this period, but there were a lot of them. The most important of these prior to the Revolution itself was called the French and Indian War, and it was started by a young man named George Washington. He was shot at by both Frenchmen and Indians countless times. For most of the colonial period, the Iroquois had a special place in these incessant rivalries, acting as a buffer between the English colonies and the French. During the Revolution, perhaps not surprisingly, the Iroquois Confederacy sided with the English against the American patriots. That confederacy launched two merciless raids in the Wyoming Valley and the Cherry Valley, in which women and children were killed. The same Michelle Guillaume Jean de Crèvecoeur, who asked the world about "the American, this new man," lived near the towns in the Wyoming Valley that were raided. He reported the scene as follows:

> It was easy to surprise defenceless isolated families who fell an easy prey to their enemies. . . . Many families were locked up in their houses and consumed [burned] with the furniture. Dreadful scenes were transacted which I know not how to retrace.

> The other party [the patriots], who had taken their flight towards their forts, were all either taken or killed. It is said that those who were then made prisoners were tied to small trees and burnt the evening of the same day.

Lest you think this was wartime propaganda, you should know that Crèvecoeur was not an American patriot nor a supporter of the Revolution.[83]

---

[83] Page Smith, *A New Age Now Begins: A Patriot's History of the American Revolution* (New York: McGraw-Hill, 1976), 2:1156-1157.

The result of these brutal raids was Washington's sending General Sullivan into the Iroquois territories to carry out what the historian Page Smith called "the most ruthless application of a scorched-earth policy in American history," comparable to Sherman's march through Georgia or the search-and-destroy missions in Vietnam.[84] After the campaign was over, there was little left of the Iroquois settlements, which had been by far the most advanced among the various native peoples of America. The purpose of our bringing this history to light is not to open up a discussion about whether the Iroquois deserved their fate or to stir up the many academic controversies concerning European, American, and Indian hostilities. The purpose is rather to raise the question whether anyone living in the year 1790, who had witnessed the American Revolution, would have remembered "both Europeans and Native Americans engaged in a common enterprise." Would they have characterized the literature of the period as focusing on "cross-cultural engagement and wilderness encounters"? The *engagements* in the wilderness were regularly undertaken not with quill and ink but with tomahawk and bow and musket and cannon. Can these editors be trusted?

We should offer one more perspective on this painting, which, as I say, we would not have cared too much about had the editors not made it their first image inside the book and drawn our attention to it with their dubious questions and answers. The image in the book is transposed. It is backwards. It has the Frenchmen and Indians rowing from left to right across the canvass, whereas the actual painting has them moving from right to left. Is this just a careless editorial error? Was it intentional? Or is this a symbol—that the editors of *The American Experience* have everything backwards?

The next fifteen pages offer the students and teachers an historical perspective on American literature. They are given a timeline, introduced to major themes, and asked to consider big questions, such as "What makes American literature American?" While I would not object too strongly to this background being made available, insofar as it does help to know a little about the

---

[84] Ibid., 1172. Page Smith, by the way, was not a left-leaning historian, but rather arguably the greatest narrative historian of the entire American story in the twentieth century. Like most great historians, he understood the tragic aspects of the conflicts between the English settlers and the Indian peoples.

period when someone is writing, when not used properly it only serves to undermine the stories being told or the thoughts being offered. Whenever a text is read historically, it is almost impossible not to *historicize* it. In other words, we read the words and thoughts as belonging to that time and not affecting us or being true in themselves. For example, the editors tell us that

> After a terrifying ocean voyage, the *Mayflower* sailed into harbor at Plymouth, Massachusetts, in 1620. Its passengers were religious reformers who had tried to "purify" the Church of England but thought they had a better chance in the New World. These Puritans, now called Pilgrims, gave every ounce of energy—and often their lives—to build a "city upon a hill," a model community based on the Bible.
> Puritanism gradually declined . . .

The editors are actually conflating two different groups of settlers, the Pilgrims who had fully separated from the Church of England and who landed at Plymouth, and the Puritan non-separating Congregationalists of Massachusetts. The words "city upon a hill," which originate in the Bible, derive in their American setting from John Winthrop's address, possibly given aboard the *Arbella*, called "A Modell of Christian Charity." The words come in the middle of these lines:

> We shall find that the God of Israel is among us when ten of us shall be able to resist a thousand of our enemies; when He shall make us a praise and glory that men shall say of succeeding plantations, "The Lord make it like that of NEW ENGLAND," for we must consider that we shall be as a city upon a hill. The eyes of all people are upon us, so that if we shall deal falsely with our God in this work we have undertaken, and so cause Him to withdraw His present help from us, we shall be made a story and a by-word through the world. We shall open the mouths of enemies to speak evil of the ways of God, and all professors for God's sake. . . .

It is one thing to see a tame description of what the Puritans were attempting to do. It is quite another to read about this "city upon a hill" in Winthrop's own words. What is all this talk of *enemies*, for instance? I thought the first part of American literature was supposed to be about *cooperation*.

What the editors of the textbook want to do is slap a label on the various periods of literature. Thus we can say tamely when we encounter a text that is making claims about the God of Israel (who smites the enemies of the Israelites) that, "Oh, this is Puritanism" and "Puritanism gradually declined." Doing so is a far cry from entering into the world of the Puritans and considering whether the words of Winthrop could be true. But the editors of *The American Experience* do not give us that chance since John Winthrop's "A Modell of Christian Charity," arguably the foundational work of American letters, does not appear in this book. As we found when surveying the Common Core recommended texts, this great inaugural of American letters is simply not there.

While an historical overview of a time period of literature would not be objectionable if handled the right way (i.e. by not historicizing the literature so as to render it almost irrelevant) several things about this particular introduction are seriously flawed. We are introduced to Thomas Paine in the following way: "Thomas Paine: Essayist, Hero of the Revolution . . . Father of the Internet?" Next to a silly cartoon of Paine drinking a cup of coffee and writing on a laptop, we are told that Jon Katz, writing in *Wired News* in 1995, claimed that Paine's "ideas about communications, media ethics, the universal connection between people, and the free flow of honest opinion are all relevant again, visible every time one modem shakes hands with another." Is this silly cartoon and quotation a sop to modern technology to make students "feel like" Paine is still relevant? Is this a case of our own idolatry of technology? It may actually be more than that. In the margins of the Teacher's Edition, teachers are invited to "Ask what issue Thomas Paine might sound off about if he were writing a blog on the Internet today." "**Answer**: Paine would probably be concerned with economic issues, such as distribution of income. He might also write about the seemingly unreasonable behavior of some political leaders." "Distribution of income," of course, is another way of saying, "share the wealth," stemming from the idea that income is *distributed* rather than *created* by productive human beings. Do we really need to ask, then, which political leaders are the "some" who are unreasonable? Clearly, casting Paine as father of the Internet is supposed to give rise to a discussion of present-day social issues favored by the editors of this Common Core textbook.

The next unwanted intrusion comes under the heading of "Recent Scholarship." The introductory section ends with a short essay by William L. Andrews. Professor Andrews, we are informed, "is an award-winning scholar and teacher whose work focuses on the historical links between black and white writers in the formation of American literature." He is the co-editor of *The Norton Anthology of African-American Literature* and other works of the same genre. This will not be the last time students and teachers meet this "award-winning scholar," since Professor Andrews serves as the Unit Author, who will provide "Author's Insights" throughout this period in literature. In this present essay, Professor Andrews tells us that "America Begins with a Promise and a Paradox." The paradox is best seen through Patrick Henry's demanding in 1775 "Give me liberty or give me death!" while at the same time, Professor Andrews tells us, "no one asked whether the slaves he held on his Virginia plantation deserved the same freedom he so passionately proclaimed." Professor Andrews offers a personal anecdote. When he went to school in Virginia, near Patrick Henry's estate, he learned in the sixth grade that Virginia was the "mother of presidents." "My teacher didn't mention that all of Virginia's great heroes, including Washington and Jefferson, were slaveholders as well."

What are we to make of this? Is it true that Henry and Washington and Jefferson were slaveholders? Yes. Is introducing a modern author's comments on this topic, well before students have read the Founding Fathers themselves, as an overview and central theme of the entire era, the ideal way to read literature and to handle the topic of slavery in a high-school literature class? Assuredly not.

Why, we must ask initially, should there be any modern scholar employed to color the views of the students before they have had the opportunity to read the Founding Fathers' writings and think about them on their own? Teachers are instructed to engage the topic in the following way.

1. Begin the class discussion by having students name ideals that America was founded upon, based on their background knowledge and Andrews's essay. Have a volunteer write all the responses on the board.
   Possible responses: Ideals include religious tolerance, individual liberty, and political equality.
2. Using this list, ask students to offer specific examples of how Jefferson and his contemporaries embodied these ideals. Then, ask for examples of behaviors of early American leaders that did not support these ideals.
   Possible responses: Students may point to the risks undertaken by leaders of the Revolution such as Patrick Henry as proof of their intense commitment to their ideals. They may point to these leaders' slave-holding as inconsistent with their ideals of liberty and equality.
3. Have students offer ideas or judgments about the main question: Has the United States become the country early citizens imagined? Encourage them to cite specific examples from their own knowledge to support their opinions.
   Possible responses: Answers will vary, but students should support their responses with specific examples and reasoned arguments.
4. To help conduct the discussion, use the Discussion Guide in the *Professional Development Guidebook*, page 65.

What do we expect to come out of this discussion? Unfortunately, the results are entirely predictable, despite the editors' assurance that "answers will vary." First, the students at this point have not read anything in their LITERATURE book. They are being asked to have a discussion before they have read any source from the period under review. Nor do they have any "background knowledge." If they are beginning this course alongside an American history course, the latter would not have gotten to the topic of the Founders and slavery. In fact, chances are high, based on the curriculum of many states, that students will not study the Founding period in high school but rather take a course dedicated to the "second half" of American history, the "first half" having been studied in middle school. So the view of Professor Andrews is the only one they have in front of them.

The second way of stacking the deck consists in having this discussion in a literature as opposed to a history class. It is unlikely that an English teacher will have the historical knowledge to be able to put this complex issue into perspective. (We shall leave aside the question of how many history teachers would understand the issue fully.) Would a literature teacher know that in 1787, as the Constitution was being debated, the Congress was drafting the Northwest Ordinance, which prohibited the extension of slavery into the Northwest Territories? Would she know that the issue of slavery was fiercely debated in the Constitutional Convention and that a provision which would allow for the abolition of the slave trade was adopted (Article I, section 9)? Would she know that many Founders after the Revolutionary War, among them Alexander Hamilton and Benjamin Franklin, joined manumission societies and saw to it that slavery was abolished in many of the states? Would she think to point out that slavery was an institution that had existed for thousands of years; that the only distinct voices before the Founders' against slavery were the Quakers, thought of as a marginal religious group (who also did not believe in war); that George Washington's father probably never thought twice about buying slaves but that Washington manumitted his slaves in his will; that the Founders are consistent in their writings on the evils of slavery; and that, just as Rome was not built in a day, neither could slavery be abolished in a single generation—though the men who pledged their lives, their fortunes, and their sacred honor on behalf of life, liberty, and the pursuit of happiness did more than any previous generation *in history* to oppose and reduce the institution of slavery? No, your average English teacher will not think of these things. She will not think of these things in large part because there is nothing in the Prentice Hall LITERATURE *The American Experience* text that prompts either the teacher or the students to think of these things! The book contains NONE of the Founding Fathers' many writings against the institution of slavery and makes NO mention of their many efforts to reduce slavery in their time nor their hope for the end of slavery in the ensuing decades. Instead, the teachers and students are treated to the misleading language of *inconsistency* and *paradox*, which will be translated into the word *hypocrisy* in their so-called discussions—which are really reading from a script.

Can we expect anything different? The students and teachers are simply not equipped to have a genuinely informed conversation about the complex issue of slavery that gave the Founders themselves—of all the crises they faced—the most difficulty. They will omit the historical reality that the Founders were having to address the millennia-long legacy of slavery at the same time they were fighting a war against the most powerful armed force in the eighteenth century, suffering the worst financial collapse in American history, facing a political crisis that could have wrecked the entire country, establishing the first constitutional republic in the modern world, setting up an economy (with much debate about that), and providing for basic internal order (at one point against, yes, a tax rebellion) and for a common defense against external attack (which would come in 1812). Goaded on by professors of multiculturalism, whose literary sympathies assuredly do not lie with the Founders, iconoclastic and uneducated teenagers are invited to take pot-shots at the Founding Fathers without even having to read them. And this mockery of a class discussion gets called "critical thinking." But this is not critical thinking. This is the act of *programming*. The Gates' Foundation probably knows something about that. In short, before the students of America have a chance to read the American Story, it has already been spoiled for them.

Finally, we notice that the textbook invites students to have a discussion on whether the United States has become the country its "early citizens" imagined. How could they possibly have that discussion when they have yet to read what those "early citizens" had to say about America? Is this not a case of asking students to make bricks without straw? Or is it the case that the textbook editors do not want an informed discussion but rather an uninformed political debate in which words such as *unfairness* will predictably surface?

The book formally begins with Unit 1, Part 1: Meeting of Cultures. We have as the artistic representation of this section a painting of Kee-o-kuk of the Sac and Fox peoples. This is a curious choice, given that the section only extends through the Pilgrims and the chief of the Sac and Fox lived in the nineteenth century. At any rate, we shall proceed. The reader should probably know that between each short section, the Teacher's Edition has several pages that look like a sales pitch for further Common Core "resources" used in teaching. One finds Common Core Companions and Reader's Notebooks and online features, including Spanish and English summaries, graphic organizers, and ready-made examinations. All this is to say that teachers really do not have to teach any more, nor to attend to the more laborious parts of teaching, such as making one's own examinations. The whole package is just handed to teachers—for a price. No doubt soon computers will be grading the students' papers.

The first selection of the book is called "The Earth on Turtle's Back." This is clearly an oral legend since the story is retold by Michael Caduto and Joseph Brucha. The next passage is called "When Grizzlies Walked Upright." The third following this theme is "The Navajo Origin Legend." I shall not offer a commentary on these works. They do raise a question, however. These stories are "origin myths." The Teacher's Edition tells teachers to ask "what other sources they know that take on the challenge of explaining" where the people of the earth come from. Students might answer with "sacred texts such as the Bible as well as the secular work of geneticists and molecular biologists." Indeed, those are likely answers. Yet I wonder whether there is any place in the Common Core textbooks that actually offers us the Story of the Creation from the Book of Genesis. We are being invited to read a Navajo creation story. Why then not Genesis? Would that story not give us a lot more insight into the English settlers who came to America? Recall that the Story of the Creation is not included in Appendix B of the Common Core Standards.

After these origin myths, students get to meet Susan Power. Ms. Power is an author living today who is a member of the Standing Rock Sioux Tribe of Fort Yates, North Dakota. She has written two books. At this juncture, we get to read her "personal essay" called "Museum Indians" about images of various Indians (can we say that?) in Chicago museums. Why this essay appears in the section of a LITERATURE textbook devoted to "Beginnings to 1800" is not explained. Apparently, once you have accepted Tom Paine on the Internet, you will buy anything.

After another break in the Teacher's Edition peddling Common Core paraphernalia, we get to read the Iroquois Constitution. The obvious question to ask is why the book has a copy of the Iroquois Constitution but not the U.S. Constitution, also not called for in the Common Core English Standards, as we have seen. I, for one, am happy to leave all constitutions out of literature books and to let English teachers get back to teaching stories and poetry. But if you have one constitution, should you not have at least part—say, the Preamble—of the Constitution we are presently living under?

The book offers selections written by Spanish explorers of the New World: Cabeza de Vaca and López de Cárdenas. While interesting, I still wonder whether they belong in a literature book. Ostensibly, they are pulled in since one of the great themes of American literature is the *wilderness*, which the editors think students should spend a lot of time on. Why they do not leave it to *literary* authors themselves to write about the wilderness is a question not to be asked.

On page 58 we encounter the first selection originally written in English by someone who lived before the twentieth century. It is a selection from William Bradford's famous *Of Plymouth Plantation*. Though I would prefer this great story to be taught in a history class, I shall not push too hard on this one. There is an art to historical narrative; we have fewer *literary* works from the early settlers; and it is a marvelous story. This story should largely speak for itself, but the teaching techniques employed reveal the triviality and bias of the editors. In the Teacher's Edition under the heading *Enrichment: Building Context*, teachers are instructed to "discuss the idea that some of today's immigrants to the United States also face hardships—similar to and different from those faced by the immigrants of Plymouth." To this end, students should engage in the activity of conducting research into the "obstacles immigrants face today—say, learning the language, finding housing, finding employment, and dealing with earlier settlers in the area." This is a ridiculous assignment. It features that last refuge of the standards makers: compare and contrast. It takes the students' minds off the unimaginable hardships of people trying to survive in a howling wilderness in the middle of winter only to see half of their men and women die. And it once again invites students to embark on a potentially explosive contemporary political topic at the very moment the nation is deliberating the policies of its own borders. Notice, too, that the emphasis is on the *obstacles* of immigration rather than on the *opportunities*. By the way, are Americans living today still considered "settlers"?

Where do we think such a classroom discussion will go? Those who have any insights into what happens in today's schools know exactly where it will go (as do the editors of this textbook, I'll wager). The teacher will ask the provocative question, "So class, which was harder, being an immigrant back then or now?" Students will say utterly predictable things, much of it involving technology. At least one student will plead the case of the modern immigrant. "It's like, you know, still hard to be an immigrant. People show up and there aren't any jobs. And, like, there's all this prejudice. And where are they supposed to live anyway? I mean, there's like no room left in the cities. Why haven't we figured out this stuff by now? We've got to do something! You know, we're talking about like millions of people, not just a hundred!" Obviously, with such pressing issues that must be fixed, it becomes much harder to care about a few religious refugees living so long ago.

The marginal comments do instruct teachers to engage the text itself a little. Yet the manner of doing so is questionable. The language used by the textbook editors refers to the Pilgrims' "values" and, occasionally, their faith. Bradford's language is much more direct. He invokes God. He states, "And yet the Lord so upheld these persons, as in this general calamity they were not all infected either with sickness or lameness." To such a passage, the editors invite the teacher to ask "why Bradford invokes 'the Lord' when reporting the health of some men while so many others fell ill." **Possible response:**[85] "Bradford has no other way of explaining the health of some people during the calamity, so in this piece he does not hesitate to refer to his faith time and time again, in effect stamping early American literature with a religious accent." This is an absurd way of writing about both Bradford and literature. "Has no other way": Is this the textbook's way of saying, "Bradford did not know about modern medical science, so he had to use God to explain things"? If so, the editors are following a double-standard since this kind of condescending

---

[85] The reader may wonder why I keep putting this phrase in bold type. This is the way it appears in the textbook. The words that follow this phrase, then, are the editors' expectations of what the students might say (or their signal to teachers of what to force students into saying).

language is not used to analyze the Native American myths. "In this *piece*": Note to editors: Bradford was not writing an op-ed; a narrative history is usually not called a "piece." "He does not hesitate to refer to his faith time and time again": Yes, people who believe in God tend to do that—except they usually do not say (until the modern age) "I am a religious person and I am going to refer to my faith now," but rather "God delivered us," "God saved us," and "God is watching over us." Obviously, this sort of language is not something the editors of *The American Experience* are accustomed to. "Stamping early American literature with a religious accent": Yes, that's it! While men and women were starving, while facing innumerable hardships, while establishing some form of sensible government and church polity, Bradford was attempting to *stamp early American literature* (which did not yet exist) with a religious accent. This is classic two-bit literary criticism. Whenever you get to something difficult or profound, slap a label on it. Whenever a passage of literature makes a claim on truth, dodge it.

The modern textbook translation of Bradford, then, is this:[86] "I do not really have a (modern) way of explaining why all these people are dying, but some do not die, so in this piece I am going to refer to my faith time and time again, because I am a religious person, and religious people do that sort of thing, and go out on a limb here and say that, you know, God has something to do with it, and thus I am going to put a religious stamp on early American literature, which will someday be a prominent THEME in high-school American LITERATURE textbooks." Bradford's way of writing is rather different:

> Besides, what could they see but a hideous and desolate wilderness, full of wild beasts and wild men? And what multitudes there might be of them they knew not. . . . What could now sustain them but the spirit of God and his grace? May not and ought not the children of these fathers rightly say: *Our fathers were Englishmen which came over this great ocean, and were ready to perish in this wilderness; but they cried unto the Lord and He heard their voice, and looked on*

---

[86] These are my words based upon the foregoing analysis.

*their adversity, etc. Let them therefore praise
the Lord, because He is good, and His mercies
endure forever. . . .*

Should not one fundamental aim of a literature class be to
recapture the depth and beauty of language and the force of an
argument? Should not the counterpart to that aim be to avoid like
the plague modern jargon that would blunt the meaning of a work
of literature? How does Pearson's Common Core version of
American literature fare in that regard?

But alas, www.Pearson/PrenticeHall/Achieve/CommonCore/
BillGates/DavidColeman.com is not yet done with Bradford. The
students have yet to receive their lesson in "culturally responsive
instruction." The lesson is prompted by this line in Bradford's
narrative:

> But about the 16th of March a certain Indian
> came boldly amongst them, and spoke to them in
> broken English, which they could well
> understand, but marveled at it.

This sentence is taken from the famous passage describing the
encounter with Samoset. It somehow causes offense to modern
ears. The offending word is "broken." Therefore, Prentice Hall
calls in the language police. Meet Sharroky Hollie, Executive
Director of the Center for Culturally Responsive Teaching and
Learning whose work "focuses on African American education
and on second language methodology." He is one of the many
"contributing authors" to this textbook and seems to be the person
responsible for the moments of Culturally Responsive Instruction
throughout the Teacher's Edition. In this instance, teachers are
cautioned about Bradford's choice of words:

> Bradford describes Samoset's speech as
> "broken English." Challenge students to find a
> good label to describe one's ability to learn
> English as a second language—perhaps *elemen-
> tary English, emerging English*, or *developing
> English*. The goal is to create appreciation for
> the effort required to gain fluency in a second
> language after the age of twelve or so.

In her essay "Mother Tongue," Amy Tan warns against the terms *broken* or *fractured* or *limited* English. Even though her Chinese mother never spoke perfect English, she was fully capable of reading, listening to, and understanding sophisticated financial reports in English.

Thus the words from a seventeenth-century colonial founder are deployed not to teach us how to be brave or faithful or resilient—the virtues he wanted to teach us—but rather to impose an unnecessary lesson in twenty-first-century political correctness. Where would we be without Teachers' Editions of Common Core textbooks to tell us how to address such urgent problems?

To be fair, the "Critical Reading" questions found at the end of the selection are somewhat better, though they still suffer from terminal two-bit literary criticism, and the "answers" provided in the margin of the Teacher's Edition are far weaker than an intelligent student could provide. Even these questions do not get the heart of the text, and the assignments that are suggested—including writing in a private diary as though you were a Pilgrim and pretending like Bradford could time-travel to your high school and you had to introduce him in an assembly (textbook cases of silly, Romper-Room progressivism)—limit any chance of a good discussion. All in all, this treatment of Bradford's great story, like so many other aspects of today's public schools, is a completely wasted opportunity.

Now it is time to enter the realm of the absurd, to boldly go where no LITERATURE textbook has ever gone before. Right after Bradford's *Of Plymouth Plantation* and right before Unit 1, Part 2, "The Puritan Influence," we have a "Mission Update." From page 68 to page 72 the students are, under the dubious heading "Contemporary Connection," invited into the world of Steve Squyres, scientist and Mars Blogger. That's right, Steve Squyres was the chief investigator for NASA's Mars Exploration Rover and kept a blog about the Mars landing, from which selections are (I guess) posted in the book, alongside information about Mars itself. Two basic questions emerge from this space adventure. At the moment when the students' minds ought to be on the 1620's and becoming more accustomed to the prose of the

King James' era, why would anyone want to launch the students into outer space via a modern blog? And what has Mars to do with American LITERATURE? No great *literature* has yet to emerge from Mars.

Clearly this Martian interlude is meant to chew up time. The Mars unit does not just consist in reading a few pages but invites students to engage in a series of activities far removed from the study of American literature:

> **Activity: Research** Ask students to investigate how scientists are addressing the complications of deep-space travel for humans. Students may use the Investigating Science worksheet, Professional Development Guidebook, page 241, as they do their research. Encourage students to report their findings to the class.
>
> **Differentiated Instruction**
>
> *Support for Less Proficient Readers*
> Students may need help to understand some of the technical details Squyres mentions. To clarify "superior conjunction," draw a diagram on the board showing Mars and Earth, with the much-larger Sun between them. Point out that the Sun is blocking the straight line between the two planets. Because radio signals cannot bend around the Sun, there can be no communication between Mars and Earth in this position.
>
> *Enrichment for Gifted/Talented Students*
> Challenge students to develop materials that will teach elementary-age pupils about the Mars rover project. They might build a life-size replica of a rover, diagram the orbits of the Earth and Mars to plot the rocket journey to Mars, or create a flowchart to show the communication process between the rovers on Mars and the controllers on Earth.

How much time is to be wasted in outer space? More important, what is not going on during the days or weeks these projects are being constructed? Clearly, the students will not be learning anything about the English language and great literature. How silly is it to have *English* teachers preparing lessons on planetary orbits and superior conjunction? And how much time do the editors of this textbook think literature teachers have to allow students to "report their findings to the class"? Should not the students be reading whole novels by the time this assignment would come along in the semester? This Mars Rover interlude is but a preview of things to come. It is but a "mission update" in the Common Core's committed objective of having students read 70% "informational texts" by the end of the senior year.

At last, after another sales pitch for Common Core materials, we turn to the Puritans on page 75. On the following page we find the wonderful poem by Anne Bradstreet, "To My Dear and Loving Husband." This is, by the way, the first writing that represents what used to be called *literature* in schools. If I were I teaching American literature in high school, this poem would be the first thing I would read and discuss with students on the first day of class—without a lot of preliminaries and two-bit literary criticism to clutter up their minds. The beauty of the poem speaks for itself:

> If ever two were one, then surely we.
> If ever man were lov'd by wife, then thee;
> If ever wife was happy in a man,
> Compare with me ye women if you can.

> I prize thy love more than whole mines of gold,
> Or all the riches that the East doth hold.
> My love is such that rivers cannot quench,
> Nor ought but love from thee, give recompense.

> Thy love is such I can no way repay,
> The heavens reward thee manifold, I pray.
> Then while we live, in love let's so persevere,
> That when we live no more, we may live ever.

What do the editors do with this lovely verse? They blow it. They bid teachers to ask a few simple fact-based questions and try to draw attention to some metaphors. Yet the editors invite no meaningful discussion about love or happiness or "reward." In the "critical reading" questions, they plainly fall all over themselves. They ask, "Which aspect of the speaker is more important in this poem—the private or the public self?" **Possible response**: "Most of the poem shows the speaker's concern with her <u>personal</u> self rather than with the <u>community</u>. The speaker does, however, also show that she accepts the religious community's doctrine of an afterlife." My translation: "We (the editors) cannot to save our lives figure out how this wonderful poem about love fits in with our stereotype of the Puritans as being obsessed with community rules and morals and not letting anyone have any fun—oh, and being worried about Hell all the time. But we cannot give up our stereotype, so let's say that there's some kind of tension between the *personal* and the *community* anyway." It never occurs to these editors that a Biblical people filled with the love of God (as in Winthrop's "A Modell of Christian Charity," with *charity* meaning *love*) might have *stronger* marriages and *more* love between wife and husband. And so another opportunity is missed.

The questions I would ask my students to start the discussion would be simply, "Does Anne Bradstreet understand love? And what is love?" Presumably, we would discuss whether this love is different from *falling in love*, what it means for *two* to be one, what *man* and *wife* have to do with love, why she would be prompted to *repay* her dear and loving husband for his love, and so on. You will not find such life-probing questions in the Common Core Graphic Organizers and Literary Analysis Workbooks, though.

We turn, finally, to Jonathan Edwards's famous sermon "Sinners in the Hands of an Angry God," beginning on page 87. The reader will recall that I pointed out that it did not make the list of "exemplar texts" found in Appendix B of the Common Core English Standards, a list characterized by a dearth of religiously inspired literature. Yet here it is in an official Common Core textbook. It is not clear whether its presence is a visit from the ghost of literature past which will disappear at some point, or whether it will remain a staple reading in American literature courses. In any event, we must see what our editors do with it. If we were looking only at the student version of the book—the one parents would have access to—it would appear that nothing is afoot. The same cannot be said, as we have learned, of the Teacher's Edition.

It would take us too far off course to explain orthodox Calvinist theology. The most we can do at present is to evaluate how sensitive, nuanced, and informative is the editors' handling of this famous sermon that strikes most modern people, even many

Christians, as coming almost from a different planet. Do they give Jonathan Edwards a fair hearing or not? Most likely the teacher would begin by following the advice given in the margins on page 87, which we must examine at length:

> Most students are all too familiar with the persuasive power of advertising, of peer pressure, and of other methods people use to influence the actions or attitudes of others. Have small groups brainstorm for persuasive techniques that they find especially effective. Then, engage students' interest in Jonathan Edwards's persuasive sermon by reading the following passage to them . . . Ask students to characterize Edwards's basic approach: Is it emotional or intellectual? Invite other responses to this quotation, as well as speculation about how Edwards, a conservative Puritan preacher, might attempt to persuade a congregation to accept his message about their "wickedness."

The question concerning whether Edwards's appeal is emotional or intellectual is clearly a loaded one and meant only to have one answer. Other marginal notes come back to the idea of emotions. Obviously, *emotional* in the context of public speaking is meant to have a negative connotation, while *intellectual* is supposed to elicit a positive response. That the editors begin with the ideas of *peer pressure* and *advertising*, both of which are regularly disparaged in schools, indicates that they wish to dispose us unfavorably to the sermon. That the editors encourage teachers to break students up into *groups* suggests that the editors themselves are not above using peer pressure to get *their* message across. The quotation marks around *wickedness* are clearly meant to be ironic. Thus, students are to look at Edwards's sermon only in the light of a "conservative . . . preacher" attempting to manipulate the emotions of his audience.

More coaching is needed, apparently. On the following page, the editors ask teachers to "encourage students to reflect on contemporary views of God before responding to the question: How do you think a contemporary audience would react to this type of 'fire and brimstone' biblical imagery?" **Possible**

responses: "A contemporary audience would probably be turned off by Edwards's use of biblical imagery. Today, it is more common for worshippers to view God as loving and benevolent rather than angry and capricious." This discussion prompt is a classic case of judging great texts by present-day standards rather than allowing the classics to teach us by offering an alternative view to our world. What if the tables were turned, and Jonathan Edwards could time-travel to our churches? (The editors are selective in their use of time travel.) What would he say? Might he not say our churches had become infected with "feel-good religion" and that Christianity had lost its sense of the Fall of Man? That would be my guess. That possibility will not be discussed because the editors are coercing us (by appealing to our emotions, no less) into an unfavorable opinion of this sermon.

In addition to stoking the fire of prejudice against Edwards's message, the editors also want to take the students off track. They offer a suggested assignment under the heading of "Enrichment: Investigating Religion and Myth":

> **The Afterlife**
> Edwards's belief in an afterlife is typical of the followers of most major religions. According to the ancient Greeks, people who led a good life were sent to Elysium, a paradise filled with sunny fields. Ancient Egyptians, too, believed in the afterlife as an agricultural land of plenty. In Norse mythology, heroes slain in battle went to Valhalla. In Buddhism and in Hinduism, the soul is reincarnated (reborn in another body or form) until it achieves a state of spiritual perfection.
> **Activity: Presentation** Encourage students to choose a religion or culture and investigate its beliefs about life after death. Have students examine how these beliefs express human values and emotions. Suggest that they record information in the *Enrichment: Investigating Religion and Myth* worksheet . . .

It is as important to notice what the students would *not* be doing as much as what they would be doing in an assignment of this nature.

They would not be learning anything from the Bible or theology. That would be the kind of *investigation* that would lead to a better understanding of the sermon under review. This wild-goose chase, under the cover of a research activity, is yet another instance of the editors deliberately diverting students from the study of *The American Experience* (the title of the book) and thus the sense that there might be anything unique or noble about that experience. Quite likely, the editors are subtly trying to undermine the sermon at hand. No doubt some of the students, given their teachers' prompting, will come to the conclusion that these other religions are much more *reasonable* than Edwards's religion (which happens to be Christianity).

It would be bad enough if the editors simply failed to help students understand this sermon by not taking measures to help teachers explain it—in terms Edwards would recognize. It would be far worse if the editors actually hid parts of the sermon from the students that lead to a clearer understanding. Unfortunately, that appears to be exactly what is going on. The sermon that is contained in the book is less than half of the original. We could forgive the heavy editing, perhaps, due to the length of the sermon itself, provided nothing essential were left out, particularly nothing that would contribute substantially to Edwards's argument. But that is not the case. There are two major cuts made: the first half of the sermon and passages within the text that remains. In both instances, those cuts affect the principal source of Edwards's evidence: direct quotations from the Bible.

In fact, Edwards began his sermon with a passage of Scripture, Deuteronomy 32:35: "Their foot shall slide in due time." Edwards begins his sermon

> In this verse is threatened the vengeance of God on the wicked, unbelieving Israelites that were God's visible people, and lived under means of grace . . .

Edwards, therefore, was not drawing his sermon out of thin air. He was relying on the words of Scripture to build the case that Hell does indeed threaten a sinful people. Now that casts the sermon in a little different light. It is not the view of the sermon found in Prentice Hall's Common Core textbook. That version begins with the "Application" part of the sermon, after the Biblically-based argument has been made.   Further, the elided parts of the Application itself are very curious.   Nearly all of them cut out citations from the Bible.   Among the passages that have been edited out of the Application section of the sermon are lines from Proverbs, Isaiah (multiple), Luke, Revelation, Ezekiel, and Romans.   The numbers tell the story.   In the version of the sermon I have (from *The Annals of America*, a well-known source of historical documents) I count twenty-two citations of Scripture besides the various allusions that characterize Edwards's pastoral style.   In the heavily edited version of the sermon found in the textbook, there remains only *one* quotation of Scripture.   One. And that reference to Genesis is the last line of the sermon, so the editors could not have very well left it out.

There is another interesting omission, particularly given that this is a textbook for high-school students:

> And you, young men and young women, will you neglect this precious season which you now enjoy, when so many others of your age are renouncing all youthful vanities and flocking to Christt?   You especially have now an extraordinary opportunity; but if you neglect it, it will soon be with you as it is with those persons who spent all the precious days of youth in sin, and are now come to such a dreadful pass in blindness and hardness.

Now is it not strange that this direct appeal to young people does not make it into the Common Core edition of the "Sinners in the Hands of an Angry God"?   Rather than asking in the margins whether students think a modern audience would be "turned off" by Edwards's sermon, the editors could point out that a large percentage of the converts in his congregation were young people, teenagers.   What might that piece of information do, or what discussions might be had, in high schools where all sorts of illicit activities take place, such as "sexting"?   Sinful teenagers needing redemption?   Now there's a chance for "enrichment"! **Activity**: *Imagine you are in a place, as hard as that might be, where there is a lot of sin.   You are told by a preacher that you must choose between Heaven and Hell—and that delaying your choice would only put your immortal soul in peril. . .* Who knows?   If "Sinners in the Hands of an Angry God" were actually fairly read in our American high schools, it might lead to a third Great Awakening, one the Common Core advocates are certainly not anticipating.

All kidding aside, the editors have either committed an act of gross educational and editorial negligence or they have deliberately withheld necessary information from the students. If they want to stick to the rhetorical aspects of the text, fine. That is not the best way to understand it, but it is a legitimate way. Yet the question in that case would not be a simplistic choice between *emotion* and *intellect*. Rather, the question*s* would be along these lines: "Jonathan Edwards cites many passages of Scripture in order to build his case for conversion to Christ. Based on these passages, is his argument plausible? Does the *mercy* of God balance out the *wrath* of God in his account? What is the role of Christ in Edwards's sermon? Is it fair to use emotion in order to convey the terrors of Hell? Does this argument combine both cool logic and appeals to emotion or does it lean more heavily to one side? What response is Edwards looking for in his audience?" The editors of this Common Core textbook have not offered such sensible questions. They have created a straw man, perhaps in an effort to discredit evangelical Christianity itself.

I am not suggesting advocacy one way or the other. When I teach Jonathan Edwards in my own classes I also assign Charles Chauncy, who was one of the most astute critics of the Great Awakening as it unfolded. But one of the arts of teaching, particularly when students all think one way on a text, is to play Devil's Advocate. In this case it is not the Devil, but the pastor most fervently warning people against the Devil, who could use an advocate. Without any clear guidance as to why men and women (and younger people) could have found such a sermon appealing, the students will just dismiss the text and say, "That's weird." What the editors of this textbook never consider is that Edwards *might have been right* or, at the very least, "had a point." He, along with Bradford, was not trying to "stamp" American literature with a religious accent. He was trying to move the souls of men and women toward God. There is a difference.

Now we turn to Part 3 of Unit 1: A Nation is Born. A quick glance would lead us to believe that all is well, that even the editors of a Common Core textbook could not mess up the Founding Fathers. The chapter opens with a portrait of George

Washington. The readings include writings and speeches of Patrick Henry, Benjamin Franklin, and Thomas Paine, as well as the Declaration of Independence. Surely this chapter must be one to put in the win column. Or not.

As we enter this chapter, we must remember that these sources are all widely available elsewhere, can be purchased much more cheaply, and, in the case of the longer selections, can be read in their entirety or at least in greater drafts. Further, our inquiry centers on what the editors do with these sources. Do they help teachers explain the readings fairly and accurately? Do they get to the heart of the matter or beat around the bush? Do their comments obscure or even misrepresent the authors? Would the teachers and students be better off reading these documents (or other documents of the same caliber) without the intervention of our editorial authorities?

The chapter begins with Patrick Henry's famous "Give me liberty or give me death" speech. The reader will recall that Henry has already been discredited in the introduction of the volume for his slaveholding. The treatment here, thankfully, does not repeat that accusation, but the damage may have already been done. The analysis provided at this juncture is pretty mediocre, a combination of obvious fact-based questions with several comments upon style, such as Henry's use of rhetorical questions.

The next selection is more curious: Benjamin Franklin's speech at the close of the Constitutional Convention in 1787. It is curious in several respects. First, it appears out of chronological order with respect to Franklin's other writings in this chapter and to the other Revolutionary documents. In the past, textbooks featured writings of Franklin in chronological order, with selections from his *Autobiography*, dwelling on his life before his feats as one of the leading Revolutionaries, appearing first. In this book, the small selection from the *Autobiography* comes almost at the end, and other famous writings, such as "Rules by Which a Great Empire May Be Reduced to a Small One," do not show up. In fact, though Franklin's closing speech at the Convention is well-known to teachers of history and government, it has not been considered one of the highlights in the American *literary* canon. Why, then, does it play such a prominent role here?

The answer may be found in the quotation in large font that appears right beside the portrait of Franklin on the first page of the selection. The first words the students will read of Franklin's (in

212

the entire book) are these: "*I confess, that I do not entirely approve of this Constitution at present . . .*" Wow! So that is Franklin's legacy? Not approving of the Constitution of the United States? What a coup for Progressive textbook editors! One of the two indispensable men of the Revolution (Washington being the other)—and one of the greatest men who has ever lived in history—is on record in opposing, it would seem, the Constitution, while, admittedly, asking the delegates to adopt the Constitution. What greater testimony could be discovered to promote the Progressive idea of "a living Constitution"?

Well, here is a case where context is everything. Yes, Franklin did oppose aspects of the Constitution as it was written, as did everyone in the Convention. Yet the emphasis in this address is on his own humility and how experience has shown him that often he had changed his opinion on important subjects based on "better Information or fuller Consideration." The tone of the speech, in fact, suggests the delegates to the Convention will find over time that the Constitution is much better than they now think it to be. In fact, that turned out to be the case. Many of the things James Madison argued against in the Convention he went on to champion and explain in *The Federalist*. There is also an important fact about Franklin's opposition to aspects of the Constitution. Franklin, alone among the delegates, advocated a unicameral legislature, like the one Pennsylvania then had. All other delegates knew unicameralism to be an illness of government under the Articles of Confederation, not a remedy. The French Revolution would soon enough prove the dangers of single-house legislatures. Franklin, possibly the greatest genius ever to have lived in America, was nonetheless not the Revolution's foremost *political* thinker. In light of this fact, should the featured quotation of Franklin (next to his portrait) not be some other insightful reflection? My candidate would be, "It therefore astonishes me, Sir, to find this System approaching so near to Perfection as it does." Those words are in Franklin's remarks but not given any attention by the editors.

Though it may seem a small thing, the editorial decision of what line from Franklin's speech gets highlighted makes all the difference. Teenage students (and their teachers) living in the Age of the Soundbite will grab hold of that comment and forget everything else about Franklin's speech—if they even read it. Just in case the students fail to see the quotation, teachers are urged in two separate places to drive the message home:

> **Ask** the Reading Strategy question: In his reference to "faults," is Franklin appealing to those who are happy with the Constitution or those who are not? Explain.
> **Answer**: Franklin is appealing to those who are dissatisfied with the Constitution. He acknowledges that imperfect delegates have produced an imperfect document.
>
> **Reading Check**
> What does Franklin confess as he begins his speech?
> **Answer**: Franklin confesses that he does not completely approve of the Constitution as written.

If you were to see the formatting of these two pages, you would discover that the speech has been completely encircled by seeming opposition to the Constitution: Franklin's not "entirely" approving; the "faults" of the document; the "imperfect" delegates who made an "imperfect" document; even Patrick Henry's opposition, Henry being the inaugural speaker of the "A Nation is Born" section of the book.

Some readers may think I am nitpicking. "Well, did Franklin say he didn't entirely approve or didn't he? Shouldn't students know this?" Yes, they should. I would prefer them to learn these things in a history or government class where the teacher has some degree of insight (we hope) into these complex matters. Even so, I can clearly see what the editors' aims are. Consider the "Enrichment" activity they suggest.

> **Activity: Debate** Have students conduct research on the Federalists and Anti-Federalists. . . . Have students use this information to conduct a mini-debate on the controversy between the two groups.

This is actually a fairly decent idea. I have had my students debate the Constitution in class before. I have also made them debate me when I played the part (with the accent of a Virginia gentleman) of an Anti-Federalist. There is only one small thing missing from this "activity": the Constitution! Once again the textbook editors are asking students to make bricks without straw. The Constitution does not appear in this textbook. The sage editors do not tell them to read the Constitution. They do not provide nor tell the students to read *Federalist* One or Ten or Fifty-One, which might bolster the pro-Constitution side of the argument. So what will these students end up saying? "Dude, even Franklin says he doesn't approve of the Constitution! It was made by *imperfect* people and it had a lot of faults—a lot of faults. They just adopted it because they didn't have anything better." And that is precisely the level of understanding the editors of *The American Experience* and the authors of the Common Core want our young men and women to have regarding the Constitution of the United States. Recall what my wife said about the editors wanting students to have opinions of something they know nothing about. Further, remember the supplemental documents that appear in Appendix B of the Common Core Standards on the Constitution. The fix is already in. How long will it be before one of these "experts" is brought in for a guest scholar appearance to tell students exactly what to think and to make the case (subtly but surely) that the Constitution must be *a living document*?

We move on to the Declaration of Independence. This moment in the book could be retitled "Dropping the Ball." The extent to which the ball is dropped can be easily seen by asking a simple rhetorical question. When you think of The Declaration, what words come to mind? Most likely they are, "We hold these truths to be self-evident, that all men are created equal, that they are endowed by their Creator with certain unalienable Rights, that among these are Life, Liberty and the pursuit of Happiness.—That to secure these rights, Governments are instituted among Men, deriving their just powers from the consent of the governed . . ." These are not the words that the editors of *The American Experience* attempt to explain or encourage students to study. The neglect of what might be called the *first principles* or *philosophical foundation* of the Declaration and of this nation as a whole is remarkable. On the pages in the Teacher's Edition the editors have supplied both numbers connected to questions written in the margins about the document and bracketed sections to read. *No numbers or brackets appear next to the words I just quoted.* The editors offer some background knowledge and begin their comments in earnest with "Prudence, indeed, will dictate . . ." They spend most of their time, just as does the example question in Appendix B of the Common Core Standards, with the list of charges against King George. If the teacher turns the page, he will find a short section on the "philosophical influence" of John Locke on Thomas Jefferson. A similar section also appears in the students' edition. The purpose seems largely to be to show that Jefferson got his ideas from Locke, not that these "self-evident truths" derive from "the laws of Nature and Nature's God." Thus, even if the teacher does try to explain the philosophical arguments, it will come across as "Locke said this, and Jefferson got his ideas from Locke." While true, that approach does not explain what these ideas mean. Definitions of certain words are also offered in the margins. Although the words *candid, assent, harass, tyranny,* and other terms are defined, *equal, endowed, unalienable, liberty,* and *happiness* are not. Do not think that students already know the meaning of these words. They do not. That the textbook does not define these words means that teachers are not supposed to explain them. As is the case in the Common Core Standards themselves, there is no genuine attempt to understand the Declaration.

The editors are not finished yet. They have to send the students off on yet another one of their wild-goose chases:

Enrichment: Investigating a Key Person in History
A Spreading Flame of Freedom
When representatives from the thirteen colonies signed the Declaration of Independence, they forged a path that would soon follow. France, which helped the colonists defeat Britain, soon convulsed in revolution.

In Latin America, Simón Bolívar campaigned for independence from Spain in the nineteenth century. He raised an army to liberate what are now the countries of Venezuela, Colombia, Ecuador, Peru, and Bolivia (which was named in his honor).

Activity: Discussion Have students conduct research into the role of Simón Bolívar in the liberation of Latin American countries from Spanish rule. . . . Have them use the results of their research as the basis of a discussion comparing North American and Latin American Revolutionary experiences.

Evidently, the "Key Person in History," when the subject being studied is the Declaration of Independence, is not Thomas Jefferson. This assignment is a transparent case of the editors being unwilling to teach The American Experience as in any way exceptional. If research were a desideratum (and I am suspicious of what goes by the name of research), then the students should be sent into the library (and not onto the Internet) to learn more about, yes, Thomas Jefferson and these ideas of life, liberty, and the pursuit of happiness. Clearly the sympathies of the editors of *The American Experience* lie elsewhere. By the way, when did it cease being the *teacher's* job to do *research* and then teach the students what they are supposed to know?

I shall skip over the selections of Thomas Paine (the inventor of the Internet) and of the slave and poet Phillis Wheatley, as well as still more advertising for Common Core accoutrement, in order to bring us back to the realm of the absurd. In this LITERATURE textbook we have several calls urging us to vote. The first is a pamphlet distributed by the League of Women Voters telling us to "stay informed" and offering a guide on how we are supposed to "watch a debate." It turns out that we have work to do "before the debate," questions to consider "during the debate," and ways of clarifying our thoughts about the candidates "after the debate." We are even given an illustration of a family watching a presidential debate (I think is it Bush and Kerry) on CNN. The child sitting on his mother's lap appears to be about eight months old, but I really do not recommend having children of that age up so late or watching television at all. (Nor can we approve of children's verbal habits being formed by the circumlocutions of politicians; better to watch Bugs Bunny.) This important call to citizenship is followed by a pamphlet recruiting the young people of North Texas to serve as poll workers. The support for "English learners" in the Teacher's Edition tells teachers that they must explain terms such as *polls*, *county*, and *registered to vote*. In an effort to connect "to the students' world," teachers are also told to divide the class into small groups and allow them to make manuals for various roles at school, such as that of hall monitor or equipment manager for a sports team. The groups should share their manuals with the entire class. Now this is critical thinking!

We return to Benjamin Franklin. It would be really hard to mess up Franklin, perhaps America's most beloved icon and symbol. While the editors do not entirely fail in their presentation of Franklin, they do fail in light of what ought to be taking place in a serious literature (or history) class in a serious high school. The editors offer only five-and-a-half pages taken from Franklin's *Autobiography*. Given that limited space, they choose the most memorable passage, Franklin's famous "bold and arduous project at arriving at moral perfection." The editorial questions are ho-hum. The real error, though, consists in reading Franklin's great work in such a cramped space. Should the students not have their own copy of the *Autobiography*? That book is a rare opportunity: one of America's greatest heroes explaining in detail how he educated himself, formed his character, and engaged constantly in works of civic, scientific, and moral improvement. Franklin's *Autobiography* is nothing less than an engaging, witty, inspiring course in self-government. The editors of *The American Experience* can only afford us a few pages. As a point of comparison, these are the exact pages that I had *sixth-graders* read in their study of the Enlightenment before their going on to read almost the whole *Autobiography* in high school. Were the students in that high school to follow this Common Core textbook meant for juniors, they would feel as though they were getting a demotion.

If they can afford only a few pages of Franklin, the editors of the textbook must surely be making the best use of the other pages. That brings us to the question of why the same number of pages given to Franklin would be consumed in this chapter designated "A Nation is Born" by the autobiographical account of Sandra Cisneros called "Straw into Gold: The Metamorphosis of the Everyday." Now maybe Ms. Cisneros is a talented writer. I try not to judge modern authors because I always find them inferior to the classic writers of our past. In the following critique, please do not imagine that I am saying "Straw into Gold" is not worth reading at all. It may very well be. Ms. Cisneros may be an engaging and interesting person. The photo provided shows her to be a lovely, thoughtful woman, with stylish cowboy boots and an impressive arm tattoo. The real question is whether she should be in an American literature textbook assigned to tens, or hundreds, of thousands of students whose teachers know they must teach this reading or risk sending their students into a standardized exam unprepared for what will surely appear given the predilections of the testing agency. Has Ms. Cisneros, a living author, proven that her writings belong among the gallery of the greats? Let us put her own words to the test. Here are opening lines from some of the documents appearing in this chapter, including "Straw into Gold."

Thomas Jefferson:
When in the Course of human events, it becomes necessary for one people to dissolve the political bands that have connected them with another and to assume among the powers of the earth, the separate and equal station to which the Laws of Nature and of Nature's God entitle them, a decent respect to the opinions of mankind requires that they should declare the causes which impel them to the separation.

Thomas Paine:
These are the times that try men's souls. The summer soldier and the sunshine patriot will, in this crisis, shrink from the service of his country; but he that stands it now deserves the thanks of man and woman. Tyranny, like Hell, is not easily conquered; yet we have this consolation with us, that the harder the conflict, the more glorious the triumph.

Benjamin Franklin:
It was about this time I conceived the bold and arduous project of arriving at moral perfection. I wished to live without committing any fault at any time; I would conquer all that either natural inclination, custom, or company might lead me into. As I knew, or thought I knew, what was right and wrong, I did not see why I might not always do the one and avoid the other.

Sandra Cisneros:
When I was living in an artists' colony in the south of France, some fellow Latin-Americans who taught at the university in Aix-en-Provence invited me to share a home-cooked meal with them. I had been living abroad almost a year then on an NEA grant, subsisting mainly on French bread and lentils while in France so that my money could last longer. So when the invitation to dinner arrived, I accepted without hesitation. Especially since they had promised Mexican food.

Ms. Cisneros goes on to describe the challenges of making corn tortillas as opposed to flour tortillas. She compares the difficulty of making tortillas to writing a critical essay for her MFA degree. (Benjamin Franklin for his part did not attend more than two years of school and taught himself how to write essays using Addison's *Spectator* as a model. This self-education is famously described in the *Autobiography* but does not appear in *The American Experience*, a book that occasionally attempts to instruct students how to write. Franklin also invented a stove, bifocals, the lightning rod, and desks with arm rests as now used in colleges and high schools, as well as discovering the basic principles of electricity. It is not known whether he could make either flour or corn tortillas.) In case the students do not understand the trials of tortilla-production, an illustration is provided, under the caption "Critical Viewing": "Judging from this painting by Mexican artist Diego Rivera, explain the challenges tortilla making would present to someone who had never made them." For students who do not readily see the fruitful comparisons between Sandra Cisneros's and Benjamin Franklin's experiences, another prompt reads "Are the challenges Cisneros describes similar in any way to those Franklin set for himself?" Mmm . . . That's a tough one: moral perfection or making tortillas? Establishing a fire department, lending library, philosophical society, school, militia, colonial union, and post office (to say nothing of a successful printing business), and later, the *United States of America* on the one hand, or getting a master's degree on the other?

If students were to be hooked by this modern story that hinges so much on the making of tortillas, and decided to look up Ms. Cisneros on the web, what would they find? Prentice Hall's *The American Experience* is constantly clamoring about students doing "research," and its editors are eager to prepare them for life in a technological world, so let's do a little web-surfing with teenage students in mind. A quick glance at Amazon would tell students that Sandra Cisneros has written two works of poetry, one titled *My Wicked Wicked Ways,* with an appropriately lascivious cover of herself, the other called *Loose Woman: Poems.* A *Publishers Weekly* review excerpted on the Amazon site offers a sample of Cisneros's verse:

> I am . . .
> The lust goddess without guilt.
> The delicious debauchery.
> You bring out
> the primordial exquisiteness in me.

> [And]

> Because someone once
> said Don't
> do that!
> you like to do it!

We further learn from the review that Cisneros "delves with urgency into things carnal—sequins, cigars, black lace bras and menstrual blood." Clearly, we've come a long way . . . from Anne Bradstreet.

If students were to do a little further digging by looking up Ms. Cisneros on the ever-popular destination for school "research," Wikipedia, they would discover much more about this author. They would learn that she is a "key figure in Chicana literature" whose work "deals with the formation of Chicana identity, exploring the challenges of being caught between Mexican and Anglo-American cultures, facing the misogynist attitudes present in both these cultures, and experiencing poverty." They would learn about her great breakthrough in graduate school when she realized what she should write about:

She recalls being suddenly struck by the differences between her and her classmates: "It wasn't as if I didn't know who I was. I knew I was a Mexican woman. But, I didn't think it had anything to do with why I felt so much imbalance in my life, whereas it had everything to do with it! My race, my gender, and my class!"

They would further learn of Ms. Cisneros's working out of this imbalance via becoming "the voices of marginalized people through her work, such as the 'thousands of silent women' whose struggles are portrayed in *The House on Mango Street*," perhaps her best-known work. In one dramatic scene in that collection of stories, we discover, a young female "describes her 'sexual initiation'—an assault by a group of Anglo-American boys while awaiting her friend Sally at the fairground. She feels stricken and powerless after this, but above all betrayed; not only by Sally, who was not there for her, but 'by all the women who ever failed to contradict the romantic mythology of love and sex.'" Further, we are told by the anonymous Wiki-author, who seems to be an admirer, that "Cisneros illustrates how this romantic mythology, fueled by popular culture, is often at odds with reality in *Woman Hollering Creek and Other Stories*, where multiple references to romantic telenovelas obsessively watched by the female characters are juxtaposed with the abuse and poverty they face in their own lives."

Now, admittedly, the textbook does not tell us to do this research on the work of Ms. Cisneros. A student would have to undertake such an inquiry on her own. Nonetheless, there does seem to be an advocacy of Ms. Cisneros's work in the book. More tellingly, this may not have been the first time students would have seen this author. The Common Core itself, in Appendix B, recommends a selection called "Eleven" taken from *Woman Hollering Creek and Other Stories*, one of her several books that de-mythologizes romance.[87] That selection would be read by

---

[87] Whereas two of Ms. Cisneros's works are recommended in Appendix B of the Common Core English Standards, none of Benjamin Franklin's is. The reader will recall that I mentioned yet another work of Cisneros in my preface, this one to be found in the Pearson/Prentice Hall tenth-grade literature textbook.

students between the sixth and eighth grades. Though the passage itself does not overtly assault romance, a student with an inquiring mind who liked this passage might decide to read the book. And isn't that what girls at thirteen or fourteen need more than anything: their ideas of romance to be de-mythologized?

If we view the time spent in school through the window of Franklin's maxim—"Dost thou love life, then do not waste time, for time is the stuff that life is made of"—and thus consider that every moment spent in a literature class is precious; if we truly believe that whatever young people read in school will shape their lives; if we still hope to form our students' minds through the best models of taste, principle, and command of the English language; if we want to inspire young men and women with stories of the heroic, then do we honestly think the time given to reading "Straw into Gold" would be well spent?[88] Or are the editors taking precious space that could be given to gold and turning it into straw? Would students profit more from six more pages devoted to Franklin's *Autobiography* or these taken up by Cisneros?

The reader may wonder, "What's a mere six pages? The students will still get a taste of Franklin and Paine and Jefferson." Maybe, but only a taste: half a bottle of water offered to a man coming out of a desert. The unit called "A Nation is Born" begins on page 96 and ends on page 207. If you exclude the pages that feature writings not belonging to the Founding period (League of Women Voters, Cisneros, etc.); instruction in alleged literary analysis, reading strategies, and other aspects of two-bit literary criticism; introductions of the writers; illustrations; writings of slaves; selections of the Common Core English Standards; and commentary by and a book plug for, Professor Andrews, the "award-winning scholar and teacher" who turned us off of the Founders in the introduction, then how many pages of the Founding Fathers' own writings and speeches do we end up with? Twenty-three. That's right: twenty-three out of one-hundred-eleven, or right at twenty percent. Those other eighty-eight pages your tax dollars are paying for, by the way.

There is more at stake. Whatever the merits of Cisneros's autobiographical prose, her writing has a very different purpose from Jefferson's and Paine's and Franklin's. While her purpose—

---

[88] The allusion to *Rumpelstiltskin* would be lost on students, as the story does not appear in the Common Core.

and the purpose of the editors—is to draw the reader's attention to her ethnicity and gender, the writings of the Founders were meant to be universal in nature, though manifested in a particular political order. The Founders meant to express eternal truths concerning the nature of human beings and their efforts to achieve liberty, justice, and happiness. Paine did not write, "These are the times that try Anglo-Scottish souls." Jefferson did not write, "When in the course of middle-class human events." Franklin *did* once write that in America a man is known not for "who he is" but for "what he can do." What he meant by that turn of phrase was that whereas in Europe a person is invariably categorized by what social class he comes from or by his connections, in America a man (or woman) is allowed to rise or fall according to his own merits. America is not simply a place on a map or a political entity. America is an idea that means something: the land of opportunity for anyone who wants to work hard and to live honestly. Nowadays, the self-proclaimed American intelligentsia found in the universities and in the media and in the higher ranks of the publishing industry in big companies like Pearson/Prentice Hall have done their best to suppress this foundational principle of our nation. They want people to be known foremost by who they are—as African-American, as Latino/Latina, as female, as "low-income," as somehow permanently disadvantaged or in need— rather than by what they can do. They want America to be a place where people have always been oppressed and will continue to be oppressed. Consequently, even in a literature textbook, in a chapter titled "A Nation is Born," these pseudo-guardians of our literary heritage cannot allow the Founding Fathers to speak for themselves. They cannot risk young people learning the self-evident truths on which this great nation was founded. They distort those truths whenever they can; they hide them when they must.

This transparent aim of promoting radical multiculturalism to the detriment of the universal principles of right and wrong, of liberty and happiness, on which our great nation was founded— and to the disadvantage of the exceptional history of American achievement—was already a trend in the textbook publishing over the last twenty years. It has now been given an official imprimatur by the Common Core, an unaccountable authority that controls the curriculum of forty-five states. Recall that Benjamin Franklin's name does not appear in the Common Core English Standards.

The textbooks of today feature a parity of Cisneros with Franklin, of tortillas with founding a great nation. The ghost of literature future will likely feature no Franklin at all. But maybe there will be some black lace and menstrual blood.

Prentice Hall's Common Core textbook fails on all counts. It is not a book devoted primarily to LITERATURE. It does not accurately reflect The American Experience. It is not a Teacher's Edition that any knowledgeable teacher would ever use. Its selection of readings does not put forward a true common core. And its transparent bias is one that few parents would tolerate if they knew what was really taking place in their children's schools. Anyone who takes a serious look at this book, and who could see how it is employed in classrooms across the nation, would recognize it to be not just a silly book, but a betrayal of all the important educational and human principles on which this nation was founded.

Lest anyone imagine that the absurdities, bias, and lost opportunities end with the editors' treatment of the Founding Fathers, let us not cease to submit facts to a candid world.

On page 219, next to the sketch of a pouting, Goth-like seeming adolescent with a peacock-feathered quill in her hand, a short article appears under the heading, "Emily Dickinson: Poet, Recluse . . . Gamer?" We learn that several video games exist devoted to Emily Dickinson. The creator of *The Sims* is quoted as saying, "If she (Dickinson) were alive today, she'd be an Internet addict, and she'd probably have a really amazing blog." Common Sense Question Number One: If Dickinson would be a gamer (as we are told by modern video game producers) does that mean teenagers have a license to "game" rather than read books? Common Sense Question Number Two: If Dickinson had spent her time playing video games, would she have written beautiful and memorable poetry? Common Sense Question Number Three: "There is no frigate like a gaming console": How does that fare as memorable verse?

On page 290, students are treated to a similar vignette on "Poe and Pop Culture." If you did not know that Lou Reed, Joan Baez, Judy Collins, Iron Maiden, Good Charlotte, Public Enemy, Green Day, the Alan Parsons Project, and Japanese pop star Utada Hikaru have music related to Edgar Allan Poe, now you do. Teachers are

225

urged to cater to this facet of pop culture: "You may wish to have interested students present Poe artifacts to the class. For example, students may wish to find and play examples of Poe-related songs by the musicians listed in the text." Common Sense Observation: How hard will it be for a kid on the back row to find a "Poe connection" to "Stairway to Heaven"?

Two whole chapters of *Moby Dick* appear in the section "A Growing Nation." (The complete novel has 135 chapters and an epilogue.) The first chapter, beginning with unforgettable words, "Call me Ishmael," is not one of them. In the two-page resource center/shopping mall hocking Common Core gadgets, there is no recommendation of an unabridged edition of Melville's classic. Under the category of "enrichment," students are advised to research whaling voyages in books or on the Internet, to research hunting rituals performed by "two different peoples in North America or elsewhere," to "find out more about these amazing mammals" (including information about the world's whaling population today and whether whales are in danger of extinction), to follow the research of modern cetologists (whale scientists), and to research the history of whaling in order to debate whether whaling should be prohibited internationally. Teachers, for their part, are asked to "obtain recordings of whale songs [songs sung *by* whales] to play for students." None of these sundry "enrichment" activities and invitations to "research" contemplates reading the whole book! Worse, featuring the last chapter of the book ("The Chase—Third Day") spoils the ending for anyone who might be inclined to read this great story.

Beginning on page 392, just after Thoreau's "Civil Disobedience," under the auspices of "reading for information," students are treated to the EPA pamphlet "Water on Tap: what you need to know," answering the pressing question: "Where Does My Drinking Water Come From And How Is It Treated?" That vital document is followed by a 2007 South Florida Environmental Report pertaining to the Kissimmee River Restoration and Upper Basin Initiatives. In this spine-tingler we are made aware that "Another Year of Above-Average Rainfall in the Kissimmee Basin Poses Regional Water Management Challenges." Five pages later a brief quotation of Thoreau appears with no visible trace of irony: "Give me a WILDNESS whose glance no CIVILIZATION can endure."

Out of chronological sequence, we are introduced to another contemporary scholar on pages 474-475. Like Professor Andrews (whom we meet several times in this volume), Professor Nell Irvin Painter is a specialist in African-American Studies. Although she addresses the issue of discrimination later on, at this juncture, *before* the unit on the Civil War, she deals with the topic of "periodization." Periodization refers to the organization of historical or literary periods according to certain themes, such as the Renaissance or Romanticism. Professor Painter explains how she determined the periodization of her book, *Standing at Armageddon*:

> In 1877, however, new conflicts eclipsed the focus on Southern political terrorism. . . . A nationwide strike of railroad workers occurred in 1877 that began a whole new era in which politics revolved around working people and strikes. . . . What about the end? Where should my period and my book end? . . . I found an echo of 1877's strikes and riots in 1919, the year contemporaries called the "Great Upheaval." There was the end of my period, a time in which working people and their issues once again dominated American politics.
> . . . My periodization of 1877-1919 reflects my belief that working people and their concerns lie at the heart of the politics of the era.

Common Sense Speculation Number One: Professor Painter is decidedly pro-labor, pro-union, anti-robber-baron, and anti-big-business. Common Sense Speculation Number Two: The editors of *The American Experience* are cleverly employing Professor Painter (an African-American woman and scholar of African-American Studies) to paint *labor* as the logical successor to slavery as a socio-political issue needing redress, and thereby Big Business as the logical successor to slaveholding. Common Sense Speculation Number Three: The editors of Prentice Hall's *The American Experience* will never feature as a foray into "recent scholarship" my colleague Burt Folsom and his book *The Myth of the Robber Barons*.

227

Those who consider my charge of bias in this LITERATURE book unfair should take a look at pages 550-551. Here Professor Painter gets to promote another book: *Sojourner Truth: A Life, A Symbol*. On these two pages she makes the point that Ms. Truth suffered discrimination in Washington, D.C. on a public streetcar. Professor Painter also tells us that this experience "was one she (Truth) shared with many other black people trying to get from one place to another before the middle of the twentieth century." That statement is entirely true, and students should learn about such things, though I am not entirely sure why Truth's "An Account of an Experience with Discrimination" that follows Professor Painter's introduction is not placed in a *history* class. Still more do I wonder why the other side of the story is not told. Of all the documents in this unit, except for Lincoln's Gettysburg Address (see below), none involves a white person stating that slavery is a moral and political evil. Nothing appears from William Lloyd Garrison, Horace Greeley, or another abolitionist writer we shall name later. Of course, the editors do not go back to statements by the Founding Fathers against slavery. Nor do they bother to quote the son of a Founder, John Quincy Adams, who was the most vocal opponent of slavery to have held high political office before Lincoln. The treatment of Lincoln is also strange. Although the Gettysburg Address is included (though mishandled), and his picture is displayed in several places, what we might call the culture of Lincoln is missing. Most notably, Walt Whitman's great poem "O Captain, My Captain!" which used to be a staple of American literature textbooks and plays a prominent role in *Dead Poets Society*, is inexplicably absent. Finally, although the book has a couple of famous slave spirituals ("Go Down, Moses," "Swing Low, Sweet Chariot"), nothing is said about *The Battle Hymn of the Republic*, which includes these lines:

As He died to make men holy,
Let us die to make men free;
While God is marching on.

The impression is left then that America was an entirely racist country, that no white man ever took offense at or opposed on principle slavery or discrimination, that hundreds of thousands of men who fought for the Union were not willing to "die to make men free," and that not until the civil rights movement of the

Fifties and Sixties did things begin to get better for black people in America.

These sins of omission, however, are not the most obvious case of bias in this unit on the Civil War. Rather, at the end of this vignette and promotional dedicated to Painter, teachers are instructed, under the heading "Critical Reading" and right next to a Common Core logo, to help students *integrate* their knowledge and ideas, whatever that means:

> **Integration of Knowledge and Ideas** Identify two ways in which Painter's commentary helps you better understand Sojourner Truth's experiences and reactions. [Students' Edition]
>
> **Possible response:** [in Teacher's Edition] Painter's commentary shows how the incidents Truth relates are similar to events in our own time. By mentioning other examples, the commentary also shows how innocent people suffer the effects of racial prejudice.
>
> **Integration of Knowledge and Ideas** Decide what an individual who experiences or witnesses discrimination should do. [Students' Edition]
>
> **Possible response:** [in Teacher's Edition]: Individuals experiencing or witnessing discrimination should record the name of the person doing the discriminating and report the incident as soon as possible. Witnesses should also do their best to take care of the victims if there is physical injury. They should also make it clear that they saw what happened and that it will be reported.

First, this is bad reading or a deliberate misreading. Professor Painter writes nothing about discrimination in "our own time." Second, the comments about discrimination in "our own time" are purely assertion. They suggest that America still suffers from the same kinds of racial prejudice that existed in the nineteenth century and during the civil rights struggles of the Sixties. That is, at the very least, a highly contested claim—and likely an outright falsehood. Third, the "possible responses" in the Teacher's

Edition purposely gin up teenagers to be witnesses to (and perhaps sufferers of) racial prejudice. Anyone who knows anything about teenagers knows that they are eager to take offense at the drop of a hat, even when no offense is given. Finally, this entire exchange is pure activism and not the teaching of literature. It has no place in a high-school textbook.

The treatment of Lincoln's Gettysburg Address on pages 537-539 explains why the students of today do not understand this incomparable speech. The commentary provided in the Teacher's Edition reveals the editors' utter incompetence in the face of words that are beautiful, moving, and profound. They fail to explain the language, the meaning, and the principle. Inexcusably, they do not remind teachers that the words "dedicated to the proposition that all men are created equal" are an echo of the Declaration. In fact, the editors mishandle the Gettysburg Address in much the same way they do the Declaration: by failing to discuss the important things. Their account is so brief and innocuous that there is virtually nothing to say about it.

On page 545, however, the editors do provide students with a great movie placard of *Cold Mountain*, starring Jude Law, Nicole Kidman, and Renée Zellweger. Four pages of dialogue from that movie follow.

There is no selection from Harriet Beecher Stowe's *Uncle Tom's Cabin* in the chapter called "A Nation Divided." This is nothing short of outrageous, given that it is likely the most politically influential novel ever written in this country. Perhaps if there were a recent movie version of it, the book would have gained the editors' attention. Lincoln's comment about Stowe being "the little woman who started this big war" seems not to be enough.

In Part 2, "Forging New Frontiers," *twelve* pages (out of 61 in the section, or 687, if you count the whole book) have Mark Twain's own words on them. The only complete work is "The Celebrated Jumping Frog of Calaveras County," which occupies six pages in the textbook. In this section supposedly on Mark Twain, *five* pages are given to Bill Bryson (b. 1951) and his *The Life and Times of the Thunderbolt Kid*. As pathetic as this showing is, it is more Mark Twain than is recommended in the Common Core English Standards at the high-school level, in which we find *no Mark Twain whatsoever*!

Not surprisingly, the editors feature a short story by Kate Chopin, "The Story of an Hour." For those unaware of Chopin's writings, the overviews in both the teacher's and students' editions provide insight:

[Teacher's Edition]:
Mrs. Mallard gets the unexpected news that her husband has been killed in an accident. She quickly recovers from the shock to discover that what she feels is relief. Though she mourns his passing, she delights in the freedom that will now be hers. Shut in her room, she relishes the opportunities ahead of her. When Mr. Mallard returns as unexpectedly as he supposedly died, Mrs. Mallard suffers a fatal heart attack. The doctors, mistakenly assuming that she had been grieving, attribute the death to "joy that kills."

[Students' Edition]:
BACKGROUND "The Story of an Hour" was considered daring in the nineteenth century. The editors of at least two magazines refused the story because they thought it was immoral. They wanted Chopin to soften her female character, to make her less independent and unhappy in her marriage. Undaunted, Chopin continued to deal with issues of women's growth and emancipation in her writing, advancing ideas that are widely accepted today.

The textbook does not specify which ideas are widely accepted. Is it the idea that a married woman gains freedom on the death of her husband? Or the idea that living only for oneself is the highest good? A familiarity with Chopin's works reveals that she was hardly in tune with what we now call "family values." In case teachers and students miss the transparent gist of the story, the editors offer commentary:

Ask students: Which part of the paragraph illustrates Mrs. Mallard's independence?

Answer: Her independence becomes clear when she spreads her arms to welcome the future—it is hers alone.
Ask students: What does Mrs. Mallard's action symbolize, and how does it affect readers?
Possible response: The action symbolizes Mrs. Mallard's desire for independence. Readers are forced to reflect on the negative aspects of nineteenth-century marriages.

Mmm . . . Wasn't a nineteenth-century marriage sort of like, well, marriage? It should probably go without saying that none of the "essential questions" asks the students to consider the husband's perspective or whether Mrs. Mallard reveals herself as selfish or inhumane, despite these lines in the story itself:

> She knew that she would weep again when she saw the kind, tender hands folded in death; the face that had never looked save with love upon her, fixed and gray and dead. But she saw beyond that bitter moment a long procession of years to come that would belong to her absolutely. And she opened and spread her arms out to them in welcome.
> There would be no one to live for her during those coming years; she would live for herself.

Years that "belong to her absolutely": Did the Mallards have children? Did Mrs. Mallard want children? Why did she get married in the first place? Would that the editors had told us which ideas of Chopin's are "generally accepted today." Is it a good thing that those ideas are accepted?

Lest the reader think volume two of *The American Experience* is any better we shall mention a couple of glaring items. Arthur Miller's *The Crucible* is printed in its entirety. A total of 141 pages are dedicated to Miller's play or to some aspect of McCarthyism in this "extended study." Images of Winona Ryder and Daniel Day-Lewis (from the movie) are liberally spread throughout the section as well as cautionary warnings against anti-communist witch-hunting. The section includes a script from

George Clooney and Grant Heslov's *Good Night, and Good Luck*, about Edward R. Murrow's taking on McCarthy. We do not have the space to go into the merits of *The Crucible* as literature, the attention it is given compared to the inattention towards much greater works of literature (Miller's 141 pages vs. Twain's 12), or the many factual errors contained in this textbook (e.g., overlooking the fact that there *was* an attempt on the part of communists to take over the motion picture industry). The reader will no doubt recognize this "extended study" as a transparent exercise in blasting *right-wing extremists*. The intent of the editors becomes clear when we realize that they print this entire play while *The Scarlet Letter* is wholly missing from volume one of *The American Experience*. Is Miller so much the superior author to Hawthorne? Don't forget that Demi Moore starred in the movie version of the latter's classic.

The treatment of World War II is a case of editorial malpractice that should live in infamy. Most of the section is dedicated to the bombing of Hiroshima. Nothing is said about the thousands of pamphlets dropped on the city, warning the occupants to leave. Nothing is said about how the war began. (Mysteriously, there is no movie script from *Pearl Harbor*, though Ben Affleck is the star. Obviously, John Wayne's *Sands of Iwo Jima* would not be to the editors' tastes.) Nothing appears that portrays America and the Allies in a positive light in the rest of the war. Very little is said about the war in Europe. Churchill is entirely missing. F.D.R. is mentioned only in passing. The instructions to the teachers at the beginning of the unit reveal the tone:

Selection Planning Guide
In this section, nonfiction prose and a single stark poem etch into a reader's mind the dehumanizing horror of world war. An excerpt from John Hersey's *Hiroshima* recounts the routines of ordinary people in the hours and seconds before the obliterating flash of history's first atomic bomb attack. Randall Jarrell's "The Death of the Ball Turret Gunner," in six lines, enumerates losses of youth, life, and humanity.

Think Aloud: Model the Skill
Say to students:

When I was reading the history textbook, I noticed that the writer included profiles of three war heroes, all of whom fought for the Allies. The writer did not include similar profiles for fighters on the other side. I realize that this choice reflects a political assumption: that readers want to read about only their side's heroes.

After eleven pages of Hersey's *Hiroshima*, including graphic pictures of the devastation (recall that Twain had only twelve pages and Franklin's *Autobiography* five-and-a-half), and after Randall Jarrell's short anti-heroic poem, "The Death of the Ball Turret Gunner," this "Critical Reading" question appears:

Integration of Knowledge and Ideas Take a Position:
Jarrell based his poem on observations of World War II, a war that has been called "the good war." Is there such a thing as a "good war"? Explain.

Once again, the deck has been stacked. No accounts of America's heroism in World War II appear in this section. The last line of Jarrell's poem is, "When I died they washed me out of the turret with a hose." Of the thousands of accounts of American bravery, of the scores of great speeches articulating and praising the Allies' conduct in this war, of the many moving stories about the liberation of Europe, none appears in this Common Core textbook whose editors have the audacity to call such transparent indoctrination "critical reading." Our generation grew up thinking that our grandfathers were heroes, that they had fought on the right side of the war, that they had—through their courage and sacrifice—saved Western Civilization and freedom in the world. Well, our textbook editors have come along to clean up that mess. Today's generation of children are even now being told a different story. Tomorrow's generation, who will not have met their great-grandfathers, will be appropriately ashamed for that Greatest Generation's killing of innocents in World War II—just as we modern Americans are now ashamed of our Founding Fathers.

My wife, to whom I have shown many of these educational travesties, has become sick at heart in seeing what the Common Core is up to. As a lover of literature, she looks for the meaning of life in books. She looks for hope in books. As she puts it, one of the greatest gifts of literature is that it invites us to dream. The authors of the Common Core, along with their willing accomplices the rich textbook publishers, are more than story-killers. They are dream-killers. They kill the dreams of young men and women precisely at the moment of their lives when they ought to be building their dreams and figuring out how to pursue them. It is abundantly clear that whatever dreams the arch-testers of the Common Core will allow children to have, they will not be the traditional dreams that have made this country great and flourishing and its people happy. The Common Core is clearly hostile to Christianity, to the Founding Fathers and the Constitution, to traditional ideas of manhood and womanhood, to marriage and the family, to the idea of America's unique example in the world, to any lesson about life and liberty that could be taught to us by a "dead white man." Sandra Cisneros and Kate Chopin are not just women writers. They are women writers who wholly despise the traditional family. And they are being deployed to manipulate the feelings of young women, to crush their own dreams of love and family. Professor Andrews is not a broad-minded scholar who loves black and white authors equally and happily traces the growth of black literature in America as he extols the merits of the Founders. He plainly does not like the Founding Fathers of this nation. Yet he is the scholar called in to shape our children's thoughts on the Founding Fathers and this country.

Some of the things we see in these textbooks are just laughably stupid. Others are downright treacherous. There is an evil genius at work here. And it is a cowardly one. The authors of the Common Core and the textbook editors know that they could not win an open and honest argument about what literature ought to be taught in school and how it ought to be taught. They regard us— *We the People*—as the masses, as conservative and reactionary throwbacks who have to be programmed with a sub-standard education lest we get in the way of their social planning. Yet they are the ones utterly devoid of vision and wholly without a dream— at least a happy one.

Yet another author the editors of *The American Experience* feature is Sylvia Plath. As most people know, Plath committed suicide at age thirty by putting her head in an oven. Under the banner of "protest literature," students are supposed to read "Mirror," a depressing poem about a woman looking in a mirror and seeing herself get old. Students are instructed that this poem reflects "<u>collective</u> attitudes that create pain in the lives of many people. [It] addresses the premium placed on physical appearance by society and the <u>anxiety</u> it produces in women in particular, especially as they age." So the physical beauty of women is yet another *standard* we have to give up as dictated by these so-called Standards, something to be unhappy about because it causes so much "pain in the lives of many people." What the woman in this poem does not reflect upon, interestingly, are the many elements of life that the editors of our textbook have sought to undermine. Why does she not think about God as she gets closer to death? Why does she not think about the children she has borne and raised? Why does she not think about the people she has helped—to whom she has given charity and love? Why does she not feel proud of the country she has grown up in and fortunate to have lived there? Why does she not think about her husband and how happy their lives have been together? Why does she not try to express as best she can some beautiful and noble sentiment to her "dear and loving husband" or to a "dear and loving child"? Is it the case that she did not experience those joys? Whose fault is that? In short, is this the poetry of protest or the wailing of surrender and self-indulgent self-infatuation? What *good* are young women and men to derive from it? Obviously, no "critical thinking" question prompts students to consider whether Plath's "Mirror" offers a glimpse at the modern Narcissus. After all, the students have not read the story of Narcissus.

"What is the American, this new man?" Crèvecoeur famously asked. According to *The American Experience*, there has been nothing very dear or loving about the American man, nor brave and honorable. And the American woman has been unhappy because of him and his nineteenth-century constructs of marriage. Reading literature in the way the editors of this textbook dictate may lead to young people's being "turned off" of reading great stories, poetry, and speeches altogether. It could very well turn them off of life.

Chapter Nine
A True Common Core

If the Common Core is the Brave New World of absurdity, superficiality and political bias in education, let us look to the brave *old* world of truth and common sense to revive the nation's schools. That may seem to be a paradoxical or even backward point of view in the "twenty-first-century global economy." Yet experience hath shown that revivals in education begin by embracing not so much the past but the *permanent*: the true classics, the best that has been thought and said and done and discovered. Just as the Renaissance began with a conversation with the ancient world, just as nineteenth-century British elites sent their sons to school to study Rome so they could learn to speak eloquently and to run an empire, so should *all* modern American children have the chance to study the classics of the Western tradition, the Founding of America, and the great literature emerging out of the true *American Experience*. Our children should study such things in depth, without the interference of the post-modern purveyors of perversity, pettiness, and ennui. Should students want to read the unhappy tales of our current cultural decline, they can opt to do so in college—at their own expense (at least in part) rather than on the taxpayer's dime.

So how do we do that? Well, the first thing we should do is reestablish a true common core. Perhaps the most egregious subterfuge perpetrated by the authors of the Common Core is the choice of the name. Essentially, the arch-testers have hijacked a brand name and betrayed a principle. Before 2010 everyone in the world of true school reform and most liberally educated folk knew what a common core is. The Common Core that forty-five states have been tricked into adopting is manifestly not a common core. Until we recognize the wholesale fraud that has been committed, we shall never have a chance at genuine school reform. We must relearn, then, what constitutes a true common core.

A true common core is exactly what its name implies. Certain things are read and studied *in common*. And those things are the most important—the core—the heart of the matter. Presumably, a genuine common core in American schools would be a set of books and other readings that everyone must know in order to participate in a common conversation about what it means to be an American and a human being. A common core is a remedy for the communication breakdown portrayed in the story of the Tower of Babel, a collapse in common conversation that is being repeated in this nation today. To overcome that breakdown, we cannot say that we should all read books of *similar difficulty*. We must all read the *same* books, or a number of the same books—the best books—so that we know how to talk to each other.

The new Common Core English Standards do not constitute a common core. They do not prescribe any single book or set of books. The authors of the Common Core make no claims that certain books simply have to be read for someone to consider himself an educated person and a culturally literate American. Had they done so, we as a nation could be having a much more interesting and productive discussion right now concerning school reform and the education of our children. Had they told us that all students in high school, whatever else they might study, should read just eight certain books—only two per year—that everyone in his right mind considers classics, then we could all be reading those great books and trying to understand them. We could be having a nationwide conversation about how literature ought to be taught with real books in mind, rather than paying homage to contrived, bogus "standards" that never do more than butcher great literature. Had the Common Core English Standards held up just a few great books, college professors could finally know what their incoming students had actually read. Heck, even advertisers and comedians would know what jokes they could tell about literary characters. We might be treated to a rash of witty references to Romeo and Juliet or Hester Prynne. More crucially, we would also have a much clearer idea of what the authors of the so-called Common Core want our students to be taught. In short, if the Common Core had advocated not a set of *standards* but a set of books, this nation that has in many ways lost its ability to read (due in large part to progressive education) could be reading again.

And that reading would not be confined to schools. If these books are important, not only children should be reading them. Sadly, none of this is happening. As it stands, everyone in the nation right now is equally in the dark as to what students will be taught in conformity to the Common Core.

The chief virtue of a genuine common core is that it produces clarity. Everyone who takes part in a true common core knows what is being taught. Some people may argue with this or that book being in a core, but everyone knows what the book is. If nothing else, intelligent people can then have a discussion about the merits of the book. Any testing regime that simultaneously requires no single book to be read *and* recommends potentially everything under the sun is simply not a common core. Unless the creators of the "Common Core" just stumbled into the name blindly, then, which is unlikely, we are forced to choose between one of two explanations for the egregious misnomer. Either the authors of the Common Core do not really understand what a common core is and did the best they could, given that ignorance, in producing this monstrosity, like Dr. Frankenstein working with different pieces of human matter. Or they knew exactly what they were doing and produced an educational regime that is the polar opposite of a true common core, trading on the name its philosophical opponents use to describe traditional, liberal-arts education. It is hard to say which is worse. Either the de facto controllers of public education in America are philosophical and educational lightweights, or they are astute manipulators of language and public sentiment, having appropriated a term owned by the educational traditionalists in order to institutionalize a progressive educational agenda. If we the American people do nothing to take back the public schools, and to require them to teach a true common core of great books, then we will show that we have completely lost sense of what those books are: our means of having a common conversation about the common good of human beings and citizens.

How do we get back to a true common core of classics? How do we make our children in the Age of the Internet interested in stories first told long ago about people who, in the case of literature, never existed? It might actually be easier than you think. The truly paradoxical nature of great literature is that the characters, with their interesting array of exploits and hopes and problems, often seem more *real* than much of what takes place in our day-to-day lives. That is, the characters in classic literature appear human. And human beings are interested in human things, naturally so, at least when they have not been acculturated to boredom in the public schools of this nation. So the Holy Grail of school reform everyone is supposedly looking for is really easy to find. It is to be found in the great books of our tradition. Once the books are in place, we need to find teachers who know them, who *truly* know them, to be brought into the nation's classrooms.[89] Then we will have good schools and all the blessings that come with good schools. That is all there is to it. We must, then, learn what a true common core looks like and how it works.

What follows is a high-school curriculum, mostly of my own design, that has been working wonderfully in schools for over ten years. Though we are concentrating on the high school for the moment, the reader should realize that students would have been well-prepared for this course of study by a rigorous K-8 education. In the middle school, for example, students would have read books normally delayed until high school, if read at all, such as *The Tempest, Dr. Jekyll and Mr. Hyde, A Christmas Carol, To Kill a Mockingbird, Fahrenheit 451, Animal Farm*, and *Lord of the Flies*. In addition to literature and history, there are some classes taught in the junior and senior years that bear upon those subjects, so I have listed those readings. I shall explain the curriculum a little more after the reader has digested it.

To put yourself in the right frame mind, imagine that you are fifteen and entering high school. You will be working through these books and other readings over the next four years. What would you learn?

---

[89] Currently, such teachers are not particularly welcome in the nation's classrooms. I am referring to the fraud that is teacher certification and the monopoly education schools have over that certification. That is a longer argument that we cannot go into at present.

Freshman Year:

Ancient Literature:

Homer, *The Iliad* (the whole thing)[90]
A couple of Greek plays, e.g., *Oedipus Rex*, *Antigone*
Selections from Plato's *Republic* (on the poets,
   Allegory of the Cave)
Plato, *The Apology* (or read in history)

Virgil, *The Aeneid* (the whole thing)
Roman poetry (students would also be in third-year
   Latin by ninth grade and reading some poetry)
Shakespeare, *Julius Caesar* (read in English class but
   taught when Roman Civil War studied in history)
Addison's *Cato* (if time)
Genesis 1-4

Composition:
The class focuses on grammar and composition and also
   entails the study of classic essays by Bacon, Addison,
   Swift, Johnson, Orwell, et alia

Western Civilization I (Ancient History):

Herodotus, *The Histories*, on the Persian Wars, esp.
   on the 300 Spartans at Thermopylae
Thucydides, *The Peloponnesian War*, (selections,
   esp. Pericles, "Funeral Oration," "Plague Speech";
   The Melian Dialogue; debate on Sicilian expedition)
Plutarch, Lives of Lycurgus, Solon, Pericles, Alcibiades
Plato, *The Republic*, Book VIII on the regimes (monarchy,
   aristocracy, democracy)
Plato, *The Apology* (may be read here if literature pressed
   for time), also *The Crito* may be read, time permitting

---

[90] "What about *The Odyssey*?" you may wonder. I recommend assigning *The Odyssey* for summer reading and then discussing some parts briefly in class before moving on to *The Iliad* (or reading *The Odyssey* in the summer after they have read *The Iliad*). There is a long argument for this approach, which we cannot enter into at the moment. A complete epic ought to be read, whether *The Iliad* or *The Odyssey*.

Aristotle, *The Politics*, Book I

Livy, selections on early Rome
Polybius, *The Histories*, Book VI
Plutarch, Lives of Cato the Elder, Julius Caesar, Cicero
Cicero, Catiline Oration (1st); sel. letters to Atticus and
    Quintus; *De Officiis* (selections)
Caesar, *The Commentaries* (selections)
Augustus, *Res Gestae Divi Augusti*
Tacitus and Suetonius on the Roman emperors
Marcus Aurelius, *Meditations*
Documents from the Judeo-Christian Tradition
    Ten Commandments, life of David,
    Sermon on the Mount

Sophomore Year:

British Literature:

Le Morte D'Arthur (selection) or *Beowulf*
Chaucer, *The Canterbury Tales* (three or four tales)
Shakespeare, *Hamlet* and *Macbeth*, sonnets
Sir Francis Bacon, selected essays, incl. "Of Studies"
Milton, *Paradise Lost* (books IX and X at least)[91]

Joseph Addison, select papers from *The Spectator*
Jane Austen, *Pride and Prejudice* (or *Persuasion*)
Charles Dickens, *Hard Times* (or *A Tale of Two Cities*)[92]
British Romantic poetry

---

[91] After many years of seeing students struggle through the whole of *Paradise Lost*, I have come around to the view that the Golden Rule of reading complete texts must be modified with *Paradise Lost* and that only certain key books should be read. (After all, something must be left for college.) That is also the obvious thing to do with *The Canterbury Tales*. If more Shakespeare could be read in lieu of the complete *Paradise Lost*, that would be ideal. Realize that students in such a school would have begun reading Shakespeare's plays beginning in the sixth grade.

[92] The choices reflect the time it takes to teach each book (*Persuasion* is shorter than *Pride and Prejudice* and would be read in tandem with *A Tale of Two Cities*), teacher preference, and whether other courses teach one of these books. *Oliver Twist* or *Great Expectations* would be read in the eighth grade.

242

Western Civilization II (Medieval, Renaissance,
Reformation, Enlightenment):

Tacitus, *Germania*
Acts of the Apostles (selections)
Augustine, *Confessions* (Books, I, II, VIII),
    City of God (short sel.)
Gregory I, *Account of Benedict's Life*
Rule of Saint Benedict
Einhard, *The Life of Charlemagne* (sel.)
Walter Scott, "Chivalry"
Magna Carta
Documents on the Investiture Conflict
Thomas of Celano, *Life of Saint Francis*
Thomas Aquinas, selection from *The Summa*
Petrarch's Letters (to Homer, Cicero, et al.)
Petrarch, "The Ascent of Mount Ventoux"
Vergerius, "On Liberal Learning"
Leon Battistta Alberti, *On the Family* (sel.)
Castiglione, *The Courtier* (sel.)
Vasari, *Lives of the Artists*, esp. Michelangelo, Leonardo
Art of Leonardo da Vinci, Michelangelo, et alia
Machiavelli, *The Prince* (sel.)
Luther, select documents incl. 95 Theses
Luther and Erasmus on the will
Council of Trent
The Thirty-Nine Articles (Anglican Church)
James I, *The Trew Law of Free Monarchies*
Thomas Hobbes, *Leviathan*, on the state of nature
Isaac Newton, *Principia Mathematica* (sel.)
John Locke, *The Second Treatise of Government*
    (esp. Books II-V, IX)
Adam Smith, *The Wealth of Nations*, "Of the Division
    of Labor," (chs. I and II of Book I); "Of the Expences
    of the Sovereign or Commonwealth," (ch. I of Book V)
Rousseau, *Discourse on Inequality* (if not enough time
    in sophomore year, to be read at beginning of senior
    year as prelude to French Revolution)

Junior Year:

American Literature:

Poetry of Anne Bradstreet
Benjamin Franklin's *Autobiography* (or in history)
Nathaniel Hawthorne, *The Scarlet Letter*
Herman Melville, *Moby Dick* (yes, the whole thing)

Ralph Waldo Emerson, essays, esp. "Self-Reliance"
Henry David Thoreau, selections from *Walden*
Mark Twain, *Huckleberry Finn*
Poetry of Whitman, Poe, Longfellow, Dickinson, Hughes,
    Cullen, Frost, et alia
If time, a novel of Fitzgerald or Hemingway
Poetry of T. S. Eliot
Two or three short stories of Flannery O'Connor

American History to 1900 (two semesters):

The Mayflower Compact
John Winthrop, "A Modell of Christian Charity"
Other colonial documents
Documents on the Great Awakening, including "Sinners"
Benjamin Franklin, documents on the Junto (discussion
    society), fires, education in Philadelphia, the increase
    of mankind, "The Way to Wealth," kite experiment
The Stamp Act documents
Benjamin Franklin, "Rules by Which a Great Empire
    May Be Reduced to a Small One," "An Edict by the
    King of Prussia"
Debate over Independence
Tom Paine, *Common Sense* (selections)
Virginia Declaration of Rights
The Declaration of Independence
George Washington, select letters, Circular to the States
The Northwest Ordinance
The Constitution of the United States and
    The Bill of Rights
Debates on the Constitution, including Anti-Federalists
The Federalist, nos. 1, 10, 39, 51 (overlap with Govt.)

Thomas Jefferson, on education and agriculture
Alexander Hamilton, Report on Public Credit and
Report on Manufactures (selections)
George Washington, Farewell Address, Last Will
Other documents from early national period including
Alien and Sedition Acts, Va./Ky. Resolutions and
Massachusetts Counter-Resolution (also in Govt. class)
Documents from Jacksonian period
Ante-Bellum documents, includ. Calhoun on nullification
and *Dred Scott v. Sandford*
Harriet Beecher Stowe, *Uncle Tom's Cabin* (sel.)
George Fitzhugh, *The Sociology of the South* (sel.)
Frederick Douglass, *Narrative of the Life* . . . (or read in
English)
Abraham Lincoln, "A Fragment on Slavery," Speech on
Dred Scott, "A House Divided," the Lincoln-Douglas
Debates (sel.), First Inaugural, Emancipation Procl.
Gettysburg Address, Second Inaugural
Frederick Douglass, "Self-Made Men"
Post-Civil War documents on Reconstruction, rise of
wealth, Andrew Carnegie on wealth
Documents on populism, includ. Bryan's "Cross of Gold"
Booker T. Washington, *Up From Slavery* & *The Story
of My Life and Work* (sel.)

Government (one semester):

Man as a "political animal," Aristotle, *The Politics*, Book I
Natural rights studied through John Locke, Virginia Decl.
of Rights, The Declaration of Independence
Selections from debates at the Constitutional Convention
The Constitution of the United States
More intensive look at *The Federalist*, nos. 10, 39, 51, 57,
70-74 (selections), 78
The Bill of Rights
Hamilton, Jefferson on the Constitutionality of the Bank
The Marshall Court, select cases, especially *Marbury v.
Madison*, *McCulloch v. Maryland*, *Gibbons v. Ogden*
Alexis de Tocqueville, *Democracy in America*, selections
on the energy of democracy, associations, and tyranny
of the majority

The Taney Court, esp. *Dred Scott v. Sanford*
Lincoln on *Dred Scott*
Abraham Lincoln, War Message delivered on Fourth of
    July, 1861 (argument vs. secession)
Thirteenth, Fourteenth, and Fifteenth Amendments
Plessy v. Ferguson (and, later, *Brown v. Board of Topeka*)
W. Wilson, "What Is Progress?" "The New Freedom"
Amendments XVI-XIX
Franklin Roosevelt, "The Commonwealth Club Address"
The New Deal Court, e.g. *Schechter Poultry v. U.S.*
Franklin D. Roosevelt, "A New Bill of Rights," S/U 1944
Ronald Reagan, "Encroaching Control," March 1961
Lyndon Baines Johnson, "The Great Society"

Moral Philosophy (one semester):

Alasdair MacIntyre, *After Virtue*, ch. 1.
Allan Bloom, "Our Virtue" and "Self-Centeredness" from
    The Closing of the American Mind
Aldous Huxley, *Brave New World*
C. S. Lewis, *The Abolition of Man*
Francis Hutcheson, James Q. Wilson on the moral sense
Adam Smith, *The Theory of Moral Sentiments* (selections)
Aristotle, *The Nicomachean Ethics*, on the def. of virtue
Aristotle and Pieper on the four cardinal virtues
Cicero, *De Officiis* (*On Duties*), selections
George Washington and William Manchester on civility
Cicero and C. S. Lewis on friendship
Benjamin Franklin, et alia on work and entrepreneurship
Genesis 3-4 on man and woman
Traditional and Contemporary Marriage Vows
Pride and Prejudice, Elizabeth visits Pemberley
David Fordyce, *Elements of Moral Philosophy*, marriage
    and parental duties
Richard Brookhiser, on Washington's "fatherhood"
George Washington as Cincinnatus, his sense of duty
John Adams/Thomas Jefferson correspondence (sel.)
Shakespeare, *Henry V* (read prev. as summer reading)
Douglass Adair, "Fame and the Founding Fathers"
Herbert Butterfield, "The Role of the Individual in
    History"

Senior Year:

Modern Literature:

Brief recap/discussion of literature from previous grades
Joseph Conrad, *Heart of Darkness*
Fyodor Dostoyevsky, *Crime and Punishment*
Franz Kafka, *The Metamorphosis*
George Orwell, *1984*
Modern Poetry
One or two other short works of modern literature
depending on time left in the semester.
All students write 20-page senior thesis, anchored in two
or more great books (or readings), one having to be
from grades 9-11, on a topic meant to explain some
aspect of human nature/society (e.g., heroism, faith,
love, justice, etc.)

American History Since 1900 (1st sem. of senior year):

Frederick Jackson Turner, "The Significance of the
Frontier in American History"
W. E. B. Du Bois, *The Souls of Black Folk* (sel.)
Plunkitt of Tammany Hall, "Honest Graft"
Theodore Roosevelt, *Autobiography* (sel.), "The New
Nationalism"
Woodrow Wilson, "The New Freedom"
Calvin Coolidge, speeches on the Boy Scouts, world
peace, the press, the rule of law, and the Declaration of
Independence
Franklin Delano Roosevelt, Commonwealth Club Address;
First Inaugural; State of the Union Address, 1944
Walter Lippmann, "The Dominant Dogma of the Age"
Harry S Truman, "The Fair Deal"
Congressional Rejection of the Fair Deal
Lyndon Baines Johnson, "The Great Society"
Ronald Reagan, "A Time for Choosing"
Martin Luther King, Jr., Letter from the Birmingham Jail,
"I Have a Dream"
Daniel Patrick Moynihan, "The Negro Family"

247

The Sharon Statement
The Port Huron Statement
Ronald Reagan, First Inaugural, Remarks on Tax Reform
    Act, Farewell Address

Foreign Policy (in Am. History class, mostly in senior
year)

George Washington, Farewell Address
Monroe Doctrine
W. G. Sumner, "The Fallacy of Territorial Extension"
Albert Beveridge, "The March of the Flag"
Woodrow Wilson, War Message and Fourteen Points
Charles Lindbergh, "America First"
Franklin Delano Roosevelt, War Message, December 1941
The Atlantic Charter
Winston Churchill, Address to Congress; "Iron Curtain"
    Speech, Fulton, Mo.
Harry S Truman, "The Truman Doctrine"
George F. Kennan, "The Sources of Soviet Conduct"
NSC-68, U. S. Objectives and Programs for National
    Security
Ronald Reagan, Address to the British Parliament;
    Christmas Day Radio Address, 1982; Remarks to the
    National Association of Evangelicals, 1983 ("Evil
    Empire"); Remarks at the Brandenburg Gate, 1987

Modern European History (two semesters)[93]:

Jean-Jacques Rousseau, *Discourse on Inequality*
Abbé Sieyès, "What Is the Third Estate?"
Edmund Burke and Tom Paine on the French Revolution
Maximilien Robespierre, "Principles of Political Morality"
Benjamin Constant, "Ancient and Modern Liberty
    Compared"
John Stuart Mill, *On Liberty* (selections)
British Parliament, Debate on the Ten Hours Bill
Karl Marx, *The Communist Manifesto*

---

[93] This is but a partial list of the many documents that would be read in a Modern
Europe course.

Charles Darwin, *On the Origin of the Species* (sel.)
Friedrich Nietzsche, *On the Genealogy of Morality* (sel.)
Otto von Bismarck, on German Unification
Max Weber, "On Bureaucracy"
V. I. Lenin, on Marxism, "What Is to Be Done?"
Adolf Hitler, *Mein Kampf*, selections
Winston Churchill, selected speeches incl. "Bolshevist
   Atrocities," "Lenin," "The Follies of Socialism," "Wars
   Come Very Suddenly," "Germany Is Arming" (1934),
   "A Total and Unmitigated Defeat," "Blood, Toil, Tears,
   and Sweat," "Arm Yourselves and Be Ye Men of
   Valour," "*This* Was Their Finest Hour," "Give Us the
   Tools," "Never Give In" (at Harrow), "This Is Your
   Victory"

Economics (one semester)[94]:

Adam Smith, *Wealth of Nations*, selections
F. A. Hayek, *The Road to Serfdom*, chs. II, III, VI
Milton Friedman, *Capitalism and Freedom*, chs. I-III
John Maynard Keynes, *The General Theory*. . . selections
Henry Hazlitt, *Economics in One Lesson*
George Gilder, *Wealth and Poverty*, chs. III-VI

Well, there it is. There is a true common core. It is a common
core that, by the way, the Common Core would very much
discourage, as we have seen. We should understand what this
curriculum offers and the principles that govern it.

The first thing the reader should ask himself is, "How many of
these books and other readings did I study in high school? In
college?" My guess is that many of the literary works seem to ring
a bell, but it is unlikely that they were read in full. Did you read
The Iliad cover to cover? *Moby Dick*? Did you read any
Dostoyevsky at all? For some time the standard practice in high
schools has been to read selections from many different texts but to
read very few complete works. As we have seen, the ways of
teaching these works do not lead to understanding. As for the

---

[94] Obviously, an economics textbook would be used. I am not including
textbooks used in history, either.

primary sources featured in the history courses above, the public schools rarely have the students read them and hardly seem to know that such sources exist. If a couple of paragraphs from a *Federalist* paper or Tocqueville appear in a history textbook, the teacher *may* assign them. Otherwise, it is as though Thucydides and Plutarch and Saint Augustine and Martin Luther and James Madison never existed. How about philosophy? Did you read Plato in high school? Aristotle? If you were even told their names, you were lucky.

If, as is likely the case, you were not provided with such a curriculum in high school, then you must ask, "Why not?" "Why wasn't my own school education held to a true standard of the best that has been thought, said, done, and discovered?" These days, those adults who are coming to the realization that their own education was far less than it should have been are channeling their frustration and justified anger into making sure that their children are given a much better education. For this reason, the usurpation that is the Common Core could not come at a worse time. Just as schools of choice are adopting traditional, rigorous curricula, the new regulations are reinstating the old superficiality.

The second thing the reader should realize is that this curriculum is governed by both logic and principle. This is not (as is the Common Core) a tedious list of random books and obscure articles. Rather, it is a curriculum in the true sense: a *course* of studies that starts out at a clear beginning point and takes the student in a definite direction towards a clear ending point or finish line. Believe it or not, there is a rationale behind every book or document appearing in this curriculum. And these different texts speak to each other. If you were to take something out, it could very well affect the whole. Not only do all the history texts clearly follow a tradition and a trajectory (from Aristotle to Magna Carta to the Declaration of Independence to the Gettysburg Address to "I Have a Dream"); not only is the literature arranged by time period in rough correspondence to the historical texts (ancient, British, American, modern); these readings work together to deliver the comprehensive story of human beings trying to achieve liberty and happiness through civilization.

We shall examine the overarching principles in a moment. But let us begin by taking a look at how four seemingly unrelated texts actually work together. For example, what do Aristotle, Jane

Austen, Daniel Patrick Moynihan, and free-market economists, such as Milton Friedman, have in common? On the surface, they have nothing in common. One is an ancient philosopher, one is a nineteenth-century woman novelist, one is a Democrat politician, and the others are largely libertarian (or classical liberal) advocates of the free market. Nothing in common.

Well, not so fast. Aristotle in book I of *The Politics* tells us that the polis is made up of households. The political order, then, is somehow dependent on the domestic order, the family, and we would not expect a good political order to result from ill-managed households. It just so happens that in the Sixties, a liberal scholar/politician named Moynihan warned the nation about the consequences of the breakdown of the black family when out-of-wedlock births were for black children what they now are for white. The breakdown of the family has indisputable economic consequences for children who are born into "single-parent homes," since they are almost always born into poverty. So it should not surprise us to learn that the Greek word for household—*oikos*—is the root of *oikonomos* (household manager), from which we get *economy* and *economics*. It is really plain common sense. Why do men work? For their families. When do they not work? When they don't have families. Therefore, fewer families, fewer men working. This point was brought home by George Gilder in *Wealth and Poverty* and *Men and Marriage*.[95] Furthermore, the breakdown of the family affects the political order. When fewer men work there is naturally more crime, more poverty, less real independence, and quite likely a very different political structure will emerge. So what does Jane Austen have to do with all of this? Well, does not the heart govern the relations between men and women? How men and women love each other (or fail to) affects the political order. And does not love itself have to be governed by reason and prudence lest it end in disaster? (We fail to remember that most great *romances* end in death and disaster, e.g., *Romeo and Juliet*.) That moral truth takes us back to Aristotle who explained the virtue of prudence better than any philosopher. Jane Austen, through her moving stories about men and women pursuing love and learning prudence along the way, is really the greatest modern teacher of Aristotle. Without love and prudence, there can be no family. Without family there can be no

---

[95] Originally titled *Sexual Suicide*.

thriving economy. Without a thriving economy, it is unlikely that there will be justice in the political order. Ergo, the ancient philosopher, the nineteenth-century novelist, the twentieth-century free-market economist, and the twentieth-century liberal politician (at least one) have a great deal to say to each other—and to us. What they have to say is that if we fail in love, as a people, we shall surely fail in everything else. Without an ordered curriculum and good teaching, though, our children will never be a part of that conversation and that lesson.

Creating such a conversation is not that difficult if we know what we are doing. We must simply understand the principles that hold this curriculum together. The first of those principles addresses the differences between literature and history and how those distinct though complementary disciplines must be taught. The reader may have picked up on the fact that in literature relatively few but nonetheless meaty texts are read. This curriculum makes no attempt to teach everything. That is because these stories are to be read with great care and attention, and the means of teaching them is through Socratic discussion. The teacher and students engage with all the characters by examining their words and actions carefully in all the scenes in the book. They will not resort to slapping certain labels on a work of literature (e.g., Romanticism) and then "comparing" it to a lot of other literary works, either read or not read, nor by simplistic plot-graphing and other Mickey Mouse techniques that have plagued schools for forty years. Rather, students will treat the characters as though they are real: get to know their passions, their virtues and vices, their hidden secrets. That takes time. It takes time to get to know a person. When have you ever heard a real human conversation in which one person asks another, "So, what is your characterization, setting, and plot?" Because the Socratic discussion takes time, fewer works of literature can be read. In general, two or three big novels or epics can be read in a year, in addition to a couple of plays, short stories, and poetry. The English teachers and professors who teach in this way call it the "less is more" approach. Reading fewer works overall, the students get to know those works thoroughly, thus gaining far more insight into characters and thereby into human nature.

Many more texts are read in the history classes than in literature. That is not to say that the texts are studied more superficially. Rather, shorter selections are read. Further, history teachers tend to lecture more, and the study of these texts will often consist in teachers more directly taking students through a difficult piece of historical writing. A perfect example of this is Thucydides. Whereas a fifteen-year-old reading *The Iliad* at home will "get" the outline of the story (though no doubt overlook important things), the first time a student tries to read Thucydides on his own, he will most likely "get" nothing out of it. The teacher will thus be more active in leading the discussion, but over time the students will become much better readers of political and philosophical works. Although the number of primary sources read in history may seem a little overwhelming at first, the reality is that the classes will study one or two primary sources a week that will augment the teacher's lectures. For example, in the middle of studying the Civil War, the teacher might pause to spend a whole period on the Gettysburg Address. Based on what students tell me year after year, the fifty minutes I devote to discussing the speech is about forty-five minutes longer than most high-school classes give to this great work of political poetry.

The multiplicity of texts in the history curriculum might give one the impression that it seeks to engage the students in instantaneous "problem solving" just as the Common Core purports to do. There is problem-solving going on, to be sure. But the approach is the polar opposite of the Common Core's. Rather than giving students random texts out of context, whose meaning is supposed to be surmised on the spot and a quick answer given, a true common core aims at a deep understanding of perennial human problems. For example, the selection from Plato's *Republic* on regimes introduced in the ninth grade follows an intense study of Athenian democracy. We also learn in literature class about Socrates' trial and execution through *The Apology*. When students read Plato's critique of democracy, they have already seen a democracy in action and know why the philosopher (whose own teacher was executed by the democracy) would be critical of popular rule. Reading Plato should not then turn into one of these silly discussions that many teachers like to have with their students: "So Plato's, like, critical of democracy, but that was way back then. So what do you think, and how does that make you *feel*?" On the contrary, students armed with the knowledge of Greek history and the story of Socrates will be able to understand Plato's sustained critique of democracy (as well as of monarchy and aristocracy). The students must come to understand this argument since it introduces one of the most important questions for mankind: how might people be given political power without abusing it? That will become the central question the students encounter throughout their study of history, one that prepares them two years later for an intensive reading of the Founding Fathers. The central question in political philosophy—how does a people achieve both liberty and justice through the regulation of power?—can be understood by a fifteen-year-old, but only if it is set up with a solid foundation and not some momentary opinion poll appealing to adolescent argumentativeness, as called for in the Common Core.[96]

Literature and history are different disciplines and require different ways of teaching, but since they both work on the permanent human problems, they naturally proceed in their separate, albeit complementary ways. As we have seen, the Common Core forces English classes to study "informational texts" alongside literary works. That requirement undermines the capacity of the English class to do what it must in the overall curriculum. If the English class cannot do its job, the whole education suffers as a result. To prove this, let us look at another example of how the curriculum fits together when things are going well. Here are the first lines of *The Iliad*, the first lines of literature that students would study in a truly rigorous high school:

Rage—Goddess, sing the rage of Peleus' son Achilles,
murderous, doomed, that cost the Achaeans countless losses,
hurling down to the House of Death so many sturdy souls,
great fighters' souls, but made their bodies carrion,
feasts for the dogs and birds,
and the will of Zeus was moving towards its end.
Begin, Muse, when the two first broke and clashed,
Agamemnon lord of men and brilliant Achilles.

---

[96] The reader may be disturbed by the students reading a critique of democracy. One must understand that the Founders had read Thucydides, Plato, and others on the disadvantages of an unchecked democracy and thus created a Constitutional, representative, federal republic that nonetheless derived all power from the people. That point gets lost a lot in discussions of politics these days, but it is a crucial distinction. One can hardly render popular rule both free and just without understanding its limitations.

The reason Achilles is enraged, as the students will soon learn, owes to a specific and a more general reason. The specific reason is Agamemnon's taking from Achilles a young princess whom he won as a prize by destroying a local settlement (yes, the Homeric age was brutal for women). The more general reason appears to be (it requires argument to make the case) that Achilles, the greatest of warriors, chafes at being under the command of Agamemnon, "lord of men." Agamemnon may likewise distrust Achilles (this would also require argument) and have taken the maiden from the warrior to reassert his power and authority. Thus the "two first broke and clashed." The "rage of Achilles," resulting from thwarted ambition, is so tremendous that it can doom countless men. We continue to read the story of Achilles' rage because it is gripping. We want to know the results; we want to know more about Achilles and Agamemnon, and later Hector and Paris and the beautiful Helen. That story is worth studying in its own right. Yet from that story we gain a windfall. We learn something about the nature of man that is essential to knowing man in a political setting. We learn that ambition can lead to rage, and that rage can lead to the destruction of "countless" others.

While these lessons about human beings are growing out of the careful study of great literature, the students in history would encounter a similar story with consequences no less dire. In history, the story revolves around the rivalry of two political organizations called *poleis*: Athens and Sparta. Each *polis* became great in its own way: Athens by its wealth and vibrant culture and political freedom, Sparta by its military prowess, political stability, and camaraderie among the citizens. These two *poleis* first fought as allies: to drive the formidable Persians out of Greece. Once that common crisis was gone, the two powerhouses became fatal enemies. We cannot tell that story here. Yet the analogy must be drawn. Ambition, the desire for wealth and power, which inspires great achievements, can also lead to ruin, whether the ruin of an individual or a civilization. The great stories of *The Iliad* and Athens and Sparta will not be the last time students encounter the effects of ambition. They will read about Julius Caesar in both history and literature. They will read *Macbeth*. They will read Machiavelli. They will have seen the rivalries of different men wanting the same woman, of different countries wanting the same land, of different parts of society—church and state, for example—striving for ultimate authority over the people, of different social

255

classes fighting for supremacy, of different men wanting to be king. By the time the students get to American history, they will know much of the story of human ambition. Ambition will not be a vague term they can hardly define. They will have become intimate acquaintances with some of the greatest works on the subject.

But they will not have finished that story because that story never ends. How vital is an understanding of human ambition to understanding America? Should students know something about human ambition in order to grasp fully the American frame of government, for instance? Let us allow the Father of the Constitution to answer that question.

> But the great security against a gradual concentration of the several powers in the same department, consists in giving to those who administer each department, the necessary constitutional means, and personal motives, to resist encroachments of the others. The provision for defence must in this, as in all other cases, be made commensurate to the danger of attack. *Ambition must be made to counteract ambition.* The interest of the man, must be connected to the constitutional rights of the place. It may be a reflection on human nature, that such devices should be necessary to control the abuses of government. But what is government itself, but the greatest of all reflections on human nature? If men were angels, no government would be necessary. If angels were to govern men, neither external nor internal controls on government would be necessary. In framing a government which is to be administered by men over men, the great difficulty lies in in this: you must first enable the government to control the governed; and in the next place oblige it to control itself. A dependence on the people is, no doubt, the primary control on the government; but experience has taught mankind the necessity of auxiliary precautions. [Emphasis added.]

James Madison understood ambition. He had read about it in history and great literature. He had seen it in his own day: on the part of Britain before the revolution, on the part of the states after the war, on the part of individual men he knew. He knew it would never go away. Therefore, he helped create a government in which that unruly passion would be divided and deployed to protect the individual rights of the people and to accomplish the ends, albeit limited ends, which only sound government can accomplish. Understanding our government, then, means understanding that long story of human ambition. Whenever we no longer read and understand those words—when we fail to recognize ambition—when we begin to believe that angels are governing us (and trying to educate us), then we gradually lose our liberty, and with it our happiness.

We see, then, that government is a very human thing. Mostly the story students are getting now is that government is a benevolent and ever-providing institution that saves us from poverty and hunger and disease and mankind's conspiracy against the planet and other horrible things. They have not read the Founding Fathers. Consequently, they have no idea that the Founders harbored a principled suspicion of political power, even when that power derived from the people themselves. Neither have today's students read the long story of human ambition found in the Western literary canon and in "the course of human events." If you were to ask students to explain ambition by using examples from history and literature, you would meet with a blank stare.[97] Offering examples to them would not be much help. Achilles. Huh? Athens and Sparta. Huh? Macbeth. Huh? Machiavelli. Double Huh? Consequently, students remain woefully ignorant of one of the prime movers of human civilization.

Should the study of ambition be a part of every young person's education? To find out, let us again consult one of the Founding Fathers of American public education. Thomas Jefferson thought that in order to preserve liberty the "minds of the people at large" should be illuminated with

---

[97] Of course, they would say "Hitler," their one answer, as Allan Bloom pointed out, for anything evil or menacing. The Hitler example is not sufficient, however, because it blinds us to evils on anything less than a monstrous scale.

knowledge of those facts, which history exhibiteth, that, possessed thereby of the experience of other ages and countries, they may be enabled to know ambition under all its shapes, and prompt their natural powers to defeat its purposes . . .[98]

We could go on to ask, how important is understanding ambition in one's daily life? Is ambition, in its good and bad forms, no longer relevant in a twenty-first-century global economy? We hear the word all the time, yet we hardly know what it is. Ambition is not the whole of the human story, to be sure. It is a part, but an indispensable part—no less indispensable than love. The story of ambition is just one of the stories not being told in schools today. We could name twenty more. Where are students to learn these things if not from the classics?

Once we see that this curriculum is ordered along these lines—and that it is modelled on the education the Founding Fathers had in mind for a free people—everything falls into place. The entire freshman year is devoted to the ancients: Greece in one semester, Rome in the other. In this compressed but highly productive year, students learn what the Founders themselves learned in their early years and continued to study throughout their lives (without the using the term "life-long learners"). The students will learn to admire and to lament the tempestuous souls of the ancient epic heroes, just as they will admire and lament the brilliance and turmoil of Athenian democracy. They will fight and found a state with the pious[99] Aeneas as they pause to learn from the balanced Roman Republic described by Polybius.[100] They will defeat the Carthaginians through Roman fortitude, but weep upon seeing the republic torn apart by the ambitions of men, the chief ambitions being those of Julius Caesar. So important were the Roman Civil Wars, and so important Caesar in ancient history, that the students will study Caesar through four perspectives: those of Cicero, Plutarch, Shakespeare, and Caesar himself. Further, students at a

---

[98] Thomas Jefferson, Preamble to a Bill for the More General Diffusion of Knowledge, 1778.
[99] *Pietas* is the virtue Aeneas most embodies, which refers to reverence for the gods, but also duty and love. From *pietas*, we derive the words *piety* and *pity*.
[100] See my lectures on Socrates and the Roman Republic for the Hillsdale Western Heritage course online.

school like this one would be reading Latin by the ninth grade, so they could read Caesar and Cicero (eventually) in the original. Finally, students would follow the rise of Augustus: the state restored and the old Roman liberty lost. Those students would have only just begun their march through the classics, but they would already be miles ahead of other fifteen-year-olds glued to their screens and bored to death by the slapdash "activities" and "performance tasks" of the Common Core. Besides that, the students who have studied the ancients for a year in this way will carry these memorable lessons for their entire lives: the wisdom, the wonders, and the warnings of the Greek and Roman worlds.

We shall not take the time to illustrate how the students would experience the entire curriculum: how they would in the sophomore year pray with Saint Benedict and fight by the side of Charlemagne, how they would rediscover the ancient world by reading letters that Petrarch wrote to authors a millennia or two after their deaths, or rediscover nature by ascending Mount Ventoux, just to see the view. Nor do we have time to shudder at the conscience-less political calculations of Machiavelli or see their horrendous results in the case of ambitious Macbeth following the advice of his unscrupulous wife. But all this students would do.

We should, however, stop to explain what happens in the curriculum in its transition from the tenth to the eleventh grade. If you ask nearly anyone involved in "curriculum development" in public schools why something is taught at any given moment over the course of four or twelve years, that nominal expert cannot tell you. Parents are never told the reason behind books. In this classical curriculum we have offered, *everything* has a purpose. What happens in the first two years is that the American inheritance is laid out. That inheritance consists in four separate legacies. The first is Athens and Rome, or the ancients. The second is often identified as Jerusalem, or the Judeo-Christian legacy, which is the subject of medieval Europe. The third is the British legacy, consisting in the politics, literature, and language inherited from that great people. The fourth is a specific historical moment known as the Enlightenment, which began in the 1680s and 90s with the Glorious Revolution, Newton's discoveries in physics, and Locke's inquiries into both the politics and the mind of man. These four legacies combined constituted the Founding Fathers' education. There were tensions among them—Athens with Jerusalem, revealed religion with the reason of the Enlightenment—but the tensions did not prevent, through study and conversation and experience and struggle, the Founding Fathers from offering answers to the great questions and "remedies" to the great problems of civilization. The first two years of high school provide the students with the background needed to learn from the Great American Story, and particularly from the Founding Fathers.

To this end, the curriculum in the junior year branches out, like a great tree, into related disciplines that both draw upon and inform the understanding of human nature gained from history and literature. Those disciplines are moral philosophy, government, and economics. Each of these is a human discipline, based on how humans behave. Moral philosophy teaches us about the moral constitution of human beings: what constitutes virtue and vice and thus wherein our duties lie. Government teaches us how human beings best live together—with freedom and justice under the rule of law. Economics teaches us how human beings flourish through work, innovation, and exchange, and under what political circumstances those human capacities are most fostered. To fully understand human beings, each one of these "sciences of man," as the Founders would have called them, must be studied. Yet they must be studied as *human* sciences: disciplines growing out of the humanities, the great stories found in literature and history. As we have said, the individual who does not understand Jane Austen may very well not have a very deep grasp on economics. That is not hyperbole. The founder of modern economics, Adam Smith—no less than our own Founding Fathers—both enjoyed and gained deep moral insights from reading the great works of literature.

In other words, a curriculum is not a dry list of books. It is not a set of mental agility drills purported to build some undefined "critical-thinking skills." A school curriculum is life. But it is not life as narrowly defined either by adolescents or by testing taskmasters ostensibly worried about young people getting jobs. It is the full view of life in all its wonders and struggles and joys and troubles, preparing young people for the world they will enter by seeing it through the eyes of those who have best understood human life. It invites young people to live through the great men and women—both real and imagined—before they themselves go into the "real world" and live. What better provision could we give them for working out their own greatest happiness?

260

Now we should ask ourselves a few straightforward questions. We should examine the extent to which the curriculum I have outlined here measures up to the ostensible aims of the Common Core.

If students are prepared (in the ninth and tenth grades) with the same historical and philosophical background that the Founding Fathers had; then go on to figure out how best to solve the great problem of political power vs. individual liberty through the ideas of the Founding Fathers themselves (eleventh grade); and later trace the effects of that establishment throughout American history, including the challenge to the Founders' ideas in the twentieth century (eleventh and twelfth grades); if they likewise see how different arrangements of power in Europe and throughout the world have often led to tyranny and loss of liberty (twelfth grade), then will they be *college ready*? Well, we must suppose that if colleges are still serious places where students learn about the great problems of human existence and their remedies, then, yes, colleges would be vying to attract such well-prepared students.

If students are immersed in the force and beauty of language and the English language in particular through reading the plays and poems of Shakespeare, the essays of Addison, and the parodies and satires of Swift, Franklin, and Orwell, would they have the literacy needed in a "twenty-first-century global economy"? If they have learned the art of convincing argument by reading the soaring rhetoric of Pericles and Cicero, of Tom Paine and Abraham Lincoln, would they be *career ready*? Insofar as one of the biggest complaints of today's employers is how poorly their employees write—and how little they understand even of their reading—then, yes, we must assume that those who had modeled their speech on Cicero and their prose writing on Franklin or James Madison could give a talk without being a slave to Power Point or write a memo that would define a problem and solve it.

If students have cultivated their sentiments and perceptions by deriving insights from the great characters of literature—Oedipus, Antigone, Hamlet, Elizabeth Bennet, Hester Prynne, and Raskolnikov—would they have what are now called the "people skills" and "emotional intelligence" requisite for understanding human character and perceiving the interesting differences in personalities? We must believe that understanding other human beings remains a vital part of both success in business and flourishing in our lives. Such human arts should not be trifled with by the new techno-progressives posing as education reformers who, whether deliberately or through foolish hubris, are trying to kill off the great stories and characters of literature and, with them, our human sympathies.

Here, then, is how a traditional curriculum works, how the course is followed. After a solid preparation in the earlier grades in which students would have been given an initial telling of the human story, in addition to having gained a strong command of the English language, the students would begin to study more thoroughly and systematically the story of our civilization. They would in fact be given an education quite similar to the one the Founding Fathers had, starting with the literature and history of Greece and Rome. This kind of education, called a liberal education, was essential to the making of this country and remains no less essential today. This liberal education is nothing less than *our story*. It is a story of human beings striving to find liberty, justice, peace, prosperity, love, and, most of all, happiness. It is also a story of tyranny, injustice, bloodshed, poverty, hate, and, all too often, misery. In giving ourselves over to this story, we obtain that rarest of possessions: wisdom, a working knowledge of how human beings think and act in both their private, personal lives and upon the public stage. Such wisdom is rewarding in its own right. If human beings are to live up to their self-given name of *Homo Sapiens*, then no education could be more suitable to them than one inculcating wisdom. Yet such an education is also useful. The man or woman who understands human nature and history, and who has a tolerable work ethic and a sound character, will never have trouble getting into college, nor landing a job, nor gaining a public voice, nor knowing what counts for truth, beauty, and goodness in this world. As such, that man or woman will have a much greater chance of obtaining the great end of human life: happiness—the happiness that comes from pursuing truth and living virtuously.

This kind of education, by the way, is not hard to "sell," whether to parents or to their children. In fact, it is the only kind of education that really inspires children and young people, especially teenagers. A liberal education inspires young people because it speaks directly to their minds and souls. It calls on them to study the very human things they are already interested in. You do not have to convince a sixteen-year-old girl that she needs to learn about love. You do not have to convince a boy of any age to study the nature and causes of war. You do not have to trick teenagers into learning political and theological and economic and philosophical arguments. They are teenagers. They love to argue. It only requires a teacher who knows something and a book that has something in it worth arguing about. The things worth arguing about turn out to be the same things worth both working and fighting for, the great ends of human existence: truth, beauty, love, justice, liberty, prosperity, and so many other things both desirable and good. Devoting oneself to learning these things teaches young people how to bring about beauty and order and justice in the world. First, however, they must learn how to bring order and beauty into their own souls. For while they are far from being heroes or demigods at this time of their lives, their tempestuous souls share much in common with the soul of Achilles. It should come as no shock that they are far more interested at age fifteen or eighteen with the passions of great men and women—who may be fictional, or who may have lived centuries ago—than they are in the "twenty-first-century global economy." Yet they will never be ready for the twenty-first-century economy unless they learn to discipline the passions of their own souls—souls crying out for a meaningful, liberal, literary education.

Conclusion
Whither We Are Tending

Abraham Lincoln once said, "If we could first know where we are and whither we are tending, we could better judge what to do and how to do it."[101] In this book I have tried to lay out where we are as a nation in our teaching and learning of literature and whither we are tending under the formidable authority of the Common Core. Further, I have tried to lay out, however briefly, the kind of literary education this nation should return to for her to remain "the last, best hope of earth."

Defeating the monstrosity that is the Common Core is not enough. The aims and means of teaching in the public schools were already unsound before the Common Core got to them. The literature textbooks were already corrupt. Our great stories had already been taken from us. Otherwise, no one would have thought such a sweeping reform was necessary. And, when it came, everyone—every parent, every student—would have seen it instantly for what it is. That the parents who have recognized most clearly the nature of the Common Core are those who have had their children in private, religious schools that are being harmed by the change shows just how far the district public schools had already fallen.[102] Sadly, generations that have been raised on "literary" pabulum do not notice when a little "non-fiction" pabulum is added to the mix.

---

[101] The opening to his famous "A House Divided" speech at the Illinois Republican State Convention, 16 June 1858.
[102] For example, the remarkable ladies who have led the charge in Indiana against the Common Core, Heather Crossin and Erin Tuttle, both had their children in Catholic schools that adopted the Common Core.

Returning this country to a public education worthy of the name begins with recalling the true ends of education: the deepest reasons we send our children to school. Looking to schools only for "career and college readiness," and then turning that readiness into a kind of formula, is a severe case of selling our sons and daughters short. The great and lasting purposes for sending our children to school must extend beyond the current job market or our infatuation with machines. Machines have been around for millennia. The computer, as valuable as it is, will never outdo indoor plumbing or the automobile for its utility. The difference between our time and the time of those inventions is that a century ago most sensible people did not want to throw away two-and-a-half millennia of liberal education just because they could have running water or get from place to place faster. It has been the hubris, not the virtue, of the present age to believe that we have nothing to learn from our intellectual fathers and mothers. It has been the innovation of our age to think that quick information can replace permanent knowledge. It is our arrogance that contends, against the example of Newton (no mean intellect he), that we are no longer dwarves resting on the shoulders of giants, but rather giants standing on the graves of dwarves: racist, sexist, and probably homophobic dwarves who somehow stumbled into liberty and greatness. Yet when we look at the alleged intellectuals of today—including the acclaimed new authors whose works appear in the Common Core—they appear so, so small. No doubt there is a motive behind the authors of the Common Core not wanting our children to read Jonathan Swift. Lilliputians are naturally the enemies of giants.

The reasons for sending our children to school must be human reasons. The phrase that has most often been associated with these human reasons is *liberal education*. A liberal education, as its name implies, is designed to teach young people how to be free. Throughout most of human history only a few people could afford to have this kind of education. It has been the glory of this country to try to give every citizen at least some portion of liberal learning. The Founding Fathers would not be at all surprised to learn that most children attend public schools today up to the age of eighteen. They would be surprised to learn what a poor job we are doing for the thirteen years we have students in school, and how illiberal the education in those schools is.

Liberal education treats human beings not as means but as ends. Liberal education, based upon the classics, does not promise merely to give future workers job skills so they can somehow squeeze into a name-your-century global economy. A liberal education teaches future husbands, wives, parents, citizens, friends, public servants, entrepreneurs, business leaders, and, yes, *workers* the language, mathematics, history, science, music, art, and stories they need to participate in a civil, common conversation about how to live together. A liberal education also recognizes a fundamental fact about the flourishing of a nation and an economy. Jobs do not make the human mind. The human mind makes jobs. The purpose of a liberal education, then, is more than getting into college or getting a job. Those are byproducts of a liberal education, but not the highest purpose. Study of the humanities in particular teaches young people (who have yet to venture out into the world on their own) the nature of human beings and human institutions. Such knowledge will serve them well in every walk of life and for their entire lives. A liberal education speaks to the longing that compels human beings to want an education in the first place. Humans, unlike other living creatures, are not content just to live. They want to live well.

Human beings, unlike machines, are not fittingly programmed by means of instruction manuals. Therefore our living well is not an "app" we can download. Although there is now an "app" called *self-control*[103] there is no computer program that can teach us honest-to-goodness self-control. In fact, the existence of the self-control "app" proves our lack of self-control. To find out how to live well, then, we need something else. We certainly need principles to live by. "Do unto others . . ." is a very great principle, quite likely the greatest of principles. But just as man cannot live by bread alone, neither can he live by principles alone, at least as expressed in such short phrases. Very often these principles get put into longer tracts or treatises that go by the name of philosophy. But philosophy is a very hard thing to read, especially for a child but sometimes even for a philosopher. So human beings, in order to understand themselves—and in order to learn how to live well—have created stories. This truth should not

---

[103] Which keeps us from texting while driving, of all things, thus using the same technology that distracts us to replace our courtesy, sense of safety, and plain common sense. Is this "app" ironically named?

come as a revelation. Human beings have an incredible power of mind called the imagination. They have a ceaseless interest in what other people are doing. And they find themselves living in a complex narrative. Anyone who does not know where he comes from, how his life is interconnected to the lives of countless others, how those others may depend on him, and what ultimate goods he is after, really does not know himself. He does not know his own story.

For a person to know his own story beyond what he picks up in his neighborhood, from his acquaintances, and from the television and internet, (sources that may simply project more, predictable images on the wall of the Cave) he must learn deeper, more beautiful, and often more tragic stories than those immediately available to his own experience. These stories are not hard to find, but a person must be looking. These stories are cheap to purchase, but they are not free. They come at the cost of investing time and thought into them. These stories cannot be read and digested in a day, nor put into a box called "critical thinking." These stories do not readily translate into a line on a résumé. A person who sits down to read a story expecting an immediate solution to his biggest worry in life may not find his remedy—right away. Yet the patient reader may find, like the sons in the fable who inherited their father's land, that "there is a treasure in the ground." He just has to dig for it. The great stories teach us, ennoble us, comfort us, and inspire us. A people that takes its best stories seriously will be more just and more humane. Lincoln was onto something when he called Mrs. Stowe "the little woman who started this big war." Abraham Lincoln knew the power of stories.

Over the course of this book we have seen how the Common Core ignores, chops up, misunderstands, trivializes, distorts, and spoils our greatest stories. They have done so through a combination of incompetence and false ideology. The editors of the textbooks are clearly trying to discredit our traditional stories through snarky and politically biased commentary whose clear design is to "blow out the moral lights" of the Great American Story.[104] The Common Core and the textbook editors are replacing the classic stories with post-modern tales of cynicism and ennui. These stories were written with a design not just to show characters with understandable moral failings in lamentable

---

[104] Abraham Lincoln, quoting Henry Clay, in the Lincoln-Douglas debates.

situations and dealing with troubles often of their own making. That describes all of Western literature. Rather, their design is to spread a general malaise throughout the country under the false name of literary sophistication. It is astonishing to see how little there is in the characters of the new literature that brings out our admiration, our amusement, and our sympathy.

I have called the authors of the Common Core the story-killers. For some that name may be hard to fathom. I have testified before state legislators who just don't understand. At the same time I have spent time with mothers and teachers who already see the effects: on their students' education and, at times, on the mood of the children themselves. This should not surprise us. Any mother knows the difference between a jaded child, a bored child, a prematurely cynical child on the one hand and a happy child, an engaged child, and a hopeful child on the other. The Common Core fosters the development of the first kind of child, as a classical, liberal education fosters the development of the second. We have to come to grips with this fundamental fact of education. If literature offers human beings a window into life, not only the complexity but the *quality* and the *meaning* of that literature will shape the readers' views of life. If there is nothing great in that literature, the readers will expect nothing great out of life. Are we now giving our young men and women, to invoke a Dickens' title, *Great Expectations*? Not with the Common Core.[105]

Of course, the authors of the Common Core have their charts and graphs and pseudo-science of text complexity. Right now there is no real "research" to validate what they are doing, but they will manufacture some. The real empirical evidence, however, is much broader than the latest study being churned out by a dubious research organization. We know what has emerged out of and accompanied the great stories of the Western and British and American tradition. Love. Law. Freedom. Science. Culture. Prosperity. Justice. Faith. Happiness. Similarly, we know what has resulted from the culture of malaise over the past century. Bureaucracy. Poverty. Self-induced helplessness. Sexual chaos. The breakdown of the family. Bad taste. The decline of courtesy and good manners. Self-indulgent narcissism. Self-loathing. Faithlessness. Unhappiness. And the arrogance of an incompetent, self-congratulatory, hypocritical elite.

---

[105] There is no Charles Dickens that I can find in the Common Core documents.

These two stories, the Great American Story and the postmodern story of malaise (at times interrupted by a mindless blog post in the name of whiz-bang informational savvy) are at war in the nation's classrooms. One story is on the deathbed of disuse. The other is being imposed on us by an unelected group of self-proclaimed and wholly unproven education innovators who are using the failure of the public schools—that their political progenitors brought about—to effect a control over our children's minds that will render them the political tools of an arrogant officialdom.

We know what works in schools—or we ought to. A liberal education works, and it works for a reason. The wolf in progressive sheep's clothing never works, and it fails for a reason. The key rests in the human mind and soul. Human beings want to know things. Human beings also feel things. They have a moral constitution. Both the human mind and soul long for greatness, for stories that are good and beautiful and true. If we allow our stories to die, our love of the good and the beautiful and the true will die with them.

It is high time we take our stories back. Then we should take our schools back. That may very well be the first step in taking our nation back.

Made in the USA
San Bernardino, CA
18 March 2014